Business Plans Kit For Dummies, 2nd Edition

Cheat Sheet

Key Components of a Business Plan

Don't know where to begin when it comes to creating a business plan? The following list outlines the major elements that your business plan should contain.

- ✔ **Executive summary:** The major points of your business plan in two pages or less.
- ✔ **Company overview:** Your mission, vision, values, products, unique attributes, and the business opportunity you plan to seize (Chapter 3).
- ✔ **Business environment:** An analysis of your industry, your marketplace, your customers, your competition, and how you stack up (Chapter 4).
- ✔ **Company description:** The capabilities that give you a unique advantage over your competitors — including your management, technology, operations, distribution, service, finances, and marketing (Chapter 6).
- ✔ **Company strategy:** Your roadmap to the future, including how you will seize opportunities and avoid threats, your growth plans, your marketing plan, and even your exit strategy (Chapters 5 and 7).
- ✔ **Financial review:** The state of your finances, including your income statement, balance sheet, cash flow statement, profit projection, and budget (Chapter 8).
- ✔ **Action Plan:** Steps you'll take to implement your business plan and meet your goals and objectives.

Attributes of a Winning Business Idea

Got a good idea? Not sure if it's worth pursuing? Ask yourself these questions. Then see Chapters 2 and 17 for more advice.

- ✔ Is it something you really want to spend time doing?
- ✔ Do you have the resources, connections, skills, and experience to turn the idea into a success story?
- ✔ Can you explain it in 25 words or less?
- ✔ Does it address or solve a real customer need, problem, or desire?
- ✔ Does it take advantage of a new opportunity? Is it the right idea at the right time?
- ✔ Will it make money — and how fast?

For Dummies: Bestselling Book Series f

Business Plans Kit For Dummies, 2nd Edition

Cheat Sheet

Five Business Planning Mistakes to Avoid

When putting together your business plan, you can avoid wasting time, energy, and resources by watching out for the following mistakes.

- ✔ **Failing to make time for business planning.** If you think writing a business plan is time-consuming, try running a business without one!
- ✔ **Failing to get buy-in from your staff** and those who can make your plan happen. Your plan can't inspire your team if you're keeping it secret.
- ✔ **Failing to understand your business environment** — by misreading your customers, underestimating your competitors, and ignoring the obstacles in your marketplace. What you don't know *can* hurt you.
- ✔ **Failing to set clear goals and objectives** with measurable outcomes and feet-to-the-fire timelines.
- ✔ **Failing to do your homework** to learn the size of your market, the nature of your industry, the extent of your financial needs, how long it will take to reach profitability, and how much of your sales will make it to your bottom line.

Evaluating Your Business Plan

Each time you review and revise your business plan, actively solicit suggestions and ideas throughout your company. Consider asking for answers to the following ten questions.

- ✔ Is the company doing enough to communicate its vision, mission, and strategic plan to employees? If not, how would you suggest we do a better job?
- ✔ Are the business goals and objectives outlined in the plan clear and appropriate?
- ✔ Do your own duties and responsibilities help support the company's goals and strategic direction?
- ✔ Can you suggest specific changes in the way your work is done that will help the company better meet its goals?
- ✔ Can you suggest ways to improve the company's overall operations?
- ✔ Do company procedures get in the way of your doing your best job? If so, how do you suggest changing them?
- ✔ Are you aware of changes in the industry — including our customers and our competitors — that should be addressed in our business plan?
- ✔ Can you suggest ways we can enhance the value we offer our customers?
- ✔ Can you think of additional ways to market our products and services?
- ✔ If you were in charge of revising the business plan, what other changes would you make?

For Dummies: Bestselling Book Series for Beginners

Business Plans Kit

FOR

DUMMIES®

2ND EDITION

**by Steven Peterson, PhD,
Peter E. Jaret,
and Barbara Findlay Schenck**

WILEY

Wiley Publishing, Inc.

Business Plans Kit For Dummies,® 2nd Edition

Published by
Wiley Publishing, Inc.
111 River St.
Hoboken, NJ 07030-5774
www.wiley.com

Copyright © 2005 by Wiley Publishing, Inc., Indianapolis, Indiana

Published by Wiley Publishing, Inc., Indianapolis, Indiana

Published simultaneously in Canada

For general information on our other products and services, please contact our Customer Care Department within the U.S. at 800-762-2974, outside the U.S. at 317-572-3993, or fax 317-572-4002.

For technical support, please visit www.wiley.com/techsupport.

Wiley also publishes its books in a variety of electronic formats. Some content that appears in print may not be available in electronic books.

Library of Congress Control Number: 2005927614

ISBN-13: 978-07645-9794-7

ISBN-10: 07645-9794-9

Manufactured in the United States of America

10 9 8 7 6

2B/RV/QV/QW/IN

WILEY

About the Authors

Steven Peterson and Peter Jaret wrote the first edition of *Business Plans Kit For Dummies*, which was released in 2001.

Steven Peterson is founder and CEO of Strategic Play, a management training company specializing in software tools designed to enhance business strategy, business planning, and general management skills. He's the creator of the Protean Strategist, a business simulation that reproduces a dynamic business environment where participant teams run companies and compete against each other in a fast-changing marketplace. He holds advanced degrees in mathematics and physics and received his doctorate from Cornell University. For more information, visit www.StrategicPlay.com.

Peter Jaret has written for *Newsweek, National Geographic, Health, Men's Journal, Reader's Digest,* and dozens of other magazines. He's the author of *In Self-Defense: The Human Immune System* and *Active Living Every Day.* He has developed brochures, white papers, and annual reports for the Electric Power Research Institute, Lucas Arts, The California Endowment, WebMD, BabyCenter, Stanford University, Collabria, Home Planet Technologies, and others. In 1992, he received the American Medical Association's first-place award for medical reporting. In 1997, he won the James Beard Award for food and nutrition writing. He holds degrees from Northwestern University and the University of Virginia.

Barbara Findlay Schenck built upon the great work of Peterson and Jaret as she wrote this second edition of *Business Plans Kit For Dummies,* which is updated throughout to include current business planning advice and all-new emphasis on the topics of greatest concern to today's entrepreneurs, business owners, CEOs, and investors. She's a successful business owner, marketing consultant, author of *Small Business Marketing For Dummies,* and co-writer of the Edgar Award-nominated memoir *Portraits of Guilt.* She has worked internationally in community development, served as a college admissions director and writing instructor in Hawaii, founded an advertising agency in Oregon, and has helped organizations large and small to plan and manage successful marketing and management programs. You can contact her at BFSchenck@aol.com.

Author's Acknowledgments

The first round of thanks goes to all who made the initial edition of *Business Plans Kit For Dummies* possible — most importantly authors Steven Peterson and Peter E. Jaret, who were backed by an outstanding acquisitions, editorial, and production team that included Tere Drenth, Heather Gregory, Jill Alexander, Holly McGuire, Carmen Krikorian, Travis Silvers, Cindy Kitchel, and Rick Oliver.

For making this second edition possible, I thank the many businesses whose experiences are reflected throughout this book. I also thank those who make everything in my life possible: My husband Peter, my son Matthew, my sisters, and my parents, Walt and Julie Findlay.

This book is the result of work by an unrivaled editorial team. Thanks to project editor Tim Gallan and copy editor Michelle Dzurny, two pros whose contributions are apparent on every page of this book. Thanks also to technical reviewer Ann Bastianelli and especially to acquisitions editor Stacy Kennedy who brought this project and team together.

Most of all, thanks to every small business owner or dreamer who picks up this book as a step toward creating a success story. I extend all my wishes for good luck and fortune.

— Barbara Findlay Schenck

Publisher's Acknowledgments

We're proud of this book; please send us your comments through our Dummies online registration form located at www.dummies.com/register/.

Some of the people who helped bring this book to market include the following:

Acquisitions, Editorial, and Media Development

Senior Project Editor: Tim Gallan

Acquisitions Editor: Stacy Kennedy

Copy Editors: Michelle Dzurny, Josh Dials

Technical Editor: Ann Bastianelli

Media Development Specialist: Angela Denny

Editorial Manager: Christine Meloy Beck

Media Development Manager: Laura VanWinkle

Editorial Assistants: Nadine Bell, David Lutton, Hanna Scott

Cartoons: Rich Tennant (www.the5thwave.com)

Composition Services

Project Coordinator: Adrienne Martinez

Layout and Graphics: Carl Byers, Andrea Dahl, Joyce Haughey, Stephanie D. Jumper, Clint Lahnen, Barry Offringa, Melanee Prendergast, Heather Ryan, Julie Trippetti

Proofreaders: TECHBOOKS Production Services, Leeann Harney, Jessica Kramer, Joe Niesen, Carl William Pierce

Indexer: TECHBOOKS Production Services

Publishing and Editorial for Consumer Dummies

Diane Graves Steele, Vice President and Publisher, Consumer Dummies

Joyce Pepple, Acquisitions Director, Consumer Dummies

Kristin A. Cocks, Product Development Director, Consumer Dummies

Michael Spring, Vice President and Publisher, Travel

Kelly Regan, Editorial Director, Travel

Publishing for Technology Dummies

Andy Cummings, Vice President and Publisher, Dummies Technology/General User

Composition Services

Gerry Fahey, Vice President of Production Services

Debbie Stailey, Director of Composition Services

Contents at a Glance

Table of Contents

Introduction

*T*here's no question among business advisors: When you're establishing, expanding, or reenergizing a business, the best way to start is by writing a business plan. The task may seem a little daunting, which is why we bring this kit to the rescue.

Business Plans Kit For Dummies, 2nd Edition, doesn't *tell* you how to proceed; it *shows* you how, walking you through the process with step-by-step action plans, examples, and do-it-yourself forms throughout the book and on the information-packed CD-ROM. So relax. Whether you're planning to launch a brand-new business, kick-start an idling enterprise, or take a going concern to all-new heights, this book makes the process straightforward, easy, rewarding — and even fun.

About This Book

You can find plenty of books full of business-planning theories and principles, but this book is different: It cuts through the academics and steers clear of the jargon to provide an easy-to-grasp, step-by-step approach to putting a business plan together. It also offers dozens of forms to make the task easier and includes examples from all kinds of businesses — from freelance contractors and small retailers to online marketers and nonprofit organizations.

What's more, we've updated this 2nd edition to include input and advice on the most current and pressing issues facing businesses today. In response to the fact that marketing is a top concern of today's entrepreneurs, business owners, CEOs, and investors, we dedicated an all-new Chapter 7 solely to the topic. And because investment dollars are flowing once again, a new Chapter 19 offers 10 things to know about venture capital. Plus, all the chapters incorporate lessons from the dot-com crash, opportunities presented by today's technology, and current resources, tips, and planning advice.

Why This Book Is for You

You've picked up this book, so you're probably starting or growing a business — most likely a small- to medium-size business, because that's how most companies start. Maybe you have nothing more than the glimmer of a good idea for a company; maybe you've already started a business and know that the time has come to write a plan; or maybe you're running someone else's company or a nonprofit organization and you want to set and follow a clear path to success. In any case, you're excited, ambitious, and a little nervous at the thought of creating a business plan. Being excited and ambitious is good, but you need to settle your nerves, because the task you face is doable, manageable, and even enjoyable. Honest. You don't even need previous business experience to make your way through this book, although people with experience will also find plenty of good advice.

Conventions Used in This Book

We have a few conventions in this book that you ought to know about. Important terms, which we make every effort to explain, are *italicized*. We place tangential, not-so-important information in gray boxes, also known as sidebars. And at the end of every chapter, we summarize the forms from that chapter that appear on the CD-ROM.

Speaking of the CD-ROM, all the forms on the CD appear in both Microsoft Word format and Adobe's PDF format. Use whichever file format you're comfortable with. See the appendix for more info on how to use the CD.

How This Book Is Organized

From start to finish, this book offers a simple, step-by-step approach to business planning. We realize that not everyone will begin on the first page and end on the last, so this book is organized to allow you to flip to the area you want and find information you can put to use right away. To get you oriented, here's an overview of the contents.

Part 1: Laying the Foundation for Your Plan

The three chapters in this part form the business foundation upon which you write your plan for success. Chapter 1 provides an overview of what's involved in the business-planning process and what makes it so important. Chapter 2 offers advice on how to brainstorm business ideas and how to seize great business opportunities when you uncover them. Chapter 3 helps you establish the mission, vision, values, and goals for your company and gives you advice for putting your principles into action.

Part II: Developing Your Plan's Components

This part of the book gets right down to the nitty-gritty details of business planning. Chapter 4 helps you understand your business environment so that you have a clear idea of exactly what you're up against in terms of competition and the marketplace. Chapter 5 guides you in charting a strategy that capitalizes on your strengths and the opportunities that surround you. Chapter 6 helps you analyze all aspects of your company and its capabilities in order to make sure you concentrate on what you do best and improve where you see weaknesses. Chapter 7 walks with you through the development of your marketing strategy — considered by most business advisors to be the heart of your business plan. Finally, Chapter 8 is all about deciphering and making sense of your financial situation, including how to create the financial reports and projections you need to start, run, and grow a company.

Part III: Tailoring a Business Plan to Fit Your Needs

This part zeroes in on the special planning issues that different kinds of businesses face. Chapter 9 looks at the planning needs of self-employed individuals in one-person shops. Chapter 10 focuses on small-business planning, but it applies to established businesses big and small who face growth opportunities or turnaround issues. Chapter 12 tackles the special issues involved in putting together a nonprofit organization. And Chapter 13 is full of advice for online companies or for companies adding an online component to their brick-and-mortar establishments. Browse through all five chapters and combine advice to match your unique business situation.

Part IV: Making the Most of Your Plan

Chapter 14 tackles the nuts and bolts of putting your written plan together, with advice on assembling a planning team, compiling the components, and writing a concise and reader-friendly document. Chapter 15 is all about getting the most out of your business plan by making it an integral part of your company's organization and operations.

Part V: The Part of Tens

Okay, so you won't find 10 dating no-nos or 10 tips to a slimmer, trimmer you. But you will find 10 ways to know whether your plan needs an overhaul, 10 ways to evaluate a business idea, 10 ways to get your business plan funded, 10 things to know about venture capital, and 10 ways to use your business plan.

Icons Used in This Book

What would a *For Dummies* book be without the margin icons alerting you to all sorts of useful stuff? Here are the icons you find in this book:

 Tried-and-true approaches to help save you time or trouble.

 Business-planning essentials you don't want to forget.

 Common problems or pitfalls to avoid.

 Real-life examples that provide useful lessons on business planning.

 A heads-up that the form or resource we bring up also appears on the CD-ROM.

 An alert that the research, analysis, or strategy we describe should definitely show up in your written business plan.

Where to Go from Here

You can start anywhere you want in this book, but here's some insider advice: Chapter 1 is a good place to begin because it provides a quick overview of the contents of the whole book. And Chapter 2 is a good place to go next, because it helps you fine-tune your business idea. If your idea is already polished and ready to go, the chapters in Part II help you shape your great idea into an even better business plan. The chapters in Part III help you tailor your plan to your unique business structure. Think of it this way: Cover-to-cover is a great approach to follow, but you can use the index to jump quickly to the exact information you need at any time. If you end up with a written business plan, the system worked!

Part I
Laying the Foundation for Your Plan

The 5th Wave — By Rich Tennant

"But boss, the proposal was so well written..."

In this part . . .

Having a business plan — which means *writing* a business plan — is the best way to turn a good idea into a thriving company.

The chapters in this part make you a business plan convert. They present the case for why a plan is important, walk you through the process, and guide you as you take the first steps toward creating a company with a long and prosperous future.

If you want great tips on how to come up with a winning business idea, I provide steps for conducting a reality check to make sure your idea is worth pursuing, help kick off your business planning process, and offer a guided tour through the essential process of creating your company's mission, vision, goals, and objectives.

Chapter 1

Starting Your Planning Engine

In This Chapter

▶ Understanding the contents, use, and value of a business plan

▶ Identifying the people who will read your plan

▶ Setting your business time frame and milestones

▶ Launching the business-planning process

*B*ecause you're holding this book, the task of writing a business plan has probably made its way to the top of your to-do list. Now you want to know what's involved in the process and which actions to take first when writing your business plan.

Well, that's exactly what this first chapter of *Business Plans Kit For Dummies,* 2nd Edition, is all about. It confirms your hunch that business planning is not only important, but also essential — when you start your business and at every growth stage along the way. Plus, it helps you think clearly about why you need a business plan, who your business plan is for, what key components you need to include, and what kind of time frame is reasonable.

Writing a business plan is a big task, but this book makes it manageable, and this chapter provides a quick and easy overview to get you oriented and on your way to business-planning success.

Committing to the Business-Planning Process

With a thousand issues clamoring for the precious hours in your day, committing time to plan your company's future isn't easy. But operating without a plan is even harder — and even more time-consuming in the long run. You took the most important step when you made the decision to write a business plan. Now you need to convert that decision into action — starting by dedicating your time and effort to the process.

As you carve time out of your calendar, these two steps will keep you motivated:

- ✔ Define your business situation and how a business plan can help you move your business from where it is to where you want it to be.
- ✔ List the ways that a business plan can heighten your company's odds of success.

The next two sections lead the way.

Defining your business-planning situation

To get your business where you want it to go, you need a map to follow, which is what your business plan is all about. It starts with a description of your current situation; describes your future plans; defines your opportunities; and details the financial, operational, marketing, and organizational strategies you'll follow to achieve success.

Take a minute to think of your company as a ship about to set sail on an ocean voyage. Your business plan defines your destination and the route that you'll follow. It details the supplies and crew you have on board as well as what you still need to acquire. It forecasts the cost of the voyage. It describes the weather and sea conditions you're likely to encounter along the way and anticipates the potential dangers that may lurk over the horizon. Finally, your business plan identifies other ships that may be attempting to beat you to your destination.

The same kind of planning is necessary back on dry land. To navigate a new course for your company, you need to start with an assessment of where your business is right now — in other words, what current business situation you want to address or overcome. You need to define where you want to arrive and what strategies you'll follow to get there.

To define your current business situation, use Form 1-1 on the CD-ROM. It lists some of the many situations that companies face as they embark on the planning process. Take a few minutes to check off the situations that apply to your circumstances.

Write a plan; make more money

For proof that a business plan is important, consider this example. When the Kauffman Center for Entrepreneurial Leadership surveyed the annual winners of its Entrepreneur of the Year Award, it found that companies with written business plans had 50 percent greater sales growth and 12 percent higher gross profit margins than companies without plans. How's that for incentive?

TYPICAL BUSINESS-PLANNING SITUATIONS

☐ *We think we have a good idea, but we're not sure if we're being overly optimistic.*

The process of putting together a business plan can be a powerful reality check. While crafting your plan, you'll put your good idea to the test. Does your business proposition make sense? Are the assumptions you're making, in fact, true? Does your strategy fit in with prevailing business conditions? Do you have the resources you need? Will you really be able to attract customers? Can you actually make a profit? Do you have contingency plans in place if things go wrong?

☐ *We know we have a great idea. We're just not sure how to turn it into a real business.*

Turning a great idea into a successful business is exactly what a business plan is all about. One key part of your plan is likely to be a business model, for example, which describes exactly how your business intends to take in and make money. (Planning a not-for-profit? Your business model will describe where the money's coming from and how you plan to allocate it.) Most business plans also include detailed goals and objectives, which together create a road map for exactly how to turn that great idea of yours into a going — and growing — concern.

☐ *We need to convince investors that our great idea can make them lots of money.*

The only way to convince investors is with a solid business plan. Sure, you can point to a time in the heady days of the Internet boom when investors may have written a check simply because an idea sounded good or the entrepreneurs were energetic and talked the talk. But booms never last very long. Most of the time, investors want to see a strong and convincing business plan — one that makes a persuasive case that your company can turn a profit. They will take an especially close look at your business model and your financials. And the same goes for lenders. A complete and convincing business plan can help you get the loans you need to get your business up and running.

☐ *We're having a tough time attracting talented people in a highly competitive labor market.*

A strong business plan will help. Prospective employees need to feel confident that they're signing on with a company that knows what it needs to do to succeed. They also need to share in your vision and excitement. If your business plan points clearly toward an attractive destination, you'll have a very good chance of enlisting the kind of skilled and enthusiastic people you're looking for. If the plan also helps inspire new hires with a strong vision and mission, all the better.

Form 1-1: This form lists typical business-planning situations that may match your circumstances.

☐ *I'm thinking of going into business for myself, but I'm not sure where to start.*

Sole proprietors going into business on their own are often less likely than bigger companies to take the time to write a detailed business plan. But they really have as much or more to gain. Writing a business plan — particularly creating a detailed set of goals and objectives — gives you a simple framework to think about where to begin and how to follow through. If you're going into business on your own for the first time, a plan can help you sidestep problems and focus clearly on what you do best. Most important of all, a detailed and well-thought-out business plan gives you the confidence you need to go out and start your own business in the first place.

☐ *Our company has hit a few big bumps in the road, and we're struggling to get back on track.*

Part of the business-planning process involves an analysis of your own strengths and weaknesses as well as a recognition of the opportunities and threats in your business environment. Establishing specific goals and objectives as part of a coherent, overall plan is especially important when your company is in trouble. An effective business plan ensures that all your employees are focused on the same goals when you most need them to be.

☐ *We've had a few financial and personnel problems lately, and staff morale is low.*

A strong and inspiring business plan can bring your employees back together and boost morale. Two key parts of a good business plan — the mission statement and the vision statement — help make clear to employees not only what the company does, but also why it's in business. The two statements express both your purpose and what the company wants to become in the future. Many businesses use their mission and vision statements to inspire their people, boost productivity, and sharpen their competitive edge.

☐ *We want to sell off part of the company so we can focus on what we're good at.*

You have two good reasons to write a business plan. One of the purposes of your plan will be to get the part of the company you're spinning off in shape and ready to sell — at the best price. The other purpose of your plan will be to help you set out goals and objectives for the remaining part of the company, allowing you to focus your efforts on what you do best. Whenever a company undergoes the kind of sweeping change you describe, it really becomes a new company. That's why writing a new business plan in this situation is so important.

Page 2 of Form 1-1.

> ☐ *We have the opportunity to grow our business, but we're worried about growing too fast.*
>
> Success can be a double-edged sword. It's great while the money keeps rolling in, but the pressure to grow has also derailed many a company. Effective planning can help you chart the best way for your own business to grow. A solid business plan will also help ensure that you have the necessary resources in place to support and power your growth.

> ☐ *We're thinking about introducing a new product or service, but we need some guidance.*
>
> Introducing a new product or service — or entering a brand new market with a product or service you already have — is very much like starting a business. You need to think through all the same issues, from whom your customers and competitors are likely to be to avoiding threats and seizing market opportunities. The process of creating a business plan helps you develop a strategy for introducing your new product or service, and then ensures that it becomes a successful part of the larger business.

Page 3 of Form 1-1.

Buying into the value of business planning

The time you invest in your business plan will pay off many times over. Following are some of the most obvious benefits you'll gain from business planning:

- ✔ A clear statement of your business mission and vision
- ✔ A set of values that can help you steer your business through times of trouble
- ✔ A description of your *business model,* or how you plan to make money and stay in business
- ✔ A blueprint you can use to focus your energy and keep your company on track
- ✔ A clear-eyed analysis of your industry, including opportunities and threats
- ✔ A portrait of your potential customers and their buying behaviors
- ✔ A rundown of your major competitors and your strategies for facing them
- ✔ An honest assessment of your company's strengths and weaknesses
- ✔ A road map and timetable for achieving your goals and objectives
- ✔ A description of the products and services you offer

- An explanation of your marketing strategies

- An analysis of your revenues, costs, and projected profits

- An action plan that anticipates potential detours or hurdles you may encounter

- Benchmarks you can use to track your performance and make mid-course corrections

- A "handbook" for new employees describing who you are and what your company is all about

- A "résumé" you can use to introduce your business to suppliers, vendors, lenders, and others

Identifying Target Audiences and Key Messages

Your business plan is the blueprint for how you plan to build a successful enterprise. It's a comprehensive document that covers a lot of territory and addresses all sorts of issues. To help focus your efforts, consider which groups of people will have the greatest impact on your success. Those groups will be the primary audiences for your business plan.

For example, if you need capital investment, investors will be your primary audience. If you need to build strategic alliances, you want to address potential business partners. After you know *who* you want to reach with your business plan, you can focus on what those readers will want to know and what message you want them to receive. This section helps you to define your audience and your message before you begin to assemble your plan.

Your audience

All the people who have an interest in your business venture — from investors and lenders to your employees, customers, and suppliers — represent different *audiences* for your business plan. Depending on the situation you face and what you want your company to achieve through its plan, certain audiences will be more important than others:

- If your company seeks investment capital, your all-important target audience is likely to be filled with potential investors.

- If your plan includes the introduction of stock options (possibly in lieu of high salaries), your current and prospective employees will be a primary target audience.

> ✔ If you're launching a business that needs clients, not cash, to get up and running — the sooner the better — potential customers will comprise your plan's primary audience.

> ✔ If you're a self-employed freelancer, your plan may be for you and you alone to focus your efforts, chart your course, and anticipate problems before they arise.

Form 1-2 presents a list of the most common audiences for a business plan. Check off the groups that you think will be most important to your business success, given your current situation.

Your message

After you target the audiences for your plan, the next step is to focus on the key messages you want each group to receive. People with different stakes in your business will read your business plan with different interests and values. For example:

> ✔ A person who owns shares in a company wants to read about growth plans.

> ✔ A banker considering a loan request wants to see proof of strong revenue and profit prospects.

> ✔ Employee groups want to see how they'll benefit from the company's growth and profits.

> ✔ Regulators focus on operational and financial issues.

For advice on targeting and talking to your key audiences, including information on which parts of the business plan various audiences turn to first and how to address multiple audiences with a single plan, turn to Chapter 14.

But for now, do some preliminary planning, using Form 1-3 on the CD-ROM:

1. **Identify the three most important audiences you intend to address with your business plan.**

   For help, refer to the list of common audiences in Form 1-2.

2. **Jot down key points you need to make to each target audience.**

   Writing down your key points doesn't require fancy prose; just get your ideas down on paper so you can refer to them when you begin writing your business plan.

CHECKLIST OF COMMON BUSINESS PLAN AUDIENCES
☐ Yourself
☐ Your Board of Directors
☐ Investors and lenders
☐ Senior management team
☐ Current employees
☐ New hires
☐ Independent contractors
☐ Vendors and suppliers
☐ Customers or clients
☐ Donors (for not-for-profits)
☐ Distributors
☐ Regulators
☐ Advocacy groups
☐ Others _____

Form 1-2: Use this checklist to identify the primary audiences for your business plan.

The Anatomy of a Business Plan

Written business plans are as varied as the companies that compile them. Some plans run almost 100 pages, whereas others barely fill a few sheets. Some plans start with executive summaries, and others plunge right into detailed descriptions of products and services. Some companies print their business plans on paper, and some publish their plans exclusively on the Web. Some plans include page after page of financial projections, and others list only anticipated costs, expected revenues, and projected profits.

Every business plan is written for a different reason and to obtain a different outcome. Still, some plans are better than others. The following information helps you write a plan that will win high marks.

Business-plan contents from beginning to end

Business plans come in all shapes, sizes, formats — even colors — but they all share a similar framework. The following components, presented in the order they generally appear, are common elements in most business plans:

- **Table of contents:** This element is a guide to the key sections in your business plan and is especially useful if your plan exceeds ten pages.

- **Executive summary:** This section is a summary of the key points in your business plan. You should incorporate it if your plan runs more than ten pages and you want to convey important information upfront. Because many readers dig no deeper than your executive summary, you want to keep it clear, captivating, and brief — in fact, try to keep it to two pages or less.

- **Company overview:** This section describes your company and the nature of your business. It may include your company's mission and vision statements as well as descriptions of your values, your products or services, ways your company is unique, and what business opportunities you plan to seize. (Turn to Chapter 3 for help defining your business purpose and developing your company overview.)

- **Business environment:** This section includes an analysis of your industry and the forces at work in your market; an in-depth description of your direct and potential competitors; and a close look at your customers, including who they are, what they want, and how they buy products or services. Think of this section this way: It describes everything that affects your business that's beyond your control. (Count on Chapter 4 to help you zoom in on your environment and develop your analysis.)

✓ **Company description:** In this section, include information about your management team, your organization, your new or proprietary technology, your products and services, your company operations, and your marketing potential. Focus on areas where you have real advantages over your competition. (Check out Chapter 6 for help in writing your company description.)

✓ **Company strategy:** Here's where you detail your road map to the future. This section brings together the information about your business environment and your company's resources and then lays out a strategy for going forward. Included in this section is your analysis of the opportunities, threats, and uncertainties that your business faces along with the ways you plan to avoid pitfalls and take advantage of opportunities. (As you prepare this section, you'll find Chapter 5 an indispensable resource.)

✓ **Marketing plan:** This section is where you describe how you plan to reach prospects, make sales, and develop a loyal clientele. Because customers and sales are essential to your company's success, this section is a major component of your business plan. (Chapter 7 is devoted exclusively to helping you develop your marketing plan.)

✓ **Financial review:** This section includes a detailed review of dollars and cents, including the state of your current finances and what you expect your financial picture to look like in the future. It typically contains financial statements, including an income statement, your balance sheet, and a cash-flow statement. (If any of these terms seem foreign to you, or if you want step-by-step financial planning advice, see Chapter 8 for all the details.)

✓ **Action plan:** In this section, you detail the steps involved in implementing your business plan, including the sequence of actions and how they align with your goals and objectives. (Flip to Chapter 3 for advice on establishing goals and objectives, and then turn to Chapters 14 and 15 for information on how action plans ensure that you'll put your business plan to work.)

✓ **Appendixes:** This section includes detailed information that supports your business plan. It may include analyses, reports, surveys, legal documents, product specifications, and spreadsheets that deliver a rounded understanding of your business plan but which are of interest to only a small number of your readers.

The preceding list of the major components of a typical business plan is featured in Form 1-4 on the CD-ROM. As you get down to the business of writing your plan, use the items on Form 1-4 as a checklist, ticking off the major components as you complete them.

Not all business plans include all the components we list. In fact, you won't find a textbook example of a written business plan. For that reason, we don't provide any rigid business-plan model in this book. Instead, you find information on how to develop each of the major components, advice for how business plans tend to work for different kinds of businesses, and ways you can organize and present materials in your written plan.

Frequently asked business-plan questions

If you're like most people who get this far into the business-planning process, you have some questions right about now. You may even be at the hand-wringing stage. Well, you can put your mind to rest because, in this section, we answer the most frequently asked questions about writing business plans.

Do I really need to include all these sections?

Nope. Your business plan should include only what's important to you and your company. If your plan is short — or written mostly for your own purposes — you can dispose of the executive summary, for example. And if you're a company of one, you probably don't need a section describing the organization of your business (unless you want to give yourself a plan for how to get organized yourself!).

For most businesses, however, the more complete your business plan is, the better off you are. If yours is a one-person operation, for example, you may figure you can do without the company overview section because you already know what your business is all about, right? Well, you may find that by compiling that section — by putting your mission, vision, values, product offering, and unique attributes into words — you uncover new ideas about what you really plan to do with your business. And that can be an extremely valuable exercise for any company, no matter how big it is.

Do I really need to write it all down?

The one-word answer is yes. Creating a written plan forces you to face tough issues that you may otherwise ignore, such as

- How big is my market?
- Why will customers come to me and not my competition?
- How much money do I honestly need to get the business off the ground?
- When can I realistically expect to make a profit?
- What other opportunities can I take advantage of?
- What threatens my business?

By putting your thoughts down on paper, you give each question the attention it deserves. For example, when you write your business plan, you define your customers and your strategy for reaching out to them; you also analyze your competition and how your offerings compare to theirs; you uncover market opportunities to seize and threats to buffer yourself against; and you establish a set of goals and objectives — along with your action plan for achieving success. And when you're done, you have it all in writing for quick, easy, and frequent reference.

How long should my plan be?

The simple answer: as long as it needs to be and not a single word longer. A business plan as thick as a Stephen King novel doesn't impress anyone. In fact, it's likely to scare them off. What really impresses investors, clients, employees, and anyone else who may read your plan is clear, straightforward, and to-the-point thinking. Don't go overboard in the cutting room or leave anything important out of your plan purely for the sake of keeping it brief, but do condense every section down to its most important points. Even comprehensive plans usually fit on 20 to 30 pages, plus appendixes. And that makes many 100-page business plans about 75 pages too long!

Establishing Your Plan's Time Frame

Your *time frame* represents how far out into the future you want to plan. You want your business to grow successfully for years and years into the future, but that doesn't mean your current business plan goes all the way to forever. Each business plan covers a unique planning period. Some are designed to get a company to a defined sales level, a funding objective, or the achievement of some other growth goal. A good business plan covers a time frame that has a realistic start and finish, with a number of measurable checkpoints in between.

Committing to a schedule

How far out should your planning horizon go? Your answer depends on the kind of business you're in and the pace at which your industry is moving. Some ventures have only six months to prove themselves. At the other end of the spectrum, organizations that have substantial endowments, such as nonprofits, are in for the long haul with business plans that look at five- or ten-year horizons. Typical business plans, however, tend to use one-year, three-year, or five-year benchmarks (odd numbers are popular, for some reason).

Business planning is an ongoing process. From year to year — and sometimes more often than that — companies review, revise, and even completely overhaul their plans. As you establish your time frame, don't worry about casting it in cement. Instead, think of your schedule as something you commit to follow unless and until circumstances change and you make a conscious decision to revise it.

Defining milestones

Setting goals and establishing measurable objectives is a critical part of business planning. (Take a look at Chapter 3 to find out more about setting goals and objectives.) But knowing your goals and objectives isn't enough. You can't just say you'll get around to achieving them; you need to establish and hold yourself accountable to a schedule that includes specific milestones along the way.

Figure 1-1 shows how a retail store specializing in digital equipment (cameras, recorders, and other devices) answered five basic questions in order to establish a reasonable time frame for its expansion plans. Based on their answers, the owners determined that the business would need one year to open new stores and achieve profitability. Over that yearlong planning period, they defined a number of milestones:

- **Month 1:** Complete business plan
- **Month 2:** Secure business loans
- **Month 3:** Begin search for retail space
- **Month 5:** Lease and develop retail space; begin hiring
- **Month 7:** Open shops; run holiday ads
- **Month 8:** Holiday shopping season begins
- **Month 12:** New stores become profitable

To establish a time frame for your business plan, look over the questions on Form 1-5 on the CD-ROM and answer the questions that are relevant to your situation. Your responses will help you set a time frame that includes your key milestones and takes into account your business trends and cycles and the competitive and financial realities of your business.

Preparing for the Real World

You're about ready to dive into the business-planning process. By now you're pretty certain about the purpose and benefit of your plan, and you have a fairly clear idea of who you want to read your opus when it's ready and what you want them to find out and do as a result. You may even have a preliminary idea of your planning timeline. (If any of that sounds like Greek, look back at the preceding sections in this chapter.)

Figure 1-1:
The
questions
included in
this form
help
determine
an
appropriate
time frame
for your
business
plan.

BUSINESS PLAN TIME FRAME QUESTIONNAIRE

1. **Identify three milestones that represent essential steps you need to take to get your business off the ground or to the next level of achievement. Estimate a time frame for each.**

- **Milestone 1:**   Secure business loans.   (2 months)
- **Milestone 2:**   Lease and develop four locations.   (5 months)
- **Milestone 3:**   Get all shops up and running.   (8 months)

2. **Is the success of your business tied to a major business trend? If so, what is the time frame?**

The emerging market for digital devices — already underway, with new products scheduled for release every quarter   (5 months)

3. **Is your business seasonal in nature? When do you need to have your product or service available to take advantage of the peak season?**

Holiday sales represent 50 percent of our revenue.   (8 months)

4. **How soon do you need to make your product or service available to stay ahead of your competition?**

Consumer electronics is extremely competitive.   (ASAP)

5. **When do you absolutely need to start making a profit or meet your profit projection?**

Moderate financial pressure on the company.   (Within 1 year)

Before you turn to Chapter 2 and dive into the planning process, however, take a minute to become aware of some of the many resources you can turn to for additional tips and tools along the way.

Locating informative resources

You're certain to have questions as your business planning gets underway. For instance, you may want to find out about trends in your industry or marketplace or obtain information on your customers or competitors. Maybe you need more information before you develop your marketing plan or need help with your finances. Luckily, you have plenty of places to turn to for help. Here's a list of the places you can check out for more information:

✔ **The Internet:** You can dig up information on markets, customers, competition — you name it. When using search engines, enter your best-guess term for what you want to find, and you'll be amazed at the results. You can also visit industry Web sites for goldmines of information. And, by all means, go to the sites of your leading competitors to read company overviews, news releases, and all kinds of other information.

- ✔ **Your local college or university library:** The periodical section of your library has business journals and other useful publications, and the reference shelves contain books on market demographics, industry trends, and other factual resources.

- ✔ **A nearby business school:** Many schools offer seminars or night classes open to the public, and professors are usually happy to answer your questions.

- ✔ **Industry trade journals:** Yes, the subscriptions are sometimes pricey, but they're often well worth the investment.

- ✔ **Newspapers:** No matter what your business, *The New York Times, The Wall Street Journal,* and a local paper keep you on top of issues you should follow.

- ✔ **Trade shows and industry symposiums:** These gatherings are usually great places to get news about products, services, customers, and your competitors — all under one roof.

- ✔ **U.S. Small Business Administration (SBA):** A rich resource for just about everything you want to know about starting and running a small business. Look online at www.sba.gov.

- ✔ **Search and research companies:** Using these resources comes with a price, but sometimes a LEXUS/NEXUS search or a market-research study is the only place to find must-have data.

- ✔ **Professional groups:** Almost every profession has a professional group, from the American Medical Writers Association to the Society of Wetlands Scientists. Find the group that serves your business arena and check out the Web site and membership requirements.

- ✔ **Local business networking groups:** These groups are comprised of members with experience, insights, and even business referrals to share.

- ✔ **Your local chamber of commerce:** This organization is a good vehicle for networking and staying abreast of local and state issues and can serve as a resource for all sorts of business and regional information.

Seeking expert advice

When you can't find the answers to specific questions, ask for advice. For example, if you're thinking of starting a retail business in town, ask other retailers to fill you in on what you need to know. If you want to break away from the corporate grind and go into business for yourself, schedule a lunch with someone who has made a similar move to discover what it takes. You're sure to get an earful of useful firsthand advice to implement in your business planning.

As you interview industry contacts — or people with experience in similar businesses — follow these steps:

- ✔ **Prepare your questions in advance.** With a little advance planning, you won't forget to discuss something really important.

- ✔ **Explain exactly why you're asking for help.** You can't expect people to be open with you if you aren't honest with them.

- ✔ **Be prepared to listen.** Even if you hear something you don't want to know, listen anyway. Anybody who warns you about potential obstacles is doing you a big favor.

- ✔ **Keep the conversation open-ended.** Always ask whether you should be thinking about other issues or addressing other topics.

- ✔ **Build your network of contacts.** Ask for introductions to others who may be helpful or for suggestions for sources of useful information.

- ✔ **Be grateful.** Pick up the lunch or dinner tab. Write a quick thank-you note. Remember: You may need to turn to the same people later for additional advice or help.

Sharing the load

Unless you want to feel overwhelmed and burdened, you need to identify the key people who can help you during the business-planning process:

- ✔ If you're in business on your own, chances are you have to shoulder most of the business-planning efforts yourself. But that doesn't mean you can't enlist the help of friends or colleagues to read over what you've written and tell you whether it makes any sense. Outsiders bring a new perspective to your plan. Just remember one thing: You need honest opinions, so make sure the people you choose feel free to praise and criticize. The last thing you want is a yes-person giving you guidance.

- ✔ If you're part of a business team, enlist the help of others in your company. For one thing, people with different backgrounds have different perspectives that add breadth and depth to your business plan. What's more, by involving key people in the planning process, you ensure that they have a strong stake in getting results after you finish the written plan.

- ✔ If you're in a big company, you may delegate a lot of the work involved in creating and writing a business plan. Some companies even hire consultants to handle parts of the process. The downside of sourcing the work to outsiders is that you may end up with a plan that doesn't really reflect what's happening in your company. Worse yet, you may fail to win the commitment of the managers who are ultimately responsible for putting the plan into action. To get inside, make sure that your senior management team plays a central role. The marketing team, for example, may be

charged with writing the company-strategy section, and the Chief
Financial Officer (CFO) is an obvious choice for completing the financial
review. And think about asking someone in corporate communications
to write a crisp, clear, to-the-point executive summary (but wait until all
the other parts of the plan are completed and ready to be summarized).

Staying on track

To organize your business-planning process, use Form 1-6 on the CD-ROM. It
lists the major components of a typical business plan and provides spaces
for you to assign names and dates. If you intend to delegate, you can use this
form to keep track of who's in charge of which business plan component and
when it's due. If you're planning all by yourself, you can use the form to track
your progress.

BUSINESS PLAN TRACKER		
Plan Component:	*Who's In Charge:*	*When It's Due:*
Executive Summary		
Company Overview		
Business Environment		
Company Description		
Company Strategy		
Marketing Plan		
Financial Review		
Action Plan		
Appendixes		

Form 1-6: Use this form to assign tasks and organize your business-planning process.

When you enlist help in putting together a plan, you're probably asking the people around you to take on more than their usual workloads. To avoid over-whelming the office, create a reasonable schedule for getting the work done. And to keep everyone motivated, share the importance of the planning process. (See the section "Buying into the value of business planning" earlier in this chapter if you need ammunition.) If you're asking people to put in overtime, reward them for their efforts. A dinner out to celebrate important milestones in the planning process can go a long way toward keeping enthusiasm high.

Because business planning involves a lot of brainstorming, discussion, vision, and revision, it generates a lot of paperwork. To keep track of it all, name one person to be the keeper of a loose-leaf notebook containing all the materials related to your plan. If you're on your own, that person is you. If you're head-ing up a planning team, make sure to assign a person who's a natural-born organizer.

Finally, consider using computer software to help you through the process. Enter "business planning software" in your search engine to find all sorts of available tools — from freeware and shareware programs to full-service soft-ware. Also, count on the CD-ROM in this kit to supply you with nearly a hundred forms to use as you develop your business plan. See the Appendix for details.

Forms on the CD-ROM

Check out the following forms on the CD-ROM designed to help you get ready to start the business-planning process:

Form 1-1	**Typical Business-Planning Situations**	A variety of situations that typically prompt business-planning activity
Form 1-2	**Checklist of Common Business Plan Audiences**	Examples of groups and individuals who may have a stake in your busi-ness plan
Form 1-3	**Business Plan Target Audiences and Key Messages**	A form for listing the key audiences for your business plan and the mes-sages you want each to receive
Form 1-4	**Major Components in a Typical Business Plan**	A checklist of the most common sec-tions found in a typical business plan
Form 1-5	**Business Plan Time Frame Questionnaire**	Questions to help you determine the best time frame to use for your business planning
Form 1-6	**Business Plan Tracker**	A form you can use to keep track of who's in charge of each business plan component and when it's due

Generating a Great Business Idea

Writing a business plan is one of the most important steps in moving a new business venture into reality — but it isn't the first step.

The first step is generating a great business idea.

Maybe you already have an idea that you're planning to move from concept to reality. Or maybe your idea is almost there, but you're not quite certain whether or not you're heading in the right direction. Or maybe you're still struggling to find a venture that matches your interests and abilities with a product or service solid enough to make it in the big, cold business world.

Count on the following pages to fuel your idea-generating process with tips and tools for taking stock of your personal resources, asking others for advice, brainstorming ideas alone or in a group, putting your possibilities through a make-it-or-break-it reality check, and, finally, weighing the likelihood that investors, customers, and colleagues will want to buy into your business proposition.

Brainstorming Business Ideas

From technologies, to careers, to personal tastes, the world is moving faster than it's ever moved before. The pace of change can be dizzying for sure, and it brings with it plenty of uncertainty and risk. But all that change also leads to big opportunities for visionaries who can foresee market wants and needs and respond with precisely matched product and service solutions.

The next time you catch yourself saying "Why didn't I think of that?" or "How in the world did they come up with that idea?" stop and realize that although great ideas may look lucky or random, when you look a little closer, you're likely to find that considerable time and effort went into making them happen.

To count yourself among the successful innovators, start with a brainstorm. The following sections provide you with tried-and-true methods for revving your creative engine — whether alone or in a group — and snaring great ideas for your next business venture.

Using the do-it-yourself idea blender

Humans are a creative bunch. We invented the airplane, bendable straws, computers, the sports bra, snowboards, light bulbs, the jitterbug, disposable diapers, the safety pin, and *Star Wars*. Motives for invention vary from person to person:

- **We invent to save lives:** The polio vaccine, air bags, and fat-free cheesecake

- **We invent to express our deepest thoughts:** Poetry, painting, filmmaking, dance, and music

- **We invent just for fun:** Game shows, rollerblades, and professional wrestling

The greatest thing about creativity is that no one holds the corner on great ideas. You may not become a creative genius overnight, but with a little time and effort and by following a few basic steps, you can become a lot more creative than you may have thought!

To see what you can accomplish on the creativity front all by yourself, put the *idea blender* to the test. Take the following easy steps:

1. **Gather a pair of dice, a couple of sheets of paper, and Forms 2-1, 2-2, and 2-3 on the CD-ROM.**

2. **Grab Form 2-1 on the CD-ROM (and check out Figure 2-1) and fill out the rows as follows:**

   - In the first row, list things about yourself — for example, "I love kids," "I'm good with computers," "I'm a detail person," "I work best alone," or "I conceptualize well."

   - In the second row, list things you like to do. Include hobbies like playing videos, listening to classical music, skydiving, refinishing antiques, or reading.

- In the third row, list great products or services that you enjoy using. Maybe you're really into personal organizers, online banking, doggy daycare, or stair machines.

- In the fourth row, dream up products or services that you would like to see come to life. Solar-powered cellphones or electric sports cars, anyone?

3. Use Form 2-2 on the CD-ROM to blend the items from the rows.

See what you come up with, as Figure 2-2 illustrates. Here's how:

- Roll the dice and enter the number that comes up into the top box marked *a*.

- Roll again and enter the new number into the box marked *b*.

MY FAVORITE THINGS

Three important things about myself:

1.	2.	3.
I love to travel	I'm an organizer	I shop a lot

Three things I really like to do:

4.	5.	6.
Triathlons	Play with computers	Collect folk art

Three products or services I enjoy using a lot:

7.	8.	9.
Specialty catalogs	Online travel sites	Hybrid bicycles

Three products or services I would like to see:

10.	11.	12.
Digital cash	Briefcase bikes	Instant holograms

Figure 2-1: Use Form 2-1 on the CD-ROM to identify your personal traits and interests.

- Continue rolling and writing the resulting numbers into the remainder of the boxes in columns *a* and *b*.

- Flip back to Form 2-1 to see which of your interests and ideas correspond to the numbers you've written into Form 2-2. Combine the two items in each row and write the resulting idea in column *c,* as shown in Figure 2-2.

Bear with this step, because you're randomly mixing and matching based on the throw of the dice. Some of your results will combine traits you have with products you like. Some results will combine two traits. Others will bring two products or two services together. Some of the results will be new and innovative, and some will make no sense at all. Finish the exercise anyway. The process will get you thinking *out of the box* and allow you to see the world around you in completely new ways.

Bright ideas often sound a bit peculiar when first expressed. (Think of online chat rooms and skateboards, for example. And who would've jumped at the notion of a pet rock?) Another thing to remember is that most creative ideas emerge by combining familiar pieces of the world around you in new and different ways (think of TV dinners and car radios, for example).

4. Pull at least two promising business ideas out of this process.

THE IDEA BLENDER — MIXING AND MATCHING YOUR INTERESTS GRID

a.	b.	c.
10	3	I like to shop and would like to see digital cash.
6	11	I collect folk art and would like to see portable bikes.
7	5	I enjoy computers and specialty catalogs.
2	9	I'm an organizer and like hybrid bikes.
8	4	I enjoy online travel sites and do triathlons.

Figure 2-2:
Form 2-2 puts the idea blender to work, mixing your interests to form business ideas.

Figures 2-1 and 2-2 show the idea blender at work. The first two dice rolls recorded in Figure 2-2 tell you to blend numbers 10 and 3. Flipping back to Figure 2-1, you see that number 3 corresponds with the personal attribute "I like to shop," whereas number 10 corresponds with the desire for digital cash. Put those ideas together, and the idea blender leads to the finding "I like to shop and would like to see digital cash."

Okay, not all blender concoctions are winners. "I collect art and would like to see portable bikes" is just a little weird. But, "I enjoy online travel sites and do triathlons" just may lead to the creation of a travel site for triathletes.

Figure 2-3 shows two pretty good concepts that came out of this idea blender example.

See how the idea blender works? After you have the hang of it, pull it out every now and then, using new personal traits and new rolls of the dice for all new possibilities. Involve friends, or turn the idea blender into an after-dinner game. Be prepared to record resulting bright ideas whenever they hit you.

Figure 2-3:
Use Form
2-3 to
record a
few good
ideas each
time you use
the idea
blender.

THE IDEA BLENDER — YOUR BUSINESS IDEA BRAINSTORMS
Brainstorm #1:
An Internet emporium of specialty shops from around the world with a centralized ordering and payment system.
Brainstorm #2:
A tour company specializing in travel adventures created around sporting competitions and catering to the amateur athlete.

Inspiring team creativity (with or without donuts or bagels)

Put a few heads together and you may whip up a mental hurricane. The creative outcome depends on the nature of the group of individuals you assemble (the more dynamic, inspired, and innovative, the better) and the communication skills that the session leader brings into the room.

Boost your personal creativity quotient

Where do creative ideas originate? As part of an informal survey, innovative individuals named their top idea-generating activities. The most frequently cited answers lead off the following list:

In the shower	Exercising	During a business meeting
Commuting	Meditating	Reading
Going to sleep	Walking	Sitting at the desk
Just waking up	Talking with friends	While under pressure
During quiet moments	While vacationing	Napping
Actively thinking	During the night	Dreaming

Identify the activities that get your creative juices going, and over the next few weeks, devote a little more time to those pursuits. Watch for a boost in your creativity as a result.

The quickest way to kill an idea is to say anything akin to any of the following:

- ✔ It won't work.
- ✔ We're not ready for that.
- ✔ It isn't practical.
- ✔ It's already been done.
- ✔ That's just plain stupid.

The group you assemble needs to remain open to all ideas presented in order to develop a healthy idea-generating environment.

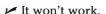

Applying the LCS system to nurture new ideas

You don't want to squash brand-new ideas before they have a chance to develop, so you should react by using the three-part *LCS system:*

- ✔ *L* is for *likes,* as in, *"What I like about your idea . . ."* Begin with some positive comments to encourage people to let loose with every creative idea that comes to mind.

- ✔ *C* is for *concerns,* as in, *"What concerns me about your idea . . ."* Sharing concerns begins dialogue that opens up and expands the creative process. As you point out a concern, someone else in the group is likely to offer a creative solution.

- ✔ *S* is for *suggestions,* as in, *"I have a few suggestions . . ."* Offering suggestions moves the brainstorming session along and may lead to the generation of a brand-new set of ideas.

Assembling a brainstorming session

With the LCS system fresh in your brains, your group can take on a brain-storming session following these steps:

1. **Start with a small group of people you trust and admire.**

   You can turn to friends, relatives, professional acquaintances — anyone you think may contribute a new and useful perspective.

2. **Invite a couple of ringers.**

   Consider inviting a few people who can stretch the group's thinking, challenge assumptions, and take the group in new and unexpected directions, even if these individuals may make you feel a bit uncomfortable.

3. **Choose the right time and place.**

   To inspire creativity, change the scene. Go to a park, a coffeehouse, or a hotel lobby. The same old places can lead to the same old thinking, so be inventive.

4. **Establish ground rules.**

   Explain what you want the group to achieve. Introduce the LCS system (see the previous section) so that participants have a tool that allows them to make positive contributions to the session.

5. **Act as the group's conductor.**

   Keep the process moving without turning into a dictator. Use these tactics:

   - Encourage alternatives: *How else can we do that?*
   - Stimulate visionary thinking: *What if we had no constraints?*
   - Invite new perspectives: *How would a child see this?*
   - Ask for specifics: *What exactly do you mean?*
   - Clarify the next steps: *How should we proceed on that?*

6. **Record the results.**

   Designate a person to take notes throughout the session, or record the session to review later. Remember, the best ideas are often side comments, so capture the offbeat comments as well as the mainstream discussion.

7. **Review your notes and thoughts while they're still fresh.**

   Set aside time after the brainstorming session to distill the discussion down to three or four ideas that you want to continue working on.

Transplanting a great idea

A successful business doesn't necessarily require an original idea.

A few years back, a California chef who was vacationing in Spain discovered the joy of *tapas,* the traditional finger food that Spaniards eat during the supper hour. On the spot, he knew that people in Los Angeles would go wild for tapas. What's more, he knew they'd love the look and feel of the tapas bars that thrive in cities like Barcelona. He decided to import traditional Spanish food to southern California, opening a series of tapas bars around Los Angeles and launching a U.S. dining rage.

Putting your personal stamp on an existing idea can be as bold as importing an idea like tapas bars or as simple as transplanting a successful business concept into your market area — like the countless entrepreneurs who followed the California chef's lead and opened tapas bars in cities and towns across the United States.

Think about the do-it-yourself pottery painting studios that you see practically everywhere these days. The idea migrated from do-it-yourself porcelain painting, which was born out of necessity by a young housewife who reportedly couldn't afford matching china. She decided to paint her own and wanted to help others to do the same. Entrepreneurs adapted the idea into a range of do-it-yourself pottery-painting businesses, including hobby shops; ceramics cafes; party businesses; glass, tile, and mosaic studios; and even pottery-painting books and online stores.

Finding business ideas within your work environment

A survey of 500 of the fastest-growing companies in America showed that nearly half grew directly out of the founders' previous work environments. In other words, the founders created these companies after looking around at what they were doing and saying, "There *has* to be a better way to do this."

When considering new business possibilities, keep in mind that 99 percent of all businesses (both old and new) fall into one of three broad categories:

- ✔ Products for sale
- ✔ Services for hire
- ✔ Distribution and delivery

Consider the range of products that your industry offers:

> Can you think of innovative ways to make them better?
>
> Can you imagine a product that completely replaces them?

Consider the services that your industry offers:

> Do you notice problems with consistency?
>
> What isn't being done that should be?
>
> What do customers complain about?

Ask yourself similar questions about your distribution and delivery systems:

> What are the most serious bottlenecks?
>
> Can you think of clever ways to improve distribution?
>
> Can you envision a radically new delivery system?

Identifying Business Opportunities

According to Thomas Edison, "Genius is 1 percent inspiration and 99 percent perspiration." The same goes for business. Coming up with the idea — through brainstorming, flashes of brilliance, and industry analysis — is the inspiration part. When you begin to think about how to turn it into a business, that's when you begin to sweat.

Putting your business ideas through a first test

After some combination of brainstorming, market analysis, and a few random flashes of brilliance, you may accumulate a drawer full of promising business ideas. Following are two guidelines to help you separate the real opportunities from the fluff:

✔ **Focus on the ideas that you're really excited about.** Lifting an idea off the ground takes energy, patience, and more hours than you can begin to imagine. Your passion is what will keep you motivated on the road to success.

> ✔ **Pursue ideas that you can follow through on.** If you feel you don't have the means or the drive to take an idea from the drawing board to the real world, scrap it.

To help you choose among your ideas, use Form 2-4 to complete a Business Opportunity Evaluation Questionnaire for each possibility you're considering. Tally your answers and consider any idea with a score of 24 or higher worthy of serious consideration. The one exception to the scoring: If your promising idea scores high on every question except for number 3 (Is this the kind of business you really want to pursue?), it may be a great idea for someone else — but not for you.

Use the Business Opportunity Evaluation Questionnaire as a first test for any business idea. If the idea scores high, it still has to pass other hurdles, but at least you know that it's an idea worth pursuing.

Narrowing your choices

After you've assembled a short list of promising ventures and filled out the Business Opportunity Evaluation Questionnaire in Form 2-4 to separate the promising ideas from all the others, you need to sort a little further before you select which opportunity to run with. No magic wand exists to do the work for you, but you can simplify the task by answering some questions that reveal pretty quickly whether or not an idea has what it takes to become a real, live business.

Use the questions in Form 2-5 to fill in details and to flesh out some of the issues around your preliminary business propositions. If you give your answers some careful thought, they'll reveal to you the likelihood of an idea breaking through as your winning business concept.

If you find yourself struggling to come up with answers to the questions in Form 2-5, your idea may be too sketchy to evaluate. That doesn't mean you should abandon the idea, but you should take the time to understand the opportunity more fully before taking it to the next stage in the business development process. For example, if you can't easily describe the customer need you're filling or how you plan to make money, you still have homework to do.

BUSINESS OPPORTUNITY EVALUATION QUESTIONNAIRE

1. Describe your promising idea in two sentences.

2. Being as honest as you can, rate the idea on a scale of 1 to 10: 1 being "the only thing we could come up with in a pinch," 10 being "the best thing since sliced bread." Circle your rating.

   1   2   3   4   5   6   7   8   9   10

3. Think seriously about what you would have to do to turn your idea into reality. Is this the kind of idea — and the kind of business — you really want to pursue? Rate your interest on a scale of 1 to 10 by circling the appropriate number: 1 for "so-so" and 10 for "very high."

   1   2   3   4   5   6   7   8   9   10

4. Imagine sitting down and persuading an investor to put down hard-earned cash to help turn your idea into a real business. How easy would it be to convince a skeptical outsider that your idea has the potential to make money? Circle your answer from 1 meaning "very difficult" to 10 meaning "a breeze."

   1   2   3   4   5   6   7   8   9   10

5. Being as objective as you can, ask yourself what odds your idea has of becoming a real business venture. Rate your chances from 1, meaning "it's a long shot," to 10, meaning "it's a guaranteed overnight success."

   1   2   3   4   5   6   7   8   9   10

Form 2-4: Evaluate each new business idea by completing this questionnaire.

BUSINESS OPPORTUNITY FRAMEWORK
1. Describe your business opportunity in two sentences.
2. List the three most important features of the product or service you propose.
3. What basic customer needs does your product or service fill?
4. Briefly describe who is likely to buy your product or service.
5. List two or three existing products or services that already meet a similar need.
6. Why would customers choose your product or service over others?
7. How will you reach your customers?
8. How do you plan to make money?

Form 2-5: The questions in this form help you test the merits of each business idea that you're considering.

Doing Your First Reality Check

After you put an idea through the preliminary evaluation, expect to get hit with the gut-wrenching moment of doubt that every entrepreneur who has ever considered launching a new enterprise has experienced.

Asking questions like "Is this really such a good idea?" and "Who am I kidding, anyway?" doesn't mean you lack confidence. What it does mean is that the time has come to step back and make sure that the road you're on is leading you where you want to go. In short, you need a reality check.

In many ways, writing a business plan is a series of reality checks. By making you carefully think through every aspect of your business — from the product or service you offer to the competitors you face and the customers you serve — the business planning process brings you face-to-face with the realities of doing business. And the first step is to make sure that your preliminary plan is on track.

Getting a second opinion

To help determine whether or not you're on solid ground, discuss your business idea and preliminary plans with a trusted friend or confidant. What you're really seeking is a *mentor* with most or all of the following characteristics:

- ✔ Someone who has experience in the business area you're considering, or at least experience in a similar business.
- ✔ Someone with the courage to tell you the truth, whether it's "That's a great idea. Go for it!" or "If I were you, I'd take a little more time to think this over."
- ✔ Someone you respect and admire and from whom you can take candid criticism without feeling defensive.

Consider turning to colleagues you've worked with in the past, teachers or professors, friends from college, or other associates.

Friends and family members sometimes can offer the advice and perspective you need, but emotional ties can get in the way of absolute honesty and objectivity. If you go this route, set some ground rules in advance. Ask for suggestions, comments, and constructive criticism and be prepared to hear both the good and the bad without taking what you hear personally.

In addition to a mentor, consider designating someone to act as the devil's advocate to guarantee that you address the flip side of every issue that you're considering. This person's task is to be critical of each idea on the table — not in a destructive way, but in a skeptical, show-me-the-money, I'll-believe-it-when-I-see-it kind of way.

Conducting a self-appraisal

When you prove to yourself that you've landed on a real business opportunity, you still have one question to answer: "Do I have what it takes to turn this opportunity into a success story?"

You see some common traits among the CEOs who were multimillionaires before they turned 25 and the entrepreneurs cruising around in sports cars issuing orders on their cellphones while the value of their stock options soar: talent *and* hard work. To succeed, you must exhibit both, and to be a high-flyer or, for that matter, to be self-employed, you need discipline, confidence, and the capacity to live with the uncertainty that's part and parcel of being out on your own.

As a first step toward appraising your strengths and weaknesses, pull out the survey in Form 2-6 and respond to the 20 statements as candidly as you possibly can. There's no such thing as a perfect score. The point of the exercise is to identify your strongest and weakest areas so that you can capitalize and compensate accordingly.

As you review your responses, watch for the following:

- ✔ Areas that receive "poor" ratings represent your weakest areas. Be alert for the need to compensate for these personal shortcomings.

- ✔ Areas that receive "excellent" ratings represent your real strengths and the personal resources you can call upon when you start your business venture.

Keep in mind that not all personal strengths and weaknesses are equal contributors to business success. For example, if you plan to be a sole proprietor who works mostly alone, the ability to manage a staff doesn't matter much, but self-motivation is absolutely essential. Or, if your business will depend on face-to-face customer service, interpersonal skills will be indispensable.

As you complete Form 2-6, place a star next to the top six traits that you think are most important to the success of your business. For the moment, ignore how you rate yourself in each of those areas. If you're weak in an important area, that doesn't mean you don't have what it takes to turn your idea into a business, but it does unveil areas that will require extra work and compensation on your part. For example, if you aren't good with details, but details are important to the success of your business, this exercise alerts you to the fact that you may need to hire a personal assistant or cajole a colleague into tying up all the loose ends.

To see how your personal strengths and weaknesses apply to the needs of your proposed business, take the top six traits from Form 2-6 and align them with your personal abilities, using Form 2-7 on the CD-ROM (see Figure 2-4).

Figure 2-4:
It's important that your personal strengths align with your business idea and that you pinpoint your weaknesses early on.

PERSONAL STRENGTHS AND WEAKNESSES GRID			
Poor	*Fair*	*Good*	*Excellent*
Tending to the details of a project			Organizing a schedule and getting things done
		Setting goals and achieving them	Juggling several tasks at once
	Taking risks	Adapting to changing circumstances	

Put a copy of your personal strengths and weaknesses grid into your daily organizer or post it near your computer. Having it close by constantly reminds you of who you are, the strengths you can draw on, and the areas you need to bolster as you begin the challenge of planning your business.

PERSONAL STRENGTHS AND WEAKNESSES SURVEY

Being as honest as you can, rate your abilities in the following areas:

1. Setting goals and pushing yourself to achieve them on time:

Poor　　　　　*Fair*　　　　　*Good*　　　　　*Excellent*

2. Making decisions and completing tasks:

Poor　　　　　*Fair*　　　　　*Good*　　　　　*Excellent*

3. Organizing a complex schedule and getting things done efficiently:

Poor　　　　　*Fair*　　　　　*Good*　　　　　*Excellent*

4. Staying focused on the specific task at hand:

Poor　　　　　*Fair*　　　　　*Good*　　　　　*Excellent*

5. Juggling several tasks at one time:

Poor　　　　　*Fair*　　　　　*Good*　　　　　*Excellent*

6. Judging a person's character:

Poor　　　　　*Fair*　　　　　*Good*　　　　　*Excellent*

7. Getting along with other people and bringing out the best in them:

Poor　　　　　*Fair*　　　　　*Good*　　　　　*Excellent*

8. Listening to several sides of an issue and then making a decision:

Poor　　　　　*Fair*　　　　　*Good*　　　　　*Excellent*

9. Leading a team, even when there is disagreement among the members:

Poor　　　　　*Fair*　　　　　*Good*　　　　　*Excellent*

10. Understanding what motivates other people:

Poor　　　　　*Fair*　　　　　*Good*　　　　　*Excellent*

11. Resolving disputes among people:

Poor　　　　　*Fair*　　　　　*Good*　　　　　*Excellent*

12. Saying what you mean and meaning what you say:

Poor　　　　　*Fair*　　　　　*Good*　　　　　*Excellent*

Form 2-6: Rate your personal strengths and weaknesses, using this questionnaire.

13. Keeping your cool even when everyone else is losing theirs:			
Poor	*Fair*	*Good*	*Excellent*
14. Telling someone no:			
Poor	*Fair*	*Good*	*Excellent*
15. Tending to the details of a project:			
Poor	*Fair*	*Good*	*Excellent*
16. Looking at the big picture:			
Poor	*Fair*	*Good*	*Excellent*
17. Acting decisively under pressure:			
Poor	*Fair*	*Good*	*Excellent*
18. Adapting to changing circumstances:			
Poor	*Fair*	*Good*	*Excellent*
19. Taking risks:			
Poor	*Fair*	*Good*	*Excellent*
20. Taking responsibility, even when things go wrong:			
Poor	*Fair*	*Good*	*Excellent*

Page 2 of Form 2-6.

Forms on the CD-ROM

Form 2-1	**The Idea Blender — Your Personal Traits and Interests**	The first step in an exercise that helps you think creatively about new business possibilities
Form 2-2	**The Idea Blender — Mixing and Matching Your Interests**	The second step in an exercise that helps you think creatively about new business possibilities
Form 2-3	**The Idea Blender — Your Business Ideas**	The final step in an exercise that helps you think creatively about new business possibilities

Form 2-4	**Business Opportunity Evaluation Questionnaire**	Questions that help you decide which business ideas are worth pursuing
Form 2-5	**Business Opportunity Framework**	Questions designed to fill in some important details around your business proposition
Form 2-6	**Personal Strengths and Weaknesses Survey**	A survey designed to provide you with an honest profile of your business abilities and traits
Form 2-7	**Personal Strengths and Weaknesses Grid**	A tool that allows you to compare your abilities with qualities important to the kind of business you're considering

Chapter 3

Defining Your Business Purpose

*I*n any kind of work you can get buried in the day-to-day demands and so caught up in the details that you miss the bigger picture altogether. That's why the business-planning process is so valuable. Writing a business plan allows you to step back and think about where you've come from and where you want to go, prompting you to ask and answer questions like the following:

- ✔ Why are you in business?
- ✔ What does your business do?
- ✔ What do you want your company to become?
- ✔ How will you get where you want to go?

If you're thinking that these questions are pretty basic, you're right. But that's exactly what makes them so important. You've heard too many scary stories about companies with great promise — and often tons of money to boot — that suddenly falter and fade away. Many of these companies could've avoided a lot of trouble along the way if the people steering the organization had taken the time to address basic issues during the planning stage.

To lead your business toward success, start by really focusing on why you're in business and what you want to achieve. Put your business values and vision into words, write a clear and compelling mission statement, and set goals and objectives to turn your mission into reality. This chapter shows you how to accomplish these tasks.

Knowing What Business You're Actually In

Business history is littered with the remains of companies whose founders thought they knew what businesses they were in, only to discover that the industries weren't quite what they seemed.

- ✔ Take a look at the railroad industry's history. During their heyday, railroad tycoons assumed that they were in the railroad business. Along came powerful competitors that had nothing to do with railroads — automobile manufacturers, the interstate highway system, jet aircraft, and regional airports. The tycoons realized that railroads weren't in the railroad business after all; they were in the transportation business. Perhaps if they saw the big picture sooner, they may have had a rosier future.

- ✔ Eastman Kodak, over its long history, made most of its money processing film — so much money, in fact, that the company came to believe that it was in the chemical-imaging business. Along came the digital revolution and new ways to record images. In no time, Kodak's customers weren't interested in the photo process, but in capturing memories — on film, video, or computer. Kodak was in the memories business all along.

- ✔ In a resort town in Florida, Mom and Pop's Toys thrived for years — until Toy Mania opened right across the street. To compete, Mom and Pop's Toys reduced prices. But Toy Mania had a bright idea. The management team created a fantasyland with puppets, animated cartoon characters, giant windup toys, and a variety show that performed three times a day in the store. In short, Toy Mania realized it was in the entertainment business. Within a year, Mom and Pop's Toys closed. It couldn't compete because the owners didn't understand the business they were in.

The first step in planning for business success is to identify what business you're in. Why do customers want the solution you provide, and why do they choose your business over the competition?

How would I describe my business?

Begin by answering this question: What business are you really in?

Here are three related questions to guide you to your answer:

- ✔ What basic needs do you fulfill in the marketplace?
- ✔ Beyond specific products and services, why do customers come to you?
- ✔ What are the three nicest things your customers could say about you?

Figure 3-1 shows how a company that provides text-editing services, mainly to marketing and communications departments and mainly over the Internet, answered these questions.

BASIC BUSINESS DEFINITION FRAMEWORK
1. What basic needs do you fulfill in the marketplace?
For each of our corporate clients, we make sure that all printed and Internet text materials are grammatically correct and conform to the company's style requirements.
2. Beyond specific products and services, why do customers come to you?
The reliability and quality of our service. Peace of mind. Not having to worry that the company will look bad in print. Confidence that what's published is correct and understandable.
3. What are the three nicest things your customers could say about you?
That we're thorough and reliable. That we have excellent turnaround. That we're friendly and easy to work with.

Figure 3-1:
The three questions on Form 3-1 on the CD-ROM help you determine the business you're in.

In reviewing their answers, the owners of the text-editing business were struck by the phrase "peace of mind." Those three words helped them realize that in addition to providing a text-editing business, they were also in the insurance business — making sure that embarrassing typos and inconsistencies didn't trip up marketing and communications managers.

In response, the company changed a few of its procedures. The owners put a managing editor in place to oversee the largest projects, and they enhanced their client-service staff to provide more communication throughout the editorial process to reinforce their clients' peace of mind. Within six months, business increased dramatically.

Now you can take a shot at answering the questions. Invest some time answering the three questions Figure 3-1 illustrates, using Form 3-1 on the CD-ROM. As you consider each question, jot down whatever comes to mind. Your answers may not go directly into your business plan, but they influence almost every aspect of your business-planning process.

Where's the money?

One of the biggest lessons from the dot-com crash is that a great business idea isn't enough to ensure business success and a long life. To turn a great idea into a successful business, you need to define and develop a workable *business model,* or a method that your company uses to generate revenue, earn profits, and protect its position in the marketplace. (You find more information on the topic of business models in Chapter 5.) In this early planning stage, while you're defining your business and describing its purpose, do something very basic: Show yourself the money. Not literally, of course. But from the get-go, be clear about how you expect your business to profit.

Way too many businesses start without a clear idea of where the money will come from, or they make general broad-brush assumptions to which they give no second thought or scrutiny. Writing off the question with the flippant answer that customers will give you money in exchange for the products or services you provide is easy. Business models, however, aren't always that straightforward:

- ✔ The local movie theater gets revenue from ticket sales, but that's only the beginning. The theater also makes money by projecting billboard-style ads prior to the movie showings and from its concession stand, where it turns a tidy profit selling candy and buckets of popcorn. It also makes money from game arcades that expand the theater experience.

- ✔ Large fitness center chains make money on enrollment fees and monthly dues, but they also rake in cash by selling fitness-related supplements, exercise clothes, gym bags, and the services of personal trainers.

- ✔ Most magazines earn revenue from subscriptions and newsstand sales, but the lion's share of their income results from the sale of advertising space. However, you can find an exception to every business model. *Consumer Reports* declares in its mission that it accepts no advertising. To maintain its independence and impartiality, it supports itself entirely through the sale of information and products, contributions, and non-commercial grants.

- ✔ Some companies sell their products at a loss — making their money from the sales of related *consumables*. Gillette, for example, doesn't mind selling razors at cost, knowing it will profit from the sale of razor cartridge refills.

- ✔ Online businesses increasingly work to supplement sales revenue with revenue earned through programs such as Google AdSense (`www.google.com/adsense`), which allows information-rich Web sites with reasonable traffic counts to earn revenue by displaying ads on their Web pages.

A first step toward defining your business is to detail how it will make enough money to stay in business — for the sake of the owners, the investors, the customers, the employees, and the community of which your business is a part. The advice (and the accompanying forms) throughout the rest of this chapter helps you define where the money's coming from for your business.

Giving Your Company Its Mission

Your mission statement defines the purpose of your business and the approach you want to take to achieve success. Crafting a mission statement forces you to take a long, hard look at the key parts of your business, making the process a fundamental part of business planning. If you're still not convinced that writing a mission statement is worth the trouble, consider these factors:

✔ **If you're starting a business, a compelling mission statement can convince potential investors that you know who you are and where you want to go.** A great mission statement doesn't make up for a poor business plan, but an ill-defined or uninspired mission statement can make investors think twice about putting money on the table.

✔ **If you're a company of one, a clear mission statement keeps you focused on what you do best.** A mission statement helps keep you on track if you run into problems along the way.

✔ **If you run a growing business, a strong mission statement can help turn employees into team players.** When everyone pursues the same purpose, your team stays pointed in the right direction.

No matter what kind of business you're in, a solid mission statement communicates the purpose of your business to people inside and outside your organization. It tells them who you are and what you do.

Asking basic questions

If you're part of a small organization — and that includes a business of one — you can write your mission statement on your own, although getting an outside perspective never hurts.

If you're part of a medium-size or larger company, enlisting help is essential. You get fresh ideas and insights, and you encourage a sense of ownership in the mission statement, which helps forge a stronger business team.

Whether you move ahead on your own or enlist some outside help, get a head start on the process by jotting down your initial responses to the eight fundamental questions on Form 3-2.

One good way to answer these questions is to assemble a group of creative, energetic people, making sure that the group represents all major areas of your business if you're part of a large company. Schedule several brainstorming sessions (for information on brainstorming, see Chapter 2), following this approach:

- ✔ **Session 1:** Discuss the importance of a mission statement. Ask your team members to answer the Form 3-2 questions.

- ✔ **Session 2:** Discuss your answers in a free and open conversation that gives all responses a fair hearing. Begin to build consensus on the best answers to each question.

- ✔ **Session 3:** Using the framework in the following section, begin to outline your company's mission. If your brainstorming group is large, you may want to select a smaller group to work on the mission statement.

- ✔ **Session 4:** Review, revise, and polish the mission statement draft.

Framing your mission

Mission statements come in all shapes and sizes, each reflecting the nature of the company it represents (see the "Thumbs up, thumbs down" section in this chapter for examples). Some mission statements begin with definitions of company values; others begin with what the companies do; and others begin with descriptions of the customers the companies plan to serve.

In other words, there's no single, perfect way to frame a mission statement.

A good starting point, however, is to use Form 3-3 on the CD-ROM to assemble key ideas about what you do, who you serve, and how you plan to distinguish your company from your competitors. Together, these facts link ideas and form a framework for your mission statement. Figure 3-2 illustrates how a company that offers information and referrals for alternative medical treatments completed the form.

YOUR MISSION STATEMENT QUESTIONNAIRE
1. What exactly do we do?
2. What products and services do we offer?
3. Who is our ideal customer?
4. What customer needs do we meet, and what benefits do we provide?
5. What markets and geographic areas do we serve?
6. What sets us apart from our competition?
7. What's the best thing a satisfied customer can say about us?
8. What gets us most excited about the company's future?

Form 3-2: The eight questions on this form prepare you to write your mission statement.

Figure 3-2:
Fill in the
blanks on
Form 3-3 to
frame a
mission
statement
for your
business.

YOUR MISSION STATEMENT FRAMEWORK

OUR PRODUCT OR SERVICE IS <u>holistic health services.</u>

WE PROVIDE <u>reliable advice about alternative therapies</u>
FOR <u>people with chronic illnesses like cancer or diabetes</u>
WHO ARE DISSATISFIED WITH <u>standard medical care.</u>

UNLIKE <u>other referral networks in our area,</u>
WE OFFER <u>both information and referrals to local providers.</u>

Crafting your mission

After answering basic questions about your business and evaluating how your answers relate to one another, you're ready to transform your ideas into a mission statement.

A few dos and don'ts

Although you don't have any cast-in-cement rules to follow, here are a few guidelines to apply:

- ✔ **Describe who you are, what you do, and what sets you apart.** At the same time, keep your mission statement as short and sweet as possible.

- ✔ **Use plain language.** Your mission statement serves as a guide for people who know your business and people who don't, so make sure that everyone who reads it can understand it. If you can't explain your idea clearly (what's a *multiplatformed B-to-B integration database solution* anyway?), you aren't clear yourself, or you haven't gotten down to the basics yet.

- ✔ **Be specific.** "We will be a leading provider of software" doesn't say much. In contrast, consider the mission of Intuit, maker of Quicken software: "The company's mission is to create new ways to manage personal finances and small businesses that are so profound and simple, customers cannot imagine going back to the old way." Now that gets down to the nitty-gritty.

- ✔ **Be enthusiastic.** A mission statement is meant to sell your message and inspire your troops, so give it a strong sense of conviction and commitment.

- ✔ **Avoid hype and hyperbole.** The latest buzzwords — from "quantum leap forward" to "a mega-paradigm shift" — don't mean much to most people. Stick to simple, straightforward explanations.

Thumbs up, thumbs down

Before you finalize your mission statement, take a look at some examples from real companies, both large and small, to see which statements you find impressive, inspiring, or just plain stronger than the others. Start with the examples in Form 3-4. Whether you write your mission statement on your own or as part of a group, take time to respond to each example with a thumbs up or thumbs down, noting what you like about the winners and what you don't like about the losers. Your answers will provide a stronger sense of what you want your mission statement to look like.

Using your favorite mission statements from Form 3-4 as models, shape your own polished version. Enter your refined mission statement into the blank box provided in Form 3-5 on the CD-ROM.

Putting your mission to work

After you've written a strong, inspiring mission statement, put your words to work.

Whether you do business on your own or run a large company, proclaim your mission loud and clear. If you're a company of one, frame and display a copy of your statement to continually inspire yourself, your clients, your suppliers, and friends of your business. If your company is large, include your mission in your employee handbook. See to it that everyone in the company knows the statement by heart. Get creative: Print it on the back of business cards, post it on your Web site, and include it in company literature.

Above all, put the words into action. Ultimately, your mission statement is worth only what you (and everyone around you) make of it.

EXAMPLES OF REAL-WORLD MISSION STATEMENTS
To be the leading global provider of handheld computing products and to provide developers with the industry-standard platform for creating world-class mobile solutions. (Palm, Inc.) ☐ Thumbs up ☐ Thumbs down Why?
The mission of the Metropolitan Police Department is to prevent crime and the fear of crime, as we work with others to build safe and healthy communities throughout the District of Columbia. (Washington D.C. Police Department) ☐ Thumbs up ☐ Thumbs down Why?
Get it there. (FedEx) ☐ Thumbs up ☐ Thumbs down Why?
To explore, enjoy, and protect the wild places of the earth; to practice and promote the responsible use of the earth's ecosystems and resources; to educate and enlist humanity to protect and restore the quality of the natural and human environment; and to use all lawful means to carry out these objectives. (Sierra Club) ☐ Thumbs up ☐ Thumbs down Why?
To provide our customers with safe, good value, point-to-point air services. To effect and to offer a consistent and reliable product and fares appealing to leisure and business markets on a range of European routes. To achieve this we will develop our people and establish lasting relationships with our supporters. (easyJet.com) ☐ Thumbs up ☐ Thumbs down Why?
The NBA's mission is to be the most respected and successful sports league and sports marketing organization in the world. (National Basketball Association) ☐ Thumbs up ☐ Thumbs down Why?
To manufacture world class quality molds to fill our customers' needs, provide satisfying careers for all our employees, and to earn a fair return in order to allow continuous improvement, and thereby enable our customers, and ourselves, to succeed in the future together. (Stellar Mold & Tool, Inc.) ☐ Thumbs up ☐ Thumbs down Why?

Form 3-4: This form asks you to rate real-world mission statements to see which examples you find most impressive.

United Community Center is a human service agency providing emergency assistance, daycare, social services and recreational activities for low-income children and families at risk in inner city Atlanta, Georgia.
(United Community Center)

☐ Thumbs up   ☐ Thumbs down

Why?

To make guests happy. (Disney World)

☐ Thumbs up   ☐ Thumbs down

Why?

To create an online community, like no other, encompassing every facet of every municipality in the United States; to aid in online economic revitalization in partnership with local businesses and local, state and national government agencies; to publish, maintain and connect a network of community websites designed to entertain, educate and enlighten the residents of our great nation, while maintaining the highest standards of personal morals, business ethics and web etiquette. (A2Z Computing Services)

☐ Thumbs up   ☐ Thumbs down

Why?

Dell's mission is to be the most successful computer company in the world at delivering the best customer experience in markets we serve. In doing so, Dell will meet customer expectations of:

- *Highest quality*
- *Competitive pricing*
- *Best-in-class service and support*
- *Superior corporate citizenship*

- *Leading technology*
- *Individual and company accountability*
- *Flexible customization capability*
- *Financial stability*

(Dell Computer)

☐ Thumbs up   ☐ Thumbs down

Why?

The YMCA of San Francisco builds strong kids, strong families and strong communities by enriching the lives of all people in spirit, mind, and body. (YMCA of San Francisco)

☐ Thumbs up   ☐ Thumbs down

Why?

Page 2 of Form 3-4.

Setting Goals and Objectives

Well-chosen goals and objectives point a new business in the right direction and keep an established company on the right track. Just think about what football would be without end zones or what the Indianapolis 500 would be without a finish line.

✔ *Goals* establish where you intend to go and tell you when you get there. They help improve your overall effectiveness as a company — whether you want to increase your share of the market, for example, or improve your customer service. The more carefully you define your goals, the more likely you are to do the right things and achieve what you wanted to accomplish in the first place.

✔ *Objectives* are the specific steps you and your company need to take in order to reach each of your goals. They specify what you must do — and when.

Think of goals and objectives this way:

✔ *Goals* tell you where you want to go; *objectives* tell you exactly how to get there.

✔ *Goals* can increase your effectiveness; *objectives* back your goals and make you more efficient.

✔ *Goals* are typically described in words; *objectives* often come with numbers and specific dates.

Suppose that your goal is to double the number of people using your Web-conferencing service. Your objectives may be as follows:

✔ Gain awareness by placing print ads in four regional markets and by airing radio ads in two major markets (by June 10)

✔ Attract first-time customers by offering an online giveaway of $1,000 (by June 1)

✔ Cultivate prospects by implementing a permission-based weekly e-mail to 2,500 targeted contacts (by July 10)

✔ Convert 10 percent of prospects to clients, using e-mail reminders (beginning July 25)

Together, goals and objectives form the road map for your company's future. Without them, you risk making wrong turns and wasting precious energy.

The following sections present three ways to approach the task of writing out your goals and objectives. Experiment by using all three approaches. If you come up with more goals than you can handle, the section "Making final choices" later in this chapter can help you sort through your list to choose the most important goals.

When establishing goals and objectives, try to involve everyone who will have the responsibility of achieving those goals and objectives after you lay them out.

Approach #1: Tying goals to your mission

The first approach to specifying goals and objectives begins with a review of your company's mission statement. (Don't have one yet? See the section "Giving Your Company Its Mission" earlier in this chapter.) Use key phrases from your mission statement to define your major goals, which leads into a series of specific business objectives.

The connections between goals and your mission are easy to visualize if you use a flowchart, as shown in Figure 3-3. In this example, key phrases in the mission statement lead to major goals, which lead to specific business objectives.

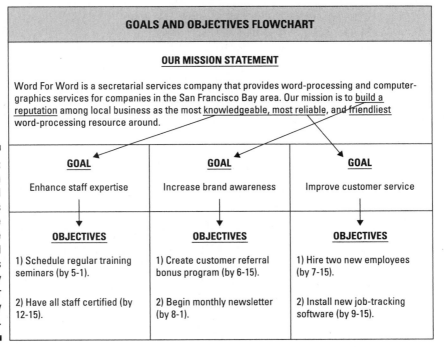

GOALS AND OBJECTIVES FLOWCHART

OUR MISSION STATEMENT

Word For Word is a secretarial services company that provides word-processing and computer-graphics services for companies in the San Francisco Bay area. Our mission is to <u>build a reputation</u> among local business as the most <u>knowledgeable, most reliable,</u> and <u>friendliest</u> word-processing resource around.

GOAL	**GOAL**	**GOAL**
Enhance staff expertise	Increase brand awareness	Improve customer service
OBJECTIVES	**OBJECTIVES**	**OBJECTIVES**
1) Schedule regular training seminars (by 5-1).	1) Create customer referral bonus program (by 6-15).	1) Hire two new employees (by 7-15).
2) Have all staff certified (by 12-15).	2) Begin monthly newsletter (by 8-1).	2) Install new job-tracking software (by 9-15).

Figure 3-3: Use Form 3-5 and follow this example to create goals and objectives tied directly to your company mission.

Use Form 3-6 on the CD-ROM to create a flowchart of goals and objectives based on your mission statement. If your mission statement doesn't suggest a list of goals, you may want to reevaluate it to see whether it really captures what your business is all about.

Approach #2: Using goal-setting ACES

Most goals define positive outcomes that you want your business to achieve, but sometimes you also want to set goals to avoid pitfalls and to eliminate a few weaknesses. To help develop goals that cover all the bases, use the acronym ACES as you tick through the following key questions:

- ✔ **A**chieve: What do you want to attain in the future?

- ✔ **C**onserve: What do you want to hang on to?

- ✔ **E**liminate: What do you want to get rid of?

- ✔ **S**teer clear: What do you want to avoid?

Figure 3-4 shows how an online shopping emporium, a small start-up company with big dreams, applied the ACES questions when creating a set of business goals.

Use Form 3-7 on the CD-ROM to apply the ACES questions to your business situation. Fill in the grid with the first thoughts that come to mind; you can revisit your responses later to see if they lead to a clear set of business goals.

Approach #3: Covering all the bases

One more way to think about business goals is to consider each of the four categories into which most goals fall:

- ✔ **Day-to-day work goals** are directed at increasing the everyday effectiveness of your company. They may involve things like order tracking, office management, or customer follow-up. As a start, name at least one change that you can make in your day-to-day operations that will make a difference in your overall effectiveness. Write it down in the form of a business goal.

- ✔ **Problem-solving goals** address specific challenges that confront your business, such as low employee morale or quality of service issues. List the two biggest problems that face your company, and then write goals that can solve them.

- ✔ **Development goals** encourage the acquisition of new skills and expertise, whether for your employees or for yourself and whether you run a large company or operate as a freelancer or an independent contractor. So, how about formulating at least one development goal for yourself or your company?

✔ **Innovation goals** help you find new ways to improve the products or services that your company offers, how you market your company, or how you distribute and deliver what your company sells. Can you identify any innovative approaches that could make your business more effective in the future? If so, formulate an appropriate goal.

GOALS AND OBJECTIVES BASED ON "ACES"	
ACHIEVE Web site up and running with at least 25 different "storefronts" Successful second round of venture capital	**CONSERVE** Strong sense of employee morale and enthusiasm Staff expertise
ELIMINATE Unnecessary duplication of efforts The competition (ha, ha)	**STEER CLEAR OF** A financial crunch Losing valued staff to other dot-com companies

SET OF BUSINESS GOALS:

- Revise business plan and financial projections.
- Review storefront vendor acquisition strategy.
- Streamline management decision-making process.
- Redesign employee benefits packages.
- Develop a new-hire training curriculum.

Figure 3-4: The four ACES questions lead to establishing business goals.

Use Form 3-8 to review common business goals. Check off any that ring true for your company and add them to your list of goals.

CHECKLIST OF COMMON BUSINESS GOALS
☐ Improve customer satisfaction
☐ Establish or increase brand awareness
☐ Find new markets for products or services
☐ Expand product or service lines
☐ Decrease time to market
☐ Improve employee satisfaction
☐ Increase management communication
☐ Reduce operational costs
☐ Generate new sources of revenue
☐ Become more entrepreneurial
☐ Increase networking with partners

Form 3-8: Sift through the common business goals listed on this form to trigger your goal-oriented thinking.

Making final choices

The three goal-setting approaches in the previous sections lead to a respectable list of goals — maybe more goals than is practical for one business plan. Select the five goals that you think are absolutely, positively essential to your business success. (If you come up with only four, don't worry. If you can't get away with fewer than six or seven, that's okay, too. Just be sure you establish a list of goals long enough to drive your success, but don't overwhelm your ability to focus on each one.)

After you decide on your list, fine-tune each goal, using these guidelines:

- ✔ Keep each goal clear and simple.
- ✔ Be specific.
- ✔ Be realistic.
- ✔ Don't be afraid to push yourself.
- ✔ Make sure that your goals are in sync with your mission.

Tie your goals to objectives, using the goals and objectives flowchart in Form 3-6 or Form 3-9, both of which are on the CD-ROM.

Your goals become part of your written business plan. Long-range goals are wrapped into your business strategy, and immediate goals drive your short-term action plans.

Exploring Values and Vision

Your mission statement and your business goals and objectives provide a road map that keeps your company moving in the right direction, but a map isn't enough by itself.

You also need a good, reliable compass — something that you can count on to keep you oriented, particularly during rocky times. You need a clear set of values and a strong vision:

- ✔ A *values statement* is a set of beliefs and principles that exists behind the scenes to guide your business activities and the way you operate.

- ✔ A *vision statement* is a precise set of words that announces to the world what your company hopes to make of itself. The vision statement defines your highest aspirations for your business. It explains why you're doing what you're doing, in terms of the greatest good you hope to achieve.

For detailed information about the roles of values and vision in businesses across a number of industries, check out *Business Plans For Dummies,* 2nd Edition, by Paul Tiffany and Steven Peterson (Wiley).

Why values matter

A company's strong sense of values can guide it through troubled times and also improve the bottom line. Studies have shown that companies that recover best from man-made catastrophes and emerge with their reputations intact are the ones with the ability to recognize their responsibilities to their customers, shareholders, employees, and the public.

Plenty of real-life examples illustrate just how important a strong sense of values can be when a company faces a crisis. Consider a few recent cases:

✔ In 1999, certain chemicals Coca-Cola products were rumored to have made several hundred people sick in Europe, and the company was slow to respond. The governments of France, Belgium, Luxembourg, and the Netherlands had to order Coke products off the shelves — and the company, scrambling to define what caused the illnesses while simultaneously working to repair its image, issued an apology that amounted to a values statement: "The Coca-Cola Company's highest priority is the quality of our products. One hundred thirteen years of our success have been based on the trust consumers have in that quality. That trust is sacred to us."

Had the company acted on those values faster, Coke could have spared tremendous damage to its reputation and image.

✔ Most oil producers have taken a wait-and-see attitude toward concerns over global climate change. Not British Petroleum (BP). The company announced a "firm overall target" to cut greenhouse gas emissions by 10 percent of their 1990 levels by 2010. This pledge made BP the first oil producer to weigh in with a measurable commitment in this area. The move, guided by the company's environmental values, also had a public relations payoff. The executive director of the Environmental Defense Fund called the announcement "a really magnificent example of a corporation acting responsibly."

✔ When customers discovered that Amazon. com required publishers to pay to have their books featured on the company's Web site, they made their opinions known in a barrage of e-mails. The company responded quickly, pledging to disclose whenever a company paid to have a book featured on its site. "We're always listening to our customers, and it was clear that our customers had a higher expectation for us than for the physical bookselling world," said a company spokesman.

These examples involve big companies, which is hardly surprising because, after all, how often does a business like Mary & Pete's Dry-Cleaning Service make the pages of *The Wall Street Journal?* However, values remain important even when you're self-employed or part of a very small company. The following is just one example:

✔ A chiropractor resigned from a large medical group, dissatisfied with the way patients were treated in the HMO setting. He opened a small practice, which soon attracted more patients than he could treat. He began to make plans to enlarge his practice, move to a larger facility, and hire two more chiropractors, but then he stopped and took stock.

The reason he established a private practice — and one of his guiding values — was his belief that patients deserved individualized, personal care. By growing his business, he realized he would spend more time managing staff and less time treating patients. The one thing he valued above all would be diminished, so he decided not to enlarge the practice. Instead, he formed a network with other chiropractors to whom he could refer patients.

Uncovering values you already hold

So, what are the values that you hold for your company and your business? You can probably come up with a list off the top of your head. People tend to take values for granted — beliefs and principles that serve as a hidden foundation for what we choose to do and how we choose to get things accomplished.

One way to uncover some of your core values is to consider how you would respond to a series of hypothetical situations — situations that call on you to make difficult decisions. Read through the scenarios presented in Form 3-10, and check the boxes that best describe what you would do. Remember, these questions don't have right or wrong answers. The whole idea of this survey is for you to get a better handle on the set of values you already hold.

Writing a values statement

Use your responses to the hypothetical situations in Form 3-10 as a guide when you draft a statement of the values you think are most important to your business. The statement doesn't have to be long and fancy. In fact, a simple list, with values written as plainly and clearly as possible, is an ideal form for a values statement. When you finalize your values, record them on Form 3-11.

Figure 3-5 presents a values statement created by a young entrepreneur who wants to combine his love of art and his commitment to folk artists into a Web-based folk-art emporium.

OUR VALUES STATEMENT

Folk Art Bazaar is dedicated to the following values:

- Using the Internet to form a community of artists and collectors
- Encouraging the preservation of folk art tools and methods
- Offering struggling folk artists a means to make a decent living
- Educating collectors about the value and importance of folk art

Figure 3-5: Your values statement can take the form of a checklist.

VALUES QUESTIONNAIRE

You discover that a product you offer poses a risk if used incorrectly. You've already dropped it from your online catalog, and the manufacturer has promised to send out warnings to everyone who's filled out a warranty card. What other steps would you take?

☐ Let the matter drop, assuming the manufacturer has taken care of things.

☐ E-mail customers who have bought the product, alerting them to the problem as well.

☐ E-mail customers with a warning and an offer of a full refund, no questions asked.

An unhappy customer asks to return an item even though it's beyond the 30-day-return and there's absolutely nothing wrong with it. If you take it back, it can't be resold. What would you most likely do?

☐ Tell them you're sorry, there's nothing you can do after 30 days.

☐ Bend the rules and refund the money, betting on repeat business.

You have meetings with two different clients, both on the opposite side of the country. They've each offered to pay your expenses as well as your fees. You plan to make only one trip to the coast. When it comes time to bill out your travel expenses, what would you do?

☐ Split the airfare evenly between the two clients, giving each a small financial break.

☐ Bill the airfare out to the client you're least interested in working with long term.

☐ Bill each client for the full airfare, assuming this is what they each agreed to.

You learn that by changing suppliers, you could substitute sustainable materials into your product, substantially improving its environmental friendliness. Unfortunately, your costs would rise by about 25 percent. What alternative would you choose?

☐ Continue producing the product in the most cost-effective way.

☐ Switch suppliers and absorb as much of the additional costs as you can.

☐ Pass the costs along after educating customers about the environmental benefits.

You discover that a long-term supplier has been consistently under-billing you for the last five years. What action would you take?

☐ Wait for the supplier to discover the error, assuming it's not your problem.

☐ Correct the current bill.

☐ Alert the supplier and offer to repay all the past under-charges.

You are faced with filling a key position in your company. Where would you most likely turn?

☐ Hire an outside person with the right job skills but no industry experience.

☐ Promote someone inside with talent and drive, and agree to train he or she in the needed skills.

Form 3-10: Describe your responses to the hypothetical situations on this form to uncover your core values.

Your are forced to let one of your team members go. Who would you tend to dismiss first?

☐ The young, inexperienced but energetic college grad who was just recently hired.

☐ The 20-year veteran, loyal and hardworking, but somewhat set in his ways.

An employee suggests that the company institute a strict recycling program. Your offices are already cramped and you worry about cutting into productivity. What's more, not all your employees want to be bothered with recycling. How would you proceed?

☐ Explain that the benefits aren't worth the costs to the company at this point.

☐ Agree to a three-month trial and then evaluate how well it's working.

☐ Ask your employees to vote on the new program and let the majority rule.

You have a smart, creative, and productive person working for you. Unfortunately, the individual is also disruptive, often flouts the rules, and is the source of many complaints in the office. What would you do?

☐ Tolerate the behavior, assuming a bit of tension is good and worth the results.

☐ Try to work with the person to get her to understand what absolutely needs changing.

☐ Terminate the employee to keep the office peace.

You are faced with a dilemma: Either work overtime and miss your child's championship soccer game, or risk letting an important business deadline slip. What would you do?

☐ Work until the project was complete, and then try to make it up to the family.

☐ Work around the soccer game, assuming things will somehow work out at your company.

An employee asks if you are willing to help defer the costs of night school courses. What would your response be?

☐ You agree, but only to reimburse courses directly related to your business needs.

☐ You agree, but only if the employee agrees to work at least a year after course work is complete.

☐ You agree to pay without any preconditions, assuming you'll have a better employee.

You're putting together a compensation package for your top managers. What sort of incentives would you most likely include?

☐ Incentives based primarily on rewarding individual effort and performance.

☐ Incentives that promote team effort and company-wide performance.

Select the top three in terms of their importance in running your business.

☐ Maximize company profits   ☐ Satisfy customers   ☐ Be as ethical as possible

☐ Create fulfilling jobs   ☐ Promote new technologies   ☐ Develop employees

☐ Win product-quality awards   ☐ Maintain long-term growth   ☐ Promote worker safety

☐ Dominate markets   ☐ Protect the environment   ☐ Beat the competition

Writing a vision statement

A *vision statement* is a short phrase or sentence that describes the enduring purpose of your business. To distinguish the vision statement from the other statements you find in this chapter, remember the following list:

- ✔ Your mission statement describes who you are and what you hope to achieve.

- ✔ Your goals and objectives set the mileposts that help you get what you want.

- ✔ Your values statement reminds you of why you're in business in the first place.

- ✔ Your vision statement expresses, in the simplest language possible, what you intend your business to accomplish. This statement captures the essential reasons you're in business: the intentions that will remain constant even when strategies and practices — and even your products and services — change in response to a changing world.

As an example, return to the business venture started by an entrepreneur whose business values are listed in Figure 3-5. His company's mission statement reads as follows:

> To create an online marketplace that brings together unique and creative folk artists from around the world with serious collectors from beginner to expert.

His enduring vision statement:

> To promote the continuing production of folk art and the livelihood of folk artists around the world through Internet technology.

Form 3-12 presents vision statements that take a range of approaches. Check the ones that really grab you. You can refer to them as you write your vision.

In 25 words or less, capture the vision you have for your company. Use the examples you like in Form 3-12 as a starting point, and then use Form 3-13 on the CD-ROM to put your statement in writing. Your vision statement makes its way into your written business plan as part of your company overview.

The vision you have for your company is something you should be very proud of. Make copies for each person you work with. Attach a copy to your computer monitor, and carry one in your daily calendar. Consider including your vision statement in your company brochure or on your letterhead to remind everyone of the essential reasons that you're in business.

Putting Your Principles into Practice

The financial and moral bankruptcies that stole headlines through the earliest years of the 2000s shifted the public spotlight back onto the term *business principles.*

Companies that remain devoted to nothing more than the bottom line will always exist. But, increasingly, companies are realizing that strong values contribute to strong businesses, and they craft their business plans accordingly.

Use your mission, vision, and values to guide the way that your business functions as a socially responsible contributor to the world around you — to your employees, your clients, your industry, and your community. And use your business plan to emphasize your company values and what they mean to all who deal with your business

Enterprise Rent-A-Car proclaims eight founding values in its corporate communications, including in its displays throughout its worldwide branch offices and on its corporate Web site under the title "What We Believe."

An "Enterprise Cultural Compass" helps employees enact the values in their everyday dealings. And, in 2003, the company introduced a Founding Values Award to recognize branches that stand out when exemplifying the company's vision.

Consider incorporating similar principles about trust, loyalty, ethics, and contribution in your values statement, and then create a plan for translating the words into actions whenever the need arises, following these steps:

1. **Whenever you encounter a difficult business or ethical situation, assess your options in light of your values.**

2. **Analyze the consequences of the various actions you can take, considering who will benefit and who will be hurt or damaged by each response.**

3. **Weigh whether your response is honest and fair.**

4. **When you're confident that your response to a difficult decision is consistent with your values and that your actions will be fair and honest, proceed with confidence.**

By knowing and remaining true to your values, when and if you encounter an ethical dilemma, you'll have a strong foundation upon which to build.

And now you know how you put your values to work.

Forms on the CD-ROM

Check out the following forms on the CD-ROM if you need help setting up the ground rules for your business:

Form 3-1	**Basic Business Definition Framework**	Questions to help you determine which business you're really in
Form 3-2	**Your Mission Statement Questionnaire**	Questions designed to generate ideas about your company's mission
Form 3-3	**Your Mission Statement Framework**	A form to help you bring ideas together into a statement of mission
Form 3-4	**Examples of Real-World Mission Statements**	Actual company mission statements along with space to record your impressions
Form 3-5	**Our Mission Statement**	A form on which you can record the final version of your company's mission statement
Form 3-6	**Goals and Objectives Flowchart**	A form to capture your company's goals and objectives as they relate to your mission statement
Form 3-7	**Goals and Objectives based on ACES**	A form to capture your goals and objectives based on things you want to achieve, conserve, eliminate, and avoid
Form 3-8	**Checklist of Common Business Goals**	A checklist of common business goals of many companies
Form 3-9	**Our Major Business Goals**	A form to record your goals
Form 3-10	**Values Questionnaire**	Situations designed to help you identify the values you already hold
Form 3-11	**Our Values Statement**	A form on which to record your values statement
Form 3-12	**Examples of Real-World Vision Statements**	A selection of actual vision statements with space to check off which ones you like
Form 3-13	**Our Vision Statement**	A form on which to record your vision statement

Part II
Developing Your Plan's Components

The 5th Wave   By Rich Tennant

"I'm writing the corporate bylaws. How do you spell, 'guillotine'?"

In this part . . .

Almost all business plans share certain features: They describe the company and what it proposes to do, closely look at the business environment, lay out business and marketing strategies, and crunch the numbers to ensure that the companies will have enough start-up money to get off the ground and enough profit to fuel success well into the future.

Use the five chapters in this part as you create the essential elements of your business plan. Chapter 4 helps you examine your marketplace — sizing up your industry, defining your customers, and checking out your competition. Chapter 5 assesses your strengths, weaknesses, opportunities, and threats and then helps you build a business model and growth strategy that capitalize on your situation. Chapter 6 examines your key business capabilities to help you focus your plan on what you do best. Chapter 7 helps you sketch your all-important marketing plan. Finally, Chapter 8 tackles the numbers, walking you through the creation of your income statement, balance sheet, cash-flow statement, financial projections, and budget.

Chapter 4

Understanding Your Business Environment

In This Chapter

▶ Investigating your industry

▶ Getting to know your customers

▶ Tracking your competition

You're writing a business plan, so it's a pretty safe bet that you're launching a new business or preparing to take an established company to all-new heights.

By now, you've probably settled on a great business idea (see Chapter 2). And maybe (hopefully) you've crafted your mission and vision statements (Chapter 3) and set crystal-clear goals, objectives, targets, and timelines (also discussed in Chapter 3) to guide your way.

But guess what: Even if your brainchild is the biggest thing since sticky notes, it isn't enough to ensure success on its own. For one thing, you need to find customers. Plus, you need to establish a pretty compelling reason (or more than one reason) for those customers to choose your offering over competing alternatives that are available around the corner or over the Internet. In short, you need to take a long, careful look at your business environment before you leap into action.

Use this chapter as you conduct a straightforward analysis of your industry, including how you fit into it and the forces that will affect your success. Take an equally close look at your customers and prospective customers — whether they're individual consumers or business clients. Finally, assess your competition, identifying exactly who and what you're up against, what competitive challenges are on your horizon, and what you have to do to move the market in your direction.

Zooming In on Your Industry

Your business may be one-of-a-kind, with products and services that are in a class by themselves, but you're also part of a larger industry: retail, telecommunications, entertainment, travel, publishing — or any of a hundred others. Even if you run a nonprofit organization (see Chapter 12), you're part of a contingent of worthy causes all seeking contributions from the same supporters. Regardless of your field, your strategy for success needs to begin with a clear sense of your industry and how you fit into it. Use this section as you figure out how you fit into your industry.

Seeing your industry's big picture

Understanding the larger forces at work in your industry is a crucial part of business planning:

- ✔ What are the long-term trends in your business arena?
- ✔ Is your industry growing fast or treading water?
- ✔ Is entering the market difficult?
- ✔ How fast are technologies, regulations, or other fundamentals of your industry changing?

Answers to questions like these are key to creating a robust business plan. By compiling a good overview of your industry, you gain a better sense of how and where your venture fits in. Chances are, along the way, you'll discover a few things you didn't know — insights that will help you sidestep trouble and chart a better course.

Complete the Form 4-1 questionnaire to summarize what you already know about your industry and, even more important, what you still need to find out.

What you don't know *can* hurt your business, so instead of leaving questions in Form 4-1 unanswered, take the time to do some research and to uncover the facts. For example, if a few suppliers control most of your industry's material costs, you can make sound decisions based on that knowledge — or you can overlook that fact and have it come back to haunt you later.

After you complete the questionnaire, look over your answers and single out areas that are most apt to influence your future:

- ✔ How serious of a competitive threat do you face?
- ✔ Who really drives your industry: customers, distributors, or suppliers?
- ✔ Will you be able to ride the rising tide of an expanding industry, or will you have to find ways to succeed in spite of a general industry slowdown?

Diamonds are forever, but what about De Beers?

For most of the 20th century, De Beers wasn't just a player in the diamond industry, but also the diamond industry's dominant force. Using both ethical and underhanded practices — including the use of West African mercenaries — De Beers controlled the world's diamond supply. The result: The company kept diamonds scarce and diamond prices high.

By the mid-1980s, however, changes that De Beers had little control over threatened the company's dominance. New diamond mines opened in Canada and Australia, conflicts in Africa led to widespread diamond smuggling, and the collapse of the Soviet Union eroded the company's influence over diamond producers in that area. In response, De Beers stockpiled billions of dollars worth of diamonds to keep supply down and prices up.

When that strategy wasn't enough to protect profits, De Beers fundamentally changed the way it did business. It began selling off its stock-piled diamonds while increasing production from mines around the world. Instead of trying to control the world market, the company decided to focus its efforts on increasing demand for diamonds worldwide.

More changes still shadow the diamond industry horizon, including the emergence of highly competitive new retailers and the introduction of diamond synthetics that even people in the industry have a hard time distinguishing from the real thing.

Time will tell how these changes affect the company's fortunes — or the price of a diamond ring. Meanwhile, this venerable old company continues to analyze its industry and adapt its business plan to fit the shifting environment. If the company is successful, De Beers, like diamonds, could be forever.

Any one of the forces, trends, or issues you identify just may be the one that holds the key to your success.

Summarize the findings from your industry analysis and include your overview in the business environment section of your written business plan.

Paying the price of admission

Most business-planning efforts are designed to seize an opportunity — either by launching a business start-up or expanding an established company into new market arenas. In either case, inevitable competitive hurdles await.

INDUSTRY ANALYSIS QUESTIONAIRE
1. How many competitors do you have? ☐ Many ☐ Some ☐ Few
2. Has a new competitor entered the market recently? ☐ Yes ☐ No
3. Have any competitors in your market area gone out of business recently? ☐ Yes ☐ No
4. How difficult is it for new competitors to enter your market area? ☐ Very difficult ☐ Difficult ☐ Easy
5. How important is technological change to your business? ☐ Very important ☐ Somewhat important ☐ Not important
6. What's the current market demand in your industry? ☐ Growing ☐ Stable ☐ Declining
7. Is there an untapped market that your industry can take advantage of? ☐ Yes ☐ Maybe ☐ No
8. What do customers care about most in your business? ☐ Price ☐ Features ☐ Service ☐ All of the above
9. How easily can customers find alternatives outside your industry? ☐ Very easily ☐ With difficulty ☐ Not at all
10. How much bargaining power do big customers have in your industry? ☐ A lot ☐ Some ☐ None
11. How much influence do large suppliers have in setting terms? ☐ A lot ☐ Some ☐ None
12. How much power do distributors wield in your industry? ☐ A lot ☐ Some ☐ None
13. What are typical profit margins like in your business? ☐ Strong ☐ Average ☐ Weak
14. What is the trend for overall costs in your industry? ☐ Declining ☐ Stable ☐ Rising
15. How would you describe the general health of your industry? ☐ Very healthy ☐ Somewhat healthy ☐ Ailing

Form 4-1: Use the questions in this form on the CD-ROM to analyze your industry.

In any industry, obstacles — known as *entry barriers* — challenge new contenders. If the barriers are low, almost anyone can join the fray. When they walls are high, entry is harder and fewer competitors make the plunge.

Consider the following examples:

✔ Suppose you're thinking about starting a printing business. Right off the bat, one entry barrier is the capital cost associated with acquiring production equipment. To overcome the barrier, you may come up with creative ways to lease the equipment or figure out how to outsource a portion of your production until you get up to full speed.

✔ If you're planning a clothing shop that eventually will have to compete with chain stores, your entry barrier is the competitive advantage of large retailers whose pricing reflects a built-in *economy of scale*. Simply put, large retailers can buy merchandise at a lower cost because they buy so much of it at a time. To overcome the barrier, you probably need to compete on attributes other than price: the quality of your fabrics, for example, or your special services or unique fashions.

✔ If you're opening a hair salon in a town with a handful of successful beauty shops, your biggest entry barrier is customer loyalty to existing stylists. To prevail, you have to give customers a reason to change; for example, you can institute a bring-a-friend-for-free haircut or onsite daycare service.

Form 4-2 presents typical entry barriers that await new competitors in a variety of industries. Check the ones that apply to your industry and marketplace. Use the space at the end of the form to add barriers unique to your business situation.

On a scale of 1 to 10, with 1 being the most significant possible impediment to your success, rank the entry barriers that you expect to encounter. Look closely at the top three barriers on your list. These barriers represent the biggest hurdles you face in getting your business up and running. When you write your business plan, acknowledge these barriers and detail how you intend to overcome the obstacles they represent.

Defining Your Customers

When you get right down to it, customers are the key to business success. Without enough of them, you don't have a business at all, so spend the time to understand precisely who your customers are, what makes them tick, and exactly what they want from your business. If you're going to succeed — which is the point of all this planning — you need to know what attracts people to your business in the first place and what makes them come back to buy again and again.

BARRIERS TO ENTRY CHECKLIST
☐ Capital costs (lots of money required up front)
☐ Distribution systems (customers are difficult to reach or product is difficult to deliver)
☐ Organization (complex operations are necessary for success)
☐ Raw materials (supplies are in high demand or are difficult to secure)
☐ New technology (sophisticated skills required)
☐ Scale economies (the bigger you are, the lower your costs)
☐ Regulations (legal obstacles)
☐ Patents (competitive hurdles)
☐ Customer loyalty (existing businesses have strong market advantage)
☐ Customer switching costs (it costs the customer to change)

Form 4-2: Use this form on the CD-ROM to flag the barriers that can affect your new business or expansion plans.

Developing your customer profile

The more you know about your customers, the more you know about where to find others just like them, how to reach them with media or other marketing communications, and what kind of messages, offers, and incentives move them toward buying.

Three key terms apply:

✔ **Geographics:** This term describes *where* your customers and your potential customers — or prospects — reside. When you know this information, you can target your marketing efforts into specific regions, counties, states, countries, or zip codes.

Building entry barriers

If your company is entering a new (to you) industry or market area, expect to face some barriers as you seek to compete profitably with companies already up and running in your business. At the same time, think about building some barriers of your own in an effort to up the ante for potential competitors who want to follow you into your business arena or market area.

Entry barriers come in a wide range of forms, including

- **Patents:** By protecting your idea and production process, you can block others from legally using your approach for a number of years. Visit the Web site of the U.S. Patent and Trademark office at www.uspto.gov for information.

- **Cost and pricing advantages:** Consider building a cash reserve to allow your business to cut prices or enhance promotions, if necessary, to force new competitors to operate at an unsustainable loss. Also, consider committing volume businesses to key suppliers to establish relationships that result in preferential pricing, which lowers the costs to your business and prices to your customers.

- **Marketing advantages:** Especially if you're the first in your market with a particular

product or service, commit adequate marketing resources to quickly build market awareness, a strong brand, and loyal customers (Chapter 7 focuses on the topic of marketing). The faster you establish your product or service as the preferred choice, the more expensive unseating you in the marketplace becomes for newcomers.

- **Regulations and trade restrictions:** Tariffs and quotas work as entry barriers to international and some domestic markets. If your industry is subject to trade restrictions, join industry associations, attend industry conferences, and follow industry news to keep up on the rules under which your business needs to operate. You should also participate in the protection of your markets from those who aren't authorized to participate.

- **Economic factors:** The price of equipment, licensing, research and development, or other mandatory expenses involved in setting up shop deter other competitors from entering your arena. As you establish your business, think in preemptive terms, selecting equipment and processes around which you can build a distinct and impenetrable advantage.

- **Demographics:** This term describes *who* your prospects are in factual terms, including age, gender, race, education level, marital status, income level, and household size.

- **Psychographics:** This term describes *lifestyle characteristics*, including attitudes, beliefs, and opinions that affect customer-purchasing patterns.

- **Behavioral:** This term describes *how* customers buy, including such product usage rate tendencies, level of loyalty, purchase occasions, and whether customers buy for price or for performance, on impulse or after careful consideration, based of personal choice or on the recommendation of others, and other such behavioral patterns.

Use Form 4-3 to develop your customer profile. If yours is an existing business, create a best-take summary of your current customers. If you're writing a plan for a new business, describe the person you believe is most apt to purchase your offering.

Conducting customer research

To paint a clear picture of your customer, undertake some research activities. Your efforts may involve highly customized efforts tailored specifically to your business clientele, or they may rely on available market analyses called *secondary research,* which you can apply to your business situation. The approaches and budgets vary widely. What never changes is the need to know exactly who's apt to buy from your business, how to reach those people, and what to say when you have their attention.

Compiling a firsthand analysis of your customer

Large companies spend huge budgets conducting customized market research. Fortunately, simpler and cheaper ways to obtain a picture of your customers are available. Consider the following ideas:

- ✔ **Stop, look, and listen.** You can discover plenty simply by observing customers. If you're in the retail business, watch where customers go inside your store and what products they linger over the longest. When you go to an industry trade show, watch which booths and exhibits attract the biggest crowds. Conduct informal surveys, asking prospects about their reactions to various products, services, and features.

- ✔ **Create a dialogue.** If you're thinking about improving a product or developing a service, invite your best customers to become part of the creative process. Ask what they like and don't like about existing offerings. What would they change? What features would they add?

  Response cards also offer a good way to obtain customer input. If you have a Web site, consider an online version. Offer a small incentive for customers to participate — a gift, membership in your company's VIP club, and a future discount are options.

- ✔ **Go virtual.** If your customers are far-flung, consider a virtual focus group by arranging for selected customers to meet in an online chat room to discuss a particular aspect of your product or service. As in a traditional focus group, offer participants a little something in return for their time and ideas.

CUSTOMER PROFILE QUESTIONNAIRE

Geographics: **Where do your customers and prospects live?** Knowing this information helps you target your marketing efforts.

List neighborhoods, zip codes, counties, states, or international regions that include concentrations of customers. (You can collect information off checks or invoices, data from credit card transactions, or zip code information at the time of purchase or using surveys.)

List the areas where inquiries come from. (Monitor the origin of incoming phone calls, ad and direct-mail responses, and Web site visitors.)

Demographics: **What are the facts about your customers?** Knowing this information helps you direct media and promotions directly at the people who match your customer profile.

Gender:	___ % Male	___ % Female	
Age:	___ % under 12	___ % 13-19	___ % 20-30
	___ % 30-40	___ % 50-60	___ % Senior citizens
Education level:	___ % High school graduates	___ % College graduates	
	___ % Advanced degrees	___ % Current students	

Household Composition: Find out if most of your customers are single, married, divorced, widowed, parents with children at home, couples with no children at home, heads of families, grandparents, recent empty-nesters, and so on.

Other facts:

Do most customers own or rent their homes?

Into which income levels do they fall?

What is their nationality? Ethnicity? Language?

What are their occupations?

Psychographics: **What makes your customers tick?** Knowing this information helps you create marketing messages that interest prospects and move them to action.

Interests: What are their favorite hobbies or pastimes? What magazines do they read? What kind of music do they prefer?

Beliefs: What opinions do they hold? Do they have strong social, religious or political affiliations? What do they value?

Purchasing patterns: Do they buy on impulse or after careful consideration? Are they loyal customers or highly susceptible to competing offers? Are they cost-conscious or are attributes, such as quality or prestige, of more importance? Do they prefer name brands? Do they use the Internet to gather information? Do they make buying decisions on their own or based on the advice of others?

Form 4-3: The questions in this form guide the development of your customer profile.

The closer you get to knowing your customers, the more success you'll experience in your marketplace.

Casting a wider net

Supplement your customer and prospect knowledge with secondary research:

- ✔ **Contact your industry association and the major media groups that serve your industry to obtain their analyses of the consumers in your market arena.** Study the findings to discover more about the profile of the people who buy products like the ones you're offering.

- ✔ **Cruise the Internet, where you can find a vast database of customer responses to everything from the latest bestseller to the most sophisticated digital equipment on the market.** Publishers and authors can track which books are selling well hour by hour. Winemakers can follow which vintages customers are snapping up. Consultants can research the hottest business topics. Digital gadget makers can survey customer reaction to cutting-edge technology as they design the next generation of electronic toys.

  To find sites relevant to your business, conduct Web searches for products like the ones you offer. In the search results, you may find sites where customers like yours weigh in on what they think. When you find such a site, visit it regularly. You're bound to get an earful — or eyeful — of useful information.

- ✔ **The reference area of your public or university library most likely has copies of the *SRDS Lifestyle Market Analyst* and the *CACI Sourcebook of ZIP Code Demographics*, which can help you locate geographic areas with concentrations of residents who match your customer profile.** This information can be invaluable as you pinpoint regions for business expansion.

Getting research assistance

If your research involves questionnaires, focus groups, or phone or in-person interviews, consider bringing in specialists to help you maintain objectivity and convey professionalism throughout the process. Contact research firms, marketing firms, and public-relations companies for help.

Another good resource is your Small Business Development Center. To find a nearby center, visit the Small Business Association Web site at www.sba.gov/sbdc and click on the Your Nearest SBDC button.

As you dive into the task of identifying and describing your customers, consider flipping through *Small Business Marketing For Dummies* (Wiley) by yours truly. It includes research instructions, such as advice regarding when and how to use the research approaches summarized in Table 4-1.

Table 4-1	Customer Research Approaches		
Method	*Purpose*	*Advantages*	*Challenges*
Questionnaires and surveys	To obtain general information	Anonymous, inexpensive, easy to analyze, and easy to format and conduct	Impersonal, feedback may not be accurate, and wording can skew results
Interviews	To obtain information and probe answers	Develop customer relationships, are adaptable to each situation, and access fuller range of information	Time consuming, reliant on good interviewers, and difficult to analyze
Observation	To document actual buyer behavior	Anonymous, immediate findings, and relatively easy to implement	Can be difficult to interpret findings and to target which behaviors to monitor; can also be expensive
Documentation review	To study factual history of clients and transactions	Readily available, not disruptive to operations, not subject to interpretation	Time-consuming, research may be incomplete, and research is limited to previously collected data
Focus groups	To find out about and compare customer experiences and reactions	Convey information to customers, collect customer impressions	Require expert facilitation and advance scheduling; difficult to analyze findings

Create an agenda for times, places, and ways to get closer to your customers. Consider it your personal customer intelligence plan. To get started, use the customer intelligence checklist in Form 4-4.

CUSTOMER INTELLIGENCE CHECKLIST
1. Places and times to observe real customers in our marketplace: • • • •
2. Ways to interact with customers around our products and services: • • • •
3. Web sites relevant to our customer feedback, behavior, and analysis: • • • •

Form 4-4: Use this form to establish an agenda for collecting customer information.

Sharpening your customer focus

Remember the old saying that knowledge is power? Well, when planning and directing your company's business activities, customer knowledge equals business power. And close is nowhere near good enough.

Consider the case of a new business specializing in online sales of lingerie. When the owners wrote their first-take customer profile, it read like this:

> We're going after Internet shoppers with a sense of style, adventure, and playfulness but who are a bit reluctant to shop for intimate apparel at a brick-and-mortar store. Our customers are women who buy our products for themselves or for significant others.

Not long after writing this profile, the owners realized that this snapshot left out some crucial aspects. How is the customer likely to find the Web site in the first place? Why would she choose to buy here rather than somewhere else? What motivates her to buy — price, quality, or special features? Is she likely to be a repeat buyer? What convinces her to come back and shop again? As the owners expanded their customer profile, here's what they added:

> Most of our customers are 18 to 35 years old and are single or recently married. They live in urban areas, especially on the East and West Coasts. They're Internet savvy, and they tend to be affluent and sophisticated. They discover our site primarily through ads placed in women's magazines and on selected Web sites. When making buying decisions, they value quality — determined by the unique designs and fine materials used in our products — more than price. The bottom line: Our products make our customers feel beautiful. By delivering on this promise, we can develop a loyal clientele of repeat buyers.

See the difference? The expanded description includes demographic characteristics — where customers live, their ages, and lifestyle information — as well as psychographic information about what drives their buying decisions.

Based on the expanded customer description, the business owners were able to hone a sharp marketing strategy. First, they realized that their customers viewed lingerie purchases as a means to an end — to looking and feeling beautiful and sensual. Knowing this information helped the owners create attention-getting ads that converted to Web-site traffic and online sales. Second, their customer snapshot revealed that the company's success relied on loyal buyers who kept coming back on their own — and referring their friends, as well. This trend sparked the decision to add an online weekly health and beauty magazine featuring columns by cosmetologists, before-and-after stories, and an interactive Q&A discussion area.

Use everything you know about your clientele to create your customer snapshot, and use Form 4-5 on the CD-ROM to condense it down to two or three plain-English sentences that describe the person most likely to buy from your business.

Make the description of your customers part of your business plan. Doing so keeps your business and its marketing efforts focused and effective.

```
┌─────────────────────────────────────────────────────────────┐
│                    CUSTOMER SNAPSHOT                          │
├─────────────────────────────────────────────────────────────┤
│                                                              │
│  Our target customers can best be described as _____   │
│                                                              │
│  _____ │
│                                                              │
│                                                              │
│  These customers are looking for _____ │
│                                                              │
│  _____ │
│                                                              │
│                                                              │
│  We will reach many of our target customers through _____ │
│                                                              │
│  _____ │
│                                                              │
│                                                              │
│  These customers will buy from us rather than our            │
│  competitors because they                                    │
│                                                              │
│  _____ │
│                                                              │
│  _____ │
│                                                              │
└─────────────────────────────────────────────────────────────┘
```

Form 4-5: Use this form on the CD-ROM to create a descriptive snapshot of your customer following this example.

Describing your ideal customer

Every customer is important to your business, but the truth is that some are simply more important than others, and a precious few are absolutely essential.

The difference between good and great customers is huge. If you're already in business, you know firsthand that some customers are more profitable, more pleasant, more apt to buy frequently, and more likely to spread good words about your business than others. And those customers are the ones you want to amass.

Separating the good from the best — and the best from the worst

Your best customers

 ✔ Ask you to do things you do well

 ✔ Appreciate what you do and willingly pay the price that you ask

> ✔ Make reasonable requests that lead to improvement and expansion of your skills and services

> ✔ Inspire your business to move in new and profitable directions

Great customers are the ones who you want to go overboard for. Heap on the special services, pile on the appreciation, and do what you can to keep them loyal to your business. You'll be doubly rewarded with repeat purchases and invaluable word of mouth.

Good customers are the ones who appreciate your offerings, buy your products, and pay your bills on time and with courtesy. But they can be transitory — here today, and gone tomorrow. And what often lures them away is a better offer. They may never become loyal patrons of your business because they value special deals more than they value long-term business relationships.

Your *worst customers* are prospects who are simply mismatched to your offerings. They're excessively negative, unreasonably demanding, and maybe even abusive to your staff and your business systems. Watch for these indicators to flag customers you're better off not having in your clientele:

> ✔ They consume considerable time and attention yet buy very little.

> ✔ They demand unreasonable concessions on pricing, service, or product alternations, and, if you consented, they would harm your business.

> ✔ They demoralize your staff.

> ✔ They refuse to pay your fair price for your offering or refuse to comply with your billing and service standards.

> ✔ They act dissatisfied no matter what you do for them.

Defining perfection

Indulge in a little fantasy. Conjure up an image of your ideal customer, whether that customer is an individual buyer or a business client (discussed later in this chapter). Imagine the sort of person who eagerly buys your products or services, raves about you to friends and colleagues, and returns to purchase from your business on a regular basis.

Get specific. Use the Form 4-6 questionnaire to detail aspects that differentiate your ideal customers from all others. List their four or five distinguishing traits on Form 4-7 on the CD-ROM.

IDEAL CUSTOMER QUESTIONNAIRE

1. What kinds of products or services do your ideal customers seek from your business? What special features do they request?

2. When your ideal customer comes to your business, what need or want is that person looking to address? Think beyond product features. Consider what product benefits the customer is seeking and what kinds of emotional outcomes the customer is hoping for.

3. When making buying decisions, what does your ideal customer value most? Cost? Quality? Features? Convenience? Reliability? Your reputation? Your unique expertise? Your after-sale support? Your product guarantee?

4. How do your ideal customers reach your business? Referrals? Ads? Direct mailings? Web site? Promotions? Cold calls? Sales presentations? By simply walking by your front door?

5. What are the buying patterns of your ideal customers? How often do they buy from your business? How large is each sales transaction? What combination of your product offerings do they purchase? Do they buy on impulse or after careful consideration? Do they buy full-priced offerings or seek discounts or sales?

6. How would you describe your ideal customer? Where does that person live? What is the person's age, gender, occupation, income level, educations level, family composition, ethnicity, and nationality?

7. How would you describe your ideal customer's lifestyle? What are his or her hobbies? Social or church affiliations? Leisure-time activities? Etc.

Form 4-6: Answer these questions, using this form on the CD-ROM, to detail what you know about the ideal customer for your business.

Segmenting your customers into buyer groups

By lumping similar customers together, companies can target their offerings to select groups of people who all respond in similar ways.

Consider the example of a new residential golf community selling homes and golf-club memberships primarily to affluent middle-age buyers. After gathering customer data, the developers found that buyers from the nearby market area wanted to upgrade their housing by buying homes with better views and amenities than they enjoyed at their previous addresses. On the other hand, buyers from out-of-area urban markets were more interested in the feeling of escape that the new community offered with its rural surroundings and wide range of nearby outdoor recreation activities.

Studying further, the developers discovered that even buyers from out-of-area urban markets broke into two segments. One segment lived fewer than six hours by car from the new community and wanted second homes to enjoy on long weekends and vacations. The segment that lived more than six hours away shopped for a dream retirement home or for a new residence from which to telecommute or to run a home-based business.

Armed with this information, the developers created direct-mail campaigns to appeal to the unique desires of prospects in each geographic market.

Analyze how your customers break into market segments. Use Form 4-8 to uncover which groups of buyers seek which kinds of products and how their interests vary from other customer groups. For an example, see Figure 4-1.

Include your market segmentation information in the business environment section of your written business plan.

Doing business with business customers

B2B is shorthand for the great contingent of businesses that sell to other businesses rather than to individual consumers.

Business and individual customers have plenty in common. They share concerns about price, quality, convenience, service, reliability, and expertise. All those aspects add up to value in their minds. But you can also expect some important distinctions in how business customers buy:

- ✔ Sales or promotional blitzes don't sway them.

- ✔ They rarely buy on impulse.

- ✔ The buying patterns of their customers and what's happening in their industries affect their buying behavior.

- ✔ Their buying decisions often rely on approval from managers, owners, financial consultants, or others.

For success selling to business customers, you really need to organize. Use Form 4-9 to create a profile for each business client and major prospect, and then circle the characteristics that the companies have in common. Use these common traits to create an ideal business customer snapshot — two or three paragraphs describing the kind of business customers you want to target. For assistance, use Form 4-5 (Customer Snapshot) on the CD-ROM.

BASIC MARKET SEGMENTATION FRAMEWORK

1. WHO is buying?

45 percent of buyers are local residents. They're almost evenly split between empty-nester couples and families with children living at home. They are affluent, active, and social.

35 percent of buyers are from areas an easy driving distance away. They are primarily 50 years old and over, with children no longer living at home. They own businesses or are in executive positions.

30 percent of buyers are from areas at least a six-hour drive away. About half are 50 years old and over and are retired or semi-retired, and half are 40-plus and self-employed.

2. WHAT do they buy?

Local residents buy upgraded residences and the region's newest and most renowned golf course and community.

Residents from nearby communities buy second homes from which to enjoy weekend and vacation retreats, golf, and outdoor recreation.

Residents from distant communities buy homes for retirement or relocation purposes.

3. WHY do they buy?

Local residents are inspired by quality, status, social setting, and premium golfing.

Residents from nearby communities are inspired by the location, quality homes, security (a gated community), and recreation — golf, skiing, river sports, and cultural offerings — that are all close enough for them to frequently enjoy.

Residents from more distant communities are inspired by the dream of a top-quality home in an ideal setting for retirement or business relocation.

Figure 4-1:
Dividing customers into market segments.

If you have a business-to-business company, include a detailed description of the kind of business customers you intend to serve in your business plan.

Sizing Up Your Competition

Unless you're very clever — and extremely lucky —your business isn't the only one on the horizon with a great idea and a serious plan to win over eager customers in your particular market.

BUSINESS CUSTOMER PROFILE ON COMPANY: _____

1. Company description:

- **Company name**
- **Industry**
- **Yearly revenue**

- **Number of employees**
- **Years in business**
- **Location**

- **Principal contact**

- **Other relevant information**

---

2. What are the major benefits you offer this company?

---

3. What are the essential qualities the company is looking for in a supplier?

---

4. Do the key decision-makers in the company tend to be engineers or marketing people?

---

5. Does this company use both small and larger suppliers?

---

6. Does the company have a policy of requiring more than one supplier?

---

7. Does the company purchase centrally, or are buyers scattered around?

---

8. Does this company require several levels of approval for purchases?

---

9. Is the company's business booming, steady, or facing increased competition?

---

10. Are there major changes inside this company that might result in opportunities for new business?

Form 4-9: If you sell to business clients, do your homework first. Use this form as you collect information.

Except for government agencies and communist states, everyone has competition. Even if your business idea launches a brand-new industry, you can expect a throng of new competitors to quickly emerge, each fighting tooth and nail to grab their slices of the market pie. Your success depends largely on how well you understand your competitors and how successful you are at distinguishing yourself from all the alternatives that exist in the minds of your potential customers. (See Chapter 7 to dig deeper into the world of competition.)

Competitors challenge you to run your business better by forcing you to distinguish yourself from the crowd. Competition isn't necessarily a bad thing — as long as you know exactly who and what you're up against.

Identify your five biggest competitors — those businesses that are most likely to take business away from you if you're not careful. Can't come up with five? Name as many as you can and record your list on Form 4-10.

Using cloak-and-dagger methods

If your plan is to open a gift shop on Main Street, scoping out your competition isn't difficult. Browse through neighboring shops that cater to the same kinds of customers you hope to attract, and inquire around — by talking to your banker, other retailers, business leaders, clerks at City Hall, and others — to see what businesses are planning to open in the near future. You can then uncover stealth competitors (see the following section), including online competitors who want to take a bite out of your market. You're ready to roll!

For many businesses, however, finding out what you need to know about the competition is a bit more complicated. You have to work harder to find out the following information:

- What products or services they offer
- Who their customers are
- What their strengths are
- Where their weaknesses are

Corporate strategists call this information-gathering effort *competitive intelligence,* or CI. Fortunately, the Internet provides a great starting point. Start at your competitors' Web sites. They can provide a goldmine of information, from product specifications to client lists. Many company sites include press-release archives, which often contain useful information about future strategies and plans.

Another resource is right down the street at your public library. Consult the *Readers' Guide to Periodical Literature* to find magazine articles about a given industry or company. You can also ask for a LEXUS/NEXUS search (the library may charge you a few bucks) to find articles that appear in newspaper business sections.

To guide you in your sleuthing, use the competitive intelligence checklist in Form 4-11.

Identifying your stealth competitors

You can usually spot direct competitors pretty easily. They look a lot like you, offer similar products or services, and go after the same markets. But you have to watch out for less-obvious competitors — known as *stealth competitors* — who can catch you off guard, winning competitive battles before you even realize they're around. Your stealth competitors go after the same customers you do, but in different, sometimes unexpected, ways.

Suppose you're starting a yoga studio. Your direct competitors are other yoga centers within, say, a 20-mile radius. But under-the-radar threats also lurk. Local fitness centers, spas, the YMCA, and the Parks and Recreation Department may also offer yoga classes. Plus, a slew of yoga videos or DVDs are available to rent or buy. And the stealth competition doesn't stop there. Think about it: Why do people sign up for yoga classes in the first place? To relax, to become more fit and flexible, and to help ease joint pains. So any place that caters to those needs — gyms that offer water aerobics classes, for example, or meditation centers — vies for your customer, too.

Imagine yourself in your customers' shoes, and consider every possible alternative — near or far — to the solution your business offers.

Traditionally, local businesses catering to local customers competed with other local businesses. But those days are gone. Here are a few examples:

- The corner bookstore that used to compete with the bookstore around the corner now goes head-to-head with the behemoth online booksellers.

- The local travel agent, once an indispensable resource for trip planners, now competes with online sites that allow travelers to book hotels, flights, car rentals — even ski equipment — on their own. Suddenly, travel agencies are lonely places, except for the forward-thinking agents who read their competitive tea leaves and focused their efforts on particular market segments and services, such as group sales or high-end, customized tour packages.

COMPETITIVE INTELLIGENCE CHECKLIST ON COMPANY: _____
☐ Mission and vision statements
☐ Years in business
☐ Organization charts
☐ Executive biographies
☐ Job postings
☐ Customer base
☐ Information on products and services
☐ Pricing data
☐ Research and development plans
☐ Distribution and delivery channels

Form 4-11: Use this form as a road map to the kind of information that's worth uncovering about your competition.

When unmasking stealth competitors, don't limit your thinking to Internet offerings. Here's an example of a business blindsided by the impact of a research breakthrough: Makers of flea collars and flea shampoos are slowly fading away because of once-a-month wonder drugs that wipe out fleas.

Scary, huh? For these reasons, you need to take extra time to come up with a list of as many potential stealth competitors as you can. Use the questionnaire in Form 4-12 so you identify competitors you may not recognize right off the bat.

After you uncover your stealth competitors, keep track of them, using Form 4-13 on the CD-ROM.

POTENTIAL STEALTH COMPETITORS QUESTIONNAIRE
1. What technologies could change your business overnight, and what companies might make them happen?
2. What businesses can you think of that may consider expanding into your markets in the future?
3. What companies may develop products and services to compete directly with you in the future?
4. Which of your customers could potentially become your competitors?
5. Which of your suppliers or vendors could turn around and compete with you?

Form 4-12: Answer the questions in this form to uncover indirect threats to your business.

Staying a step ahead

Keep in front of your competitors by anticipating and countering their next moves. Predicting the future isn't easy; you have to think through your competitors' options so you're better prepared to defend your position. Aim to emulate a chess master who routinely thinks five or six moves ahead.

Most likely, your competitors' next moves will build on their relative capabilities — areas in which they feel they have advantages over their competition. A competitor whose strength is in Research and Development may be planning to develop and introduce a new product; a competitor strong in marketing and sales may have plans to undertake a market expansion; and a competitor whose strong suit is customer loyalty may plan to grow its business by adding customers, resulting in increased market penetration or market share.

More often than not, companies compete in the following ways:

- Lower prices
- Better service
- Highly targeted customer focus
- Unique and attention-getting products or services

On Form 4-10, you record the names of your top five competitors. Now use Form 4-14 to describe each competitor's strongest suit or key capability — along with the strategic move you think each competitor is most likely to make in the next year or so. No one can hold you to your predictions, but by taking the time to think through the possibilities, you can fine-tune your business plan and prepare yourself for the competitive battles ahead.

OUR BIGGEST COMPETITORS AND THEIR LIKELY MOVES		
Competitor	**Key Capability**	**Likely Strategic Move**
1.		
2.		
3.		
4.		
5.		

Form 4-14: List the key capabilities and future moves of your biggest competitors on this form to fine-tune your business plan accordingly.

Add a general description of your competitive environment, including the strengths, capabilities, and likely moves of major competing businesses, to your business plan. This information influences all your other business planning.

Forms on the CD-ROM

To help you assess the business environment you're likely to face, check out the following forms on the CD-ROM:

Form 4-1	**Industry Analysis Questionnaire**	A list of questions designed to unveil what you know and what you don't know about your industry
Form 4-2	**Barriers to Entry Checklist**	A checklist of the hurdles new competitors face in a variety of industries
Form 4-3	**Customer Profile Questionnaire**	A list of questions to ask and answer when creating your customer profile
Form 4-4	**Customer Intelligence Checklist**	A form for collecting customer input on an ongoing basis
Form 4-5	**Customer Snapshot**	A framework for creating your customer description
Form 4-6	**Ideal Customer Questionnaire**	Questions that help you define your ideal customer
Form 4-7	**Distinguishing Traits of Ideal Customers**	A form for making side-by-side comparisons between your best customers and all the others
Form 4-8	**Basic Market Segmentation Framework**	Questions that help you group customers into market segments
Form 4-9	**Business Customer Profile**	A questionnaire to help you create a profile of your business customers
Form 4-10	**Your Biggest Competitors**	A form to record the list of your top five competitors
Form 4-11	**Competitive Intelligence Checklist**	A form to keep track of information on each of your biggest competitors
Form 4-12	**Potential Stealth Competitors Questionnaire**	Questions to help you identify potential competitors before they become threats
Form 4-13	**Stealth Competitor Tracking Form**	A form for keeping track of potential competitors
Form 4-14	**Major Competitors and Their Likely Moves**	A form to keep track of large competitors and their likely strategic moves

Chapter 5

Charting Your Strategic Direction

* *

In This Chapter

▶ Analyzing your strengths, weaknesses, opportunities, and threats

▶ Figuring out how to make money

▶ Deciding whether you want to grow bigger

* *

*I*f you've worked your way through the last few chapters, you may feel like a juggler. On the one hand, you're evaluating the industry that you're in. On the other hand, you're getting to know your customers better. All the while, you're keeping both eyes on the competition. (Chapter 4 helps you on all three fronts.)

But wait, you have more to keep track of. You need to watch what's happening *inside* your business. What are your company's strengths? Where's your company a little weak? What opportunities — and what threats — are on the horizon? How do you plan to compete and win? How will you make money? What's your long-term strategy? How will you expand and develop your company? And when the time comes to retire or move on to other ventures, what exit strategy will you follow?

The answers to these questions are essential to your business planning, and they're what this chapter is all about.

Assessing Your Capabilities, Opportunities, and Threats

In the business world, the companies with their heads in the sand are headed toward extinction. While they cling to the past or hunker down in the moment, companies with visionary leaders look around with 20/20 vision and adapt their plans to steer clear of trouble and seize the opportunities they see on the horizon.

So how do you put your business in the winning group? For starters, take an eye-opening look at your business situation by conducting a *SWOT analysis*.

In MBA lingo, *SWOT* is an acronym for strengths, weaknesses, opportunities, and threats. A SWOT analysis is an important part of business planning for one simple reason: It works.

Before you can carry out a SWOT analysis, you need to look at each of the pieces of the process separately, first by sizing up your business strengths and weaknesses and then by looking at your opportunities and threats.

Sizing up your strengths and weaknesses

Business strengths and weaknesses come in all shapes and sizes. Following are eight key *capabilities* that make up the essential elements of success:

- ✔ **Research and development (R&D):** Your ability to design and develop new products, services, or technologies

- ✔ **Operations:** Having the resources and systems necessary to produce the highest-quality products or services in the most efficient ways possible

- ✔ **Marketing:** How well you get your products or services into the marketplace and onto customers' radar screens

- ✔ **Distribution and delivery:** The ability to get your products into customers' hands

- ✔ **Customer service:** Everything you do to create a loyal clientele that supports you with purchases, repeat purchases, and praise

- ✔ **Management:** How you provide leadership, direction, and a vision for your company

- ✔ **Organization:** The procedures and company structures that enable you to make the most of your staff and resources

- ✔ **Financial condition:** The long- and short-term financial health of your company

Not all eight capabilities are equally important to every business. (For a more complete description of each, take a look at Chapter 6.) For example, a state-of-the-art distribution and delivery system may be essential to the success of one firm but not particularly important to another. Research and Development may be crucial for a computer manufacturer, but it may be of little impact to a massage business. And, if your company is a one-person business, management capabilities — at least as they apply to staffing issues — may be largely irrelevant.

Don't jump to conclusions, however. Chances are good that, in some way, shape, or form, each of the key capabilities contributes in some way to your company's ability to compete and succeed. You just may need to be a bit flexible in the way you think about how each category impacts your company.

Grading your capabilities

To rank the importance of each capability to your company's success, use Form 5-1 (see Figure 5-1) on the CD-ROM. Grade your company's strength in each area. Circle "excellent" in the areas where you know that your business excels, and give lower grades where you think your business falls short. No one is handing out gold stars for top marks; the only perfect outcome is one that's frank about your company's strengths and weaknesses.

Figure 5-1 shows how the owners of Soup's On, a gourmet catering company with plans to expand from a single outlet into a small chain, graded the company.

Here's a little background about what went into their thinking. Research and Development may not seem important to the success of a catering firm, but the Soup's On expansion strategy called for a Web site where customers could view the current selection of dishes, create personalized menus, place orders, and schedule catered events. To support this Internet strategy, the owners knew that they needed to beef up their Web presence, so they gave R&D a ranking of medium importance. They gave operational ability a ranking of high importance after deciding that their ability to accurately fill orders and prepare meals was fundamental to their success. They also gave a high ranking to "distribution and delivery," which they defined as their ability to transport food to events and to supervise setup, serving, and clean up.

Figure 5-1:
Rank the importance of key capabilities to your business success. Use Form 5-1 to assess how your company rates in each area.

COMPANY STRENGTHS AND WEAKNESSES SURVEY						
Capability	**Importance to Business**			**How Does the Company Rate?**		
Research and development	Low	(Medium)	High	(Poor)	Fair	Good	Excellent
Operations	Low	Medium	(High)	Poor	Fair	Good	(Excellent)
Sales and marketing	Low	Medium	(High)	(Poor)	Fair	Good	Excellent
Distribution and delivery	Low	Medium	(High)	Poor	Fair	Good	(Excellent)
Customer service	Low	Medium	(High)	Poor	Fair	(Good)	Excellent
Management	Low	Medium	(High)	Poor	(Fair)	Good	Excellent
Organization	Low	(Medium)	High	Poor	Fair	(Good)	Excellent
Financial condition	Low	Medium	(High)	Poor	(Fair)	Good	Excellent

Matching your capabilities to the task at hand

After you rank and assess your company's capabilities, use your findings to complete Form 5-2, the Strengths and Weaknesses Grid, which is on the CD-ROM. This form shows you, at a glance, how your business strengths and weaknesses align with the capabilities most necessary to your success.

Figure 5-2 shows how the owners of the catering company completed the grid. On the plus side, the caterers gave themselves excellent rankings in the crucial areas of operations and distribution and delivery. And they rated their customer service as good — although good isn't excellent, it's still okay.

But then red flags begin to flutter. The caterers ranked the areas of management and financial condition as highly important but gave their business only fair grades in those areas. Yikes. Plus, they found more trouble in the area of marketing. Their plan called for expansion into new geographic areas, but current sales come almost entirely from repeat business and word of mouth. In all honesty, they had to rate their marketing capability as poor. They also decided that they were no better at Research and Development. No one on staff had expertise to match the aspirations of their Internet strategy.

Thanks to their findings, the caterers called a timeout to boost capabilities in key areas before proceeding with their expansion plans.

As you study your strengths and weaknesses grid, keep the following thoughts in mind:

- ✔ Capabilities listed in the top left of the grid are essential capabilities and areas where you possess strong expertise — a great combination.

- ✔ Capabilities at the bottom left of the grid are essential to your success, but your company is weak in these areas and, therefore, is vulnerable.

- ✔ Capabilities in the middle row of the grid are of medium importance to your success. The capabilities listed in the right-hand column are of minor importance. Any poor rating is cause for concern, but when your business is weak in an area of minor importance, the deficiency is of lesser concern — at least for now.

Capitalizing on strengths and overcoming weaknesses

After you know where your business stands on key capabilities — and which capabilities matter most to your business success — you're in position to build on strengths and work on weaknesses.

As you write your business plan, don't be afraid to toot your own horn by announcing important company strengths with a full chorus of 76 trombones. After all, these strengths provide evidence that you have what it takes to succeed in your field. At the same time, acknowledge deficiencies by detailing your strategy for turning those company weaknesses around.

One more word of advice: Because your company's strengths and weaknesses are likely to change over time, return to the grid in Form 5-2 on a regular basis to take a fresh look at where you stand.

COMPANY STRENGTHS AND WEAKNESSES GRID			
How Does the Company Rate?	**Importance to Business**		
	High	*Medium*	*Low*
Excellent	• Operations • Distribution and delivery		
Good	• Customer service	• Organization	
Fair	• Management • Financial condition		
Poor	• Sales and marketing	• Research and development	

Figure 5-2: The grid provided in Form 5-2 helps you match your business expertise with the capabilities most important to your success.

Identifying opportunities and threats

After taking a hard look at your company's strengths and weaknesses, look outside your company for external forces that can ultimately shape your destiny. These include

- The appearance of new competitors
- The emergence of unique technologies
- Shifts in population and popular taste
- Changes in politics and regulations
- Fads and fashion crazes

When you're the one and only

If you're the boss and entire staff of a one-person company, you may be wondering what all this talk about capabilities has to do with your success. The answer: plenty. The same issues that confront big companies apply to a business of one — just on a smaller scale. Here's how a freelance computer-networking specialist adapted the descriptions of each capability to fit her situation:

✔ **Research and development:** This capability includes staying current with new software and hardware technologies by completing online training courses and certification programs.

✔ **Operations:** This capability covers billing, accounting, scheduling, and an answering service to field calls when I'm out and to make sure that customers can reach me in emergency situations.

✔ **Marketing:** This capability includes business cards, stationery, and maybe a Web site in the future. It also includes my ability to make calls and presentations to prospective clients.

✔ **Distribution and delivery:** This capability includes getting to and from client meetings and having the right equipment and software in the right place at the right time.

✔ **Customer service:** This capability involves establishing working relationships with clients who have information technology needs and creating loyalty through excellent service delivery.

✔ **Management:** This capability includes my ability to set and reach goals and objectives and to maintain a sense of direction and vision. I also define management as my ability to be my own boss.

✔ **Organization:** This capability includes support services for accounting, secretarial, and so on.

✔ **Financial condition:** This capability means having funds for computer hardware, software, testing equipment, cash to stay afloat until invoices are paid, and a financial cushion.

Using Form 5-3 on the CD-ROM, list the threats and opportunities facing your business, and follow these guidelines:

✔ When listing opportunities, think about emerging technologies, availability of new materials, new customer categories, market growth, new uses for old products (think about how cellphones double as cameras), new rules and regulations, new distribution or location opportunities, and other forces that can contribute to your success.

✔ When listing threats, consider the impact of shrinking markets, changing consumer trends, raw material shortages, economic downturns, new regulations, and changes in your competitive environment, including new competitors and competitive mergers and alliances. Also think about the impact of expiring patents, labor issues, global issues, and new products that may make your offering outdated or unnecessary.

If you're having a tough time getting specific, go back to the strengths and weaknesses survey in Form 5-1, and this time use it to describe the strengths and weaknesses of your leading competitor. You won't know as much about that company as you know about yours, but you probably know enough to flag areas where it's strong and weak. The competitor's strengths are potential threats to your business, and its weaknesses present you with potential opportunities

When the catering company I mention in the previous sections began planning to expand into a small chain, the owners held a retreat to consider potential threats and opportunities. Figure 5-3 shows their findings.

Looking over the list, the caterers were encouraged. Their opportunities outnumbered their threats. What's more, they were convinced that they had the capabilities to capitalize on the pluses and counter the negatives.

COMPANY OPPORTUNITIES AND THREATS	
Possible Opportunities	**Potential Threats**
• Increasing number of couples who work and have money but don't have the time to cook	• Difficulty in finding reliable staff in a very tight regional labor market
• Growing interest in healthy, organic, high quality ingredients	• Indirect competition from "do-it-yourself" catering and take-out at local grocery stores
• Growing sophistication of consumers and a demand for "true" gourmet take-out food	• Direct competitors, especially the "waiters-on-wheels" who will deliver from a number of local restaurants
• Business boom in the area, creating a strong market for catering of business events	
• Promise of the Internet to improve marketing and customer service	

Figure 5-3: Use Form 5-3 to list external forces that could present your business with opportunities and threats.

Conducting a SWOT analysis

So how do you seize business opportunities and sidestep potential threats? You conduct a SWOT (strengths, weaknesses, opportunities, threats) analysis.

A SWOT analysis helps you line up your company's capabilities with the realities of your business environment so you can direct your business toward areas where your capabilities are strong and your opportunities are great.

Think of a SWOT analysis as an easy-to-use alignment and steering tool that can help small businesses, large corporations, freelancers, schools, nonprofits, small towns, and nearly every other kind of business or organization to evaluate and align strengths, weaknesses, opportunities, and threats.

To conduct a SWOT analysis, follow these steps:

1. **Refer to your company's strengths and weaknesses (which you list on Form 5-2) and your opportunities and threats (which you list on Form 5-3).**

2. **Divide your strengths into two groups: strengths that can help you take advantage of opportunities facing your business and strengths that can help you head off potential threats.**

3. **Divide your weaknesses into two groups: one group that requires improvements before you can take advantage of opportunities and a group that includes capabilities that you need to completely overhaul and turn quickly into strengths in order to avert threats on your business horizon.**

Use Form 5-4 on the CD-ROM to record the findings of your SWOT analysis. Figure 5-4 shows how the owners of the Soup's On catering business completed the grid for their company.

COMPANY SWOT ANALYSIS GRID		
	Opportunities	**Threats**
Strengths	Use superior operations and delivery to go after increasingly sophisticated high-end take-out and catering markets CAPITALIZE ON THESE	We depend on our high quality and service, but it's harder to attract and keep good people MONITOR THESE
Weaknesses	Big growth in catered events market, but we're weak in marketing Promise of the Internet, but we have no R&D IMPROVE THESE	Our poor marketing and precarious financial condition are dangerous, given the increased competition we face ELIMINATE THESE

Figure 5-4:
Fill in the SWOT Analysis Grid on Form 5-4 to analyze your company against your business environment.

Based on the outcome of the caterers' SWOT analysis, they made some significant business decisions: They hired a marketing consultant with a background in developing restaurant chains; they researched online marketing programs to get a sense of the resources required to achieve a true Internet presence; they tightened their management structure to prepare for growth; and they recruited two investors to improve their company's financial condition.

As a result, Soup's On is ready to grow into a small chain. The owners know to expect increased competition for catering and takeout services, but they also see that growing demand will support a number of catering companies. What's more, they're confident that by focusing on quality, consistency, and sophisticated menus, they can compete successfully against grocery stores and restaurants. By investing time upfront to understand their strengths and weaknesses — and by dealing with their opportunities and threats — the caterers have increased their chances of success.

Include findings from your SWOT analysis in your business plan, addressing how you intend to

- ✔ Seize business opportunities by capitalizing on your company's strengths

- ✔ Improve capabilities in weak areas in order to take advantage of business opportunities

- ✔ Monitor potentially threatening outside forces while maintaining internal capabilities so that you're prepared to respond from a position of strength if a threat arises

- ✔ Eliminate weaknesses to protect your business from current threats

Revisit your SWOT analysis on a regular basis — at least annually and more frequently if your business is under siege, experiencing growth problems, or failing to meet goals and objectives — to see how the balance of strengths, weaknesses, opportunities, and threats may have shifted. The business environment is constantly changing, so you want to be sure that your business plan reflects the way the world around you *is,* not the way it *was.*

Defining Your Business Model

Don't reach for the balsa wood and glue. A business model isn't something you build from the ground up. And you don't need flip charts or diagrams full of circles and squares and arrows pointing every which way, either.

When management-types ask about a business model — as in, "So what's your business model?" — they really want an answer to a much more direct and basic question: "How do you plan to make money?"

Behind that question is a lineup of other questions:

- Who's your target customer?
- What customer problem or challenge do you solve?
- What value do you deliver?
- How will you reach, acquire, and keep customers?
- How will you define and differentiate your offering?
- How will you generate revenue?
- What's your cost structure?
- What's your profit margin?

During the 1990s, when the business world was buzzing with talk about a new economy and new business rules, people — even business gurus — seemed to forget the part about making money, and businesspeople sidelined the use of business models. But when the dot-com boom began to bust, suddenly everybody started asking about business models again.

Staying in the black

Sooner rather than later in the business-planning process, you need to invest a good chunk of time delving into the nitty-gritty details of your company's finances — your income statements, balance sheets, cash flow, budgeting, and all the details that can make or break your company's future. (Chapter 8 makes poring over the numbers as pain free as possible.) At this point, however, your assignment is way more basic: Figure out where the money will come from. Who will pay? How much? How often? And what portion of every sale will make its way to your bottom line in the form of — here's the magic word — *profit*.

Following are terms that you hear on your journey to profitability:

- *In the black:* If your revenues exceed your costs, you're in the black.
- *Red ink:* If you're not in the black, your company is losing money, which means that you could be drowning in red ink.
- *Fixed costs:* Your business will have plenty of costs — from renting an office and buying equipment to paying salaries and buying supplies. Some of these costs — office rental or salaries, for example — don't change often and must be paid on a regular basis, no matter how good (or bad) your company is looking. These are fixed costs or *overhead.*
- *Variable costs:* Other costs, called variable costs, fluctuate with your sales volume. They include the materials that go into producing your product or service.

To keep out of the red ink, you need enough money coming in to cover all your costs. But to break into the black, you need to price your goods and services to cover your costs *plus* a little (or more than a little) for your bottom line. That's called *profit*. Don't leave your business plan without it!

The first step toward profitability is to create a financial projection for your business. Use Form 5-5 on the CD-ROM as you estimate costs and revenues.

As you work up your numbers, refer to Figure 5-5, which shows financial projections for a restaurant with plans to open in Chicago. The owners are looking for investors, so they want to present a convincing business model as a part of their business plan. In other words, they want to show that the revenues they plan to take in will exceed their costs and deliver a profit.

On the revenue side, they calculate how much they will make on each meal and how many meals they plan to serve. On the cost side, they enter their fixed costs (rent, loans, utilities, insurance, wages) and their variable costs (food, supplies, part-time help, and so on). Their estimates show that they plan to turn a profit of $1,950 a week, or almost $8,000 a month.

Based on their experience in the restaurant business, however, the owners know that their projections won't turn into reality overnight — that's part of the reason they want investors. They project that the restaurant will incur losses during the first six months, break even during months seven and eight, and turn a profit starting in month nine. (To brush up on planning time frames, check out Chapter 1.)

Timing your future

How you expect to make money is one part of your business model, but *when* you expect the money to roll in is another important factor. Some companies run up costs and spend cash months (even years) before a revenue stream begins to flow. For that reason, your business model must include a timeline that takes the following into account:

- ✔ The upfront costs you expect to incur when setting up your business
- ✔ The source of funds to pay for your upfront costs
- ✔ A schedule showing when you expect revenues to pour in

The question of timing isn't only for big companies with factories to build and products to design. Timing can have a real impact on businesses of any size.

QUICK FINANCIAL PROJECTION WORKSHEET		
Projected Revenues		
Anticipated number of meals served:	250 / week	
Average gross revenue per meal:	$ 37.50	
Total weekly gross revenue:		$ 9,375.
Projected Fixed Costs		
Restaurant space rental:	$ 1,000. / week	
Loan payments on equipment:	$ 350. / week	
Utilities, insurance, and other costs:	$ 225. / week	
Full-time personnel costs:	$ 2,350. / week	
Total weekly fixed costs:		$ 3,925.
Projected Variable Costs		
Food / wine wholesale costs:	$ 3,000. / week	
Temporary service staff:	$ 500. / week	
Total weekly variable costs:		$ 3,500.
Expected Profits		
Total weekly profits:		$ 1,950.

Figure 5-5:
Use this form on the CD-ROM to calculate revenues and costs and to project profits for your business.

Take the example of a bed and breakfast (B&B) on Cape Cod, where the tourist season begins on June 1 and ends with the big Labor Day weekend in September. Except for a few holiday periods, the B&B brings in all its revenue during those three summer months. The owners need a business model that ensures that summer revenues are enough to cover fixed costs — mortgage, utilities, taxes, salaries, and upkeep — all year round. Timing issues apply to many retailers, too, who often make the majority of annual sales during the year-end holiday or some other single selling season.

Knowing how customers pay

An effective business model also takes into account how customers pay. When customers buy a product or service, they typically have a number of payment options. The most common choices include paying in one lump sum or spreading the purchase price over monthly installments. In some businesses, customers also have the choice to pay as they go or to prepay for unlimited use of a product or service. Other times, a company invites customers to buy or to rent, to finance their purchases, or to lease products instead of purchasing them.

Each option has financial consequences that affect your business model. As you establish the purchasing options you plan to offer customers, consider how each selection will affect your revenue picture.

Creating a business model that works

Some business models are as old as the marketplace itself; others are as new as the Internet. Some have weathered the test of time; others are almost experimental.

The simplest model involves creating a product and selling it directly to customers. Other models involve selling wholesale to retailers, selling through distributors, licensing products to other companies, selling online, selling through auctions, and countless other alternatives. No one-size-fits-all solution exists. In fact, most companies use some combination of business models to arrive at a unique model.

The questionnaire in Form 5-6 helps you think about how your company will make money. After completing it, ask two more questions:

✔ Can I spot additional potential sources of revenue that I may be able to develop in the future?

✔ Can I come up with alternative payment plans — such as membership or subscription fees — that would entice new customers, keep customers loyal to my company, and increase my revenue stream down the road?

Use your findings to adjust your financial projections, returning to Form 5-5 on the CD-ROM. Your calculations don't have to be fancy (see Chapter 8 when you're ready for some serious financial footwork); you just want a good indication of the likely success of your business model.

Your business model is the key to your business plan and the formula for your success over the long term. Describe your business model in the Executive Summary of your business plan and early in your Company Overview (see Chapter 1 for details on these sections).

Setting Growth Strategies

If your business planning works out, your company is likely to grow bigger. But simply assuming that growth will take off isn't enough. You must also map out *how* your business will grow — and how big you want it to get.

Understanding your options

After you strip away the big words and elaborate theories, you find that companies grow in three basic ways:

- ✔ **By finding more customers to buy their current products or services:** You can grow your client list by

    - Advertising to bring in additional customers

    - Encouraging good customers to buy more often

    - Finding new uses (and customers) for your offerings

- ✔ **By providing existing customers with new and different products or services:** Approaches include

    - Making changes in your product line based on customer feedback

    - Packaging your products or services in useful and unique combinations

    - Developing related products and services

- ✔ **By approaching brand-new customers with completely new products or services:** You can attract new customers by

    - Using current capabilities to develop brand-new products or services

    - Leveraging your company assets and marketing capabilities to woo brand-new customers

    - Staying patient and preparing for the long haul, because this strategy is perhaps the most difficult way to expand your business

Planning for growth

How do you plan to grow your company? Before you answer that question, review your goals and objectives (flip to Chapter 3). Chances are good that they lay the groundwork for growing your business in some way or another — by reaching more customers, expanding your product line or services, or entering new markets.

Form 5-7 lists resources you may need to develop your growth strategy.

Form 5-8 presents basic questions that guide your thinking as you plan for growth. The results of your SWOT analysis (Form 5-4) may prompt your answers.

In addition to deciding how you want to grow, define how much you want to grow. Answers vary widely. One independent contractor may want to grow her business just enough to stay busy and keep the bank account healthy — but not so much that she needs to hire employees. In contrast, another entrepreneur may want to grow big — and fast — so that he can move away from doing the work himself and concentrate on expanding his business.

BUSINESS MODEL QUESTIONNAIRE
1. List all your principle sources of revenue. (Don't forget to include things like product accessories, service agreements, upgrades, and so on.) •   • •   • •   •
2. List where you expect your fixed costs to come from. (Remember the obvious, such as utilities, a bookkeeping service, city taxes, insurance, and so on.) •   • •   • •   •
3. List the sources of your variable costs. •   • •   • •   •
4. Jot down the key timing issues your business faces. (Make sure to include the start-up interval, seasonal variations in sales, and any cost or price cycles.) •   • •   • •   •
5. Describe how customers will pay for your products or services (single or multiple payments, weekly or monthly fees, subscriptions, and so on).

Form 5-6: Answers to these questions will guide development of your business model.

Include your growth plans in the Executive Summary of your written business plan. You can also stick them in the Company Strategy section, the Financial Review, and in your Action Plans (Chapter 1 gives the lowdown on these sections).

RESOURCES FOR GROWTH CHECKLIST
☐ Raising additional capital
☐ Developing management expertise
☐ Acquiring new office space
☐ Purchasing or leasing office equipment
☐ Hiring new employees
☐ Training and developing staff
☐ Establishing human resources guidelines
☐ Installing accounting and information systems
☐ Investing in research and product development
☐ Spending on advertising and promotions
☐ Outsourcing certain functions
☐ Forming strategic alliances with other companies
☐ Acquiring other companies
☐

Form 5-7: Growing your business requires resources. Use this form to check off the needs you foresee.

PLANNING FOR GROWTH QUESTIONNAIRE
1. What are your goals for company growth over the next year? (Use revenues, profits, number of clients, market share, or any other measure that makes the most sense to you.)   •   •
2. What are your three- and/or five-year goals for growth?   •   •
3. What will it take to get your company where you want it to be? (List three or four key requirements.)   •   •   •   •
4. Which of your key strengths will be most important in helping you meet your goals for growth?
5. What company weakness could be most significant in limiting your company's growth?
6. What are the major milestones you intend to reach along the way?   •   •   •

Form 5-8: This form presents questions that help guide your thinking as you prepare for business growth.

Outlining an Exit Strategy

Here you are, a business owner all gung-ho about getting started or getting bigger, and people are already asking you about your plan for getting out.

When you're right in the middle of starting, growing, or reenergizing your company, hatching a plan for how to exit stage right is hard to do, but that's exactly what you have to take on.

An exit strategy is a plan for how you'll personally leave your business at some point in the future. Closing up shop is one option, but short of liquidating business assets, closing reaps no value from the business you've built. That's why business plans — even for start-up enterprises — should include strategies for someday selling, merging, or transitioning the company in some way to new owners when it's time for the founder to retire or move on to other ventures.

Knowing where your business is headed and how you may someday exit is a crucial part of an effective long-term plan. By planning your exit early on, you put yourself in a position to steer your business toward your desired outcome.

Businesses seeking investors with deep pockets of upfront cash have double the need for an exit strategy. An investor on the outside who's willing to put money into a company wants to know how he'll get it back — along with a handsome return on his investment. Unless you have a convincing exit strategy that describes exactly how you plan to make that happen, attracting serious investors is an uphill battle. (You can find more on this topic in Chapter 18.)

Even if you're starting a company simply to be in business — with no idea of selling or turning your business over to others when you retire — you should still take some time to think about what you're creating as you put your company together. You just may be creating something that has lasting value, even after you want to call it quits. Maybe you're creating a brand name that people recognize. Perhaps you'll attract a group of loyal customers. Maybe your network of contacts or your relationships with suppliers will have real value to someone else. If and when the time comes to close up shop, you should be aware of the intrinsic value of what you own. Don't simply throw it away.

Whatever kind of business you're in, ask yourself three basic questions:

- ✔ What are my reasons for going into business in the first place?
- ✔ How long do I plan to stay in business?
- ✔ What do I hope to end up with when I call it quits?

Form 5-9 shows some of the most common exit strategies. Put checkmarks beside ones that may be possibilities for your company. You don't know for sure that a big company will come along and acquire your little company, but if being acquired is a thought on your radar screen, it's important to plan for it along the way.

CHECKLIST OF COMMON EXIT STRATEGIES
☐ **Going public**
Your private company goes public by selling shares to be traded on a stock exchange through an initial public offering, or IPO
☐ **Being acquired**
Your company is bought by another company outright, and you may or may not have a role to play in the larger business
☐ **Being sold**
Your company is bought by an individual or group of individuals who may or may not want to keep you as part of the management team
☐ **Merging**
Your company joins forces with another existing company on an equal footing, and a joint management structure is put in place
☐ **Being bought out**
One or more of the owners of your company buys out the other owners to assume control of the business
☐ **Franchising**
You sell your business concept to others who replicate it, paying you fees for the use of the name, business model, and other assets
☐ **Going out of business**
Your company's assets are sold, the doors are shut, and the books are closed for good

Form 5-9: Set your dreams in motion by using this form to check the exit strategies you envision for your company.

For each of the exit options you consider, make a short list of the business capabilities and resources you need to have in place for the strategy to eventually become a reality.

In most cases, your written business plan at least gives a nod to your exit strategy. Sketching out how you'll personally leave your business and harvest its value at some point in the future is a first step in guiding the final chapter of your involvement to a positive conclusion.

Forms on the CD-ROM

The following forms on the CD-ROM help you explain your company's strategy in your business plan.

Form 5-1	**Company Strengths and Weaknesses Survey**	A form that helps you rank success factors and rate your abilities in each key area
Form 5-2	**Company Strengths and Weaknesses Grid**	A grid that lets you see at a glance how your abilities align with the capabilities needed for success
Form 5-3	**Company Opportunities and Threats**	A form for listing the potential opportunities and threats facing your business
Form 5-4	**Company SWOT Analysis Grid**	A grid designed to line up your company strengths and weaknesses against the business opportunities and threats you face
Form 5-5	**Quick Financial Projection Worksheet**	A worksheet for making quick financial projections as you develop your business model
Form 5-6	**Business Model Questionnaire**	Questions to help you define your business model
Form 5-7	**Resources for Growth Checklist**	Critical resources you may need as your company grows
Form 5-8	**Planning for Growth Questionnaire**	Questions to answer as you plan your company's growth
Form 5-9	**Checklist of Common Exit Strategies**	A list of the most common exit strategies for business owners

Chapter 6

Describing Your Business and Its Capabilities

Come on, you may be thinking. How hard can it be to describe who my company is and what it does? Before you tackle that question, ask a few other entrepreneurs to tell you what their companies do — and watch as they grope for answers. Describing a company isn't quite as simple as it sounds, and that's why this chapter is so important.

When a banker or potential investor is reading your business plan, the first thing that person wants to know, in a nutshell, is what your business does. Your job is to give a good description — without getting lost in the details and without lapsing into industry jargon. And you have to keep it short, too. After all, you're writing a business plan, not the great American novel.

Your business description must clearly and concisely convey the most important aspects of your company, the customers you serve, and the products and services you offer. This chapter helps you examine your company's capabilities and put into words who your company is, what your company does best, and what's most important to your company and its customers.

Introducing Your Company

Imagine that you're at your high-school reunion and a bunch of old pals ask what you're up to. As you describe your company, you want to cover the high points, and you also want to build enthusiasm by conveying that it's a really great idea.

Here's an example of what the conversation may sound like:

"I've put together a brand-new way to encourage people to contribute to worthy nonprofit organizations. The concept started when I began thinking about the success of online gift certificate sales. It occurred to me that I could use the same idea to help worthy causes — selling nonprofit gift certificates online to provide a simple way for people to donate to charities instead of exchanging gifts during the holidays.

Here's how it works: Instead of wrapping gifts for employees, a company can give $100 charitable gift certificates. Employees go to my company Web site, which shows a list of 100 handpicked nonprofits, ranging from environmental groups to medical researchers. Each employee can choose where he or she wants to contribute the money and whether to give all $100 to one organization or to divvy it up.

And the same approach works for family gifts. Instead of giving relatives $50 gifts, you can give charitable gift certificates. The cool thing is that recipients get to direct the money to causes that really matter to them. And, of course, I'm hoping that after they receive a certificate and see the site, they'll want to give charitable gift certificates rather than the ties or unwanted kitchen gadgets that end up under the tree."

The venture sounds interesting. It also sounds exciting because the speaker is so obviously enthusiastic. But what if his or her former classmates start asking questions, such as, "So how will the company support itself?" "How will people hear about your site?" "How do you choose the 100 charitable organizations?" The answers to these questions determine whether the idea gains group support or lands in a pile labeled "It's a nice idea, but . . ."

What is it you're selling, anyway?

If you're in business, you need to be ready to describe your company and the product that you're selling.

Here's a true story: An entrepreneur was presenting her business idea to a group of potential investors. The business idea involved summarizing the latest medical research into easy-to-understand short reports designed to encourage people to lead healthier lifestyles. She talked about the accelerating pace of medical research and new insights by behavioral scientists regarding how people change. She waxed eloquent on the subject of preventive healthcare and showed statistics detailing the aging of the American population. Ten minutes into her presentation, an investor interrupted to ask the simple question, "What is it you're selling, anyway?" The answer: an online health newsletter directed at people over 50. In her excitement, the entrepreneur forgot to state the obvious.

Here's the moral of this tale: When describing your company, get to the point, beginning with a clear description of your product or service. For help, use the product/service description checklist on Form 6-1, which you find on the CD-ROM. See Figure 6-1 for an example of how the founder of the online health newsletter completed the form.

Include a concise description of your company's products or services in both the Company Overview and Company Description sections of your written plan (see Chapter 3 for help describing your business and Chapter 1 for information on these sections of your plan). Too much information can confuse the very people you want to convince, so add only as much technical detail as your audience needs to make sense of your offerings. (Chapter 1 helps you identify the audience for your plan.) Features worth mentioning include size, color, design, cost, quality, capabilities, and life span of your product. Most important, tell how the features deliver valuable customer benefits.

PRODUCT/SERVICE DESCRIPTION CHECKLIST

1. Product or service summary:

"Wellness Update," an online health newsletter for people over 50

2. Key product or service features:

- Easy-to-understand summaries of key medical findings related to healthy lifestyles
- Targeted e-mail updates tailored to specific diseases or health conditions
- Personalized "health accounts" that allow users to keep track of exercise, diet, weight, and other lifestyle factors

3. Target customers:

- People 50 years and over with an interest in maintaining a healthy lifestyle
- HMOs and other health organizations with preventive health programs
- Fitness centers interested in offering clients expanded services

4. Key customer benefits:

- Getting the latest health-related news in easy-to-read capsule summaries
- Advice and practical help on making lifestyle changes
- Access to experts who will answer preventive health-related FAQs

Figure 6-1:
Know your product. Use the checklist on Form 6-1 to summarize your offering and the benefits it delivers.

Include a product photo in your business plan if you think it can help readers get a better idea of what you intend to offer. As the saying goes, a picture is worth a thousand words — and it takes up way less room than the thousand words.

How do you prepare an elevator speech?

When you're in business, you need to be ready at any moment with an answer to the question, "So what do you do?"

Marketers and venture capitalists call your response your *elevator speech*, because if you craft it correctly, you can deliver it in the time it takes to ride an elevator from the top floor to the lobby of a high-rise building. In that short span — which is just as apt to take place at a conference or a networking event — you need to

- ✔ Introduce yourself and your business in a way that makes the other people want to know more.

- ✔ Tell what you do in terms that someone outside your business or industry can easily understand.

- ✔ Describe your product or service and the benefits that it delivers.

- ✔ Define the market for your offerings.

- ✔ Set yourself apart by highlighting your competitive advantages, your unique business model (Chapter 5 has more on this key issue), and the people behind your business, such as prominent investors, board members, associations, or business partners.

- ✔ Generate interest, prompt questions, and begin to develop a relationship.

This list is a tall order for sure, and for that reason, practicing is the only way to perfect your response. Before you write your elevator speech, however, you need to keep in mind what you *shouldn't* do or say:

- ✔ Don't begin with a dull, generic introduction, such as "I sell insurance," or "I run a social service agency." Start by inspiring interest and prompting questions rather than evoking stereotypes.

- ✔ Don't dive into a sales pitch. Remember, you're presenting your company here, not the bells and whistles included in each of your products.

Use the questions in Form 6-2 as you begin your elevator speech. You won't include all your answers in your short business description, but by answering the questions in advance, you see which aspects of your business are worthy of white-hot spotlights.

An elevator speech exercise

See which of the following two elevator speeches reels in your interest.

"I'm a health-information specialist. I produce a world-class newsletter, send e-mail updates, and establish client relationships in an effort to support health and wellness for people 50 and older. Working with individuals, HMOs, physicians, and health and fitness centers, my business is a leading player in helping people maintain healthy lifestyles by providing summaries of medical advances and practical lifestyle advice, as well as access to leading medical professionals."

Or

"Our business translates medical breakthroughs into people language for the fast-growing, never-gonna-grow-old 50-plus age group. Basically, we shrink the latest medical findings into news capsules that we feature in a monthly newsletter. Paid subscribers include HMOs, clinics, and fitness centers — plus 15,000 individuals who receive targeted e-mails addressing specific health conditions. Since our launch in 2003, we've won endorsements from medical groups and advertising commitments from more than 50 marketers who value the opportunity to reach our clientele of health-conscious older Americans."

The first description starts with a bit of a clunker. The term "health-information specialist" must mean something, but the listener probably isn't quite sure what and likely cares even less. The jargon continues throughout the presentation. Plus, the two first sentences start with "I" — too self-centered to ignite a conversation. The entrepreneur doesn't include a single word that indicates that she has a business with a revenue stream. I hope the listener isn't a potential investor!

The second description starts off with a sentence that describes the company's innovative product and target clientele. The second sentence tells how the business works. The third sentence references the business model, or where revenues come from. And the fourth sentence builds credibility by presenting endorsements and proof of market acceptance. The whole message is delivered with enthusiasm and in easy-to-understand language, making it the best option of the two.

A good way to start working on your elevator speech is to imagine that you're talking to a group of longtime friends. You're apt to relax, get right to the point, and explain your company — or your new business idea — in the simplest, most persuasive language possible.

If you find yourself at a loss for words, revisit your company's mission and vision statements for inspiration. In a few phrases, they should capture what your company is all about. (Don't have a mission statement or vision statement? Chapter 3 helps you put them together.)

Jot down a first draft of your elevator speech (or use a voice recorder and transcribe it later). Your early thinking comes in handy when you sit down to write a short, compelling description of your business in the Company Overview and the Company Description sections of your plan (Chapter 1 has more on these sections). As you finalize your draft, use language that expresses enthusiasm and excitement (without gushing).

ELEVATOR SPEECH-PLANNING QUESTIONNAIRE
1. **What business are you in?**
2. **What is your product or service?** Give a broad-brush answer without getting hung up on details.
3. **Who is your target customer? How large is your market?**
4. **What benefits do your customers receive, or what problems do you help them solve?**
5. **What sets your business apart?** Think about unique technologies, special expertise, marketing potential, and the strengths of your management team, investors, board members, and industry associations.
6. **Who are your competitors and how is your business different and better?**

Form 6-2: Plan a concise, interesting description of your business, incorporating the answers to these questions.

Describing Your Business Capabilities

Every company has a set of unique assets that leverage a good idea into a thriving business. These assets are called *business capabilities,* and they're key elements of your company description. They include

- ✔ Research and Development
- ✔ Operations
- ✔ Marketing
- ✔ Distribution and delivery
- ✔ Customer service
- ✔ Management
- ✔ Organization
- ✔ Financial condition

Hopefully this list looks familiar, because these elements are the same capabilities you assess when rating your company's strengths and weaknesses. (No bells ringing? Flip to Chapter 5 for information on how your strengths and weaknesses relate to the opportunities and threats that your business faces.)

This chapter dives in deeper, taking a closer look at how your business capabilities affect your company's success. The following sections help you scrutinize your abilities in R&D, operations, distribution and delivery, management, and organization.

The reason that I don't cover marketing (including customer service) and financial capabilities in this chapter is because they're so essential to your success (and so fundamental to your business plan) that each capability gets an entire chapter to itself (see Chapters 7 and 8).

Acknowledge your key capabilities in your written business plan. If you're in business all by yourself and a few of the capabilities truly don't affect your success, you can take a pass on those areas. But don't let yourself off the hook too easily. In one way or another, each of these eight capabilities is likely to be an engine that drives you toward your business goals and objectives.

Research and development

Research and development, usually known as R&D, refers to your ability to design, develop, or enhance new products, services, or technologies. If your company is a high-tech firm, R&D is number one on the list of capabilities crucial to your long-term success.

Just because your company isn't technology based, don't assume that R&D isn't an important capability. Even a one-person consulting business needs research ability to track the competitive arena, find out about prospective customers, and keep up-to-date with industry and client news posted online. Plus, your Web site likely needs ongoing attention, which is another technology issue. In today's world, no matter what business you're in, R&D capability affects your success.

Suppose that you're starting a store that sells used books. You may think that your store doesn't require much R&D. Well, think again. The Internet opened a whole new way to market used books — from first editions and antique books to hard-to-find titles that sometimes sell for thousands of dollars. As an enterprising bookstore owner, you may want to tap into this network of booksellers to expand your market reach. Even if you opt against selling books online, you can use online resources to find out what people are paying for specific titles.

R&D may also be the key to enhancing your business skills or enlarging the portfolio of services that you offer customers. Ways to improve your R&D skills include

- ✔ Attending trade shows with R&D sessions
- ✔ Taking technology training courses
- ✔ Completing a certification program
- ✔ Updating your computer skills
- ✔ Keeping up-to-date with trade journals
- ✔ Joining an industry group
- ✔ Enlarging your business library with subscriptions to publications that broaden your awareness of technology issues and opportunities

Your business plan should include a section that addresses your R&D capabilities, including the following:

- ✔ The importance of R&D to your competitive success
- ✔ A concise description of your current R&D capacity (size and expertise of your engineering staff, for example)
- ✔ Your agenda for R&D over the next year
- ✔ Planned R&D expenditures over the next year
- ✔ Your long-term R&D goals

Operations

In the lineup of key business capabilities, the term *operations* describes the processes and resources that you use to produce the highest-quality products or services as efficiently as possible.

Business operations typically include four key areas:

- **Location:** Where you do business
- **Equipment:** The tools you need to get the job done
- **Labor:** The human side of business operations
- **Process:** The way you get business done

The importance of each of these areas depends on the nature of your company. Location is absolutely critical to a retail outlet that lives or dies by walk-in customers. An Internet company may decide that location doesn't matter a bit — unless business depends on highly skilled talent or the kinds of resources that cluster in places like Silicon Valley.

The CD-ROM includes four forms to help you evaluate the importance of the four key operational areas — location, equipment, labor, and process — to your company. Take time to complete Forms 6-3, 6-4, 6-5, and 6-6 on the CD-ROM.

Growing pains

Even for a small company, operations can be critical to success. A talented San Francisco florist watched his small business blossom as the local economy boomed. At the beginning, he managed all the designs and arrangements himself. He bought new inventory at the flower market early in the morning and finished the bookkeeping late at night.

But those daily tasks all changed as the company expanded. The florist found that he could no longer do everything himself, so he scrambled to hire and train employees. In the rush to meet growing demand, he failed to establish a clear set of operational procedures. The result: a business breakdown. Suddenly, his company had no mechanism for quality control. Flower arrangements were delivered to customers before receiving approval, and no single person was put in charge of going to the flower market.

For a brief, rocky period, a number of influential and unhappy clients threatened to find other suppliers. Just in the nick of time, the florist sat down with a consultant and worked out a new way of doing business based on the larger staff size. The new operational procedures spelled out each person's duties and responsibilities. They described the process of filling customer orders from the first telephone call to the last bill. To his surprise, the florist discovered that, thanks to the new procedures, he had more time to do what he did best — the creative end of the business — and still meet the growing demand.

If your plan is for a start-up company, include a description of how you plan for each of the four key operational areas, using your responses to Forms 6-3, 6-4, 6-5, and 6-6. For established companies, detail what operational changes are necessary to achieve the new goals and objectives detailed in your business plan and how you plan to implement and fund an expansion of your operation.

Distribution and delivery

How you get your products and services into your customers' hands is what *distribution and delivery* is all about. Not all businesses are equally concerned with distribution and delivery systems, of course. If you're a psychologist whose clients come to your office for counseling; if you run a freelance design business; or if you provide a dog-walking service, a telephone, e-mail access, and a means for personal transportation may be the extent of your distribution and delivery needs.

For some businesses, however, capabilities in distribution and delivery are important, if not downright critical, to success. Consider these examples:

✔ Every time the holiday season rolls around, catalog companies and online retailers face the same nail-biting challenge: How to ensure that customer orders reach their destinations in time for the big day. Some retailers absorb overnight express delivery costs in order to meet promises. A few companies have seen their reputations plummet — and their customers disappear — when they haven't been able to get deliveries out on time.

✔ One of the biggest challenges for a new magazine is getting distributors to give the magazine valuable shelf space on newsstands. The same goes for food manufacturers. With grocery store shelves already overcrowded with thousands of products, getting a new breakfast cereal or snack chip some face time isn't an easy hurdle to clear.

✔ Even businesses in service industries sometimes have to focus on distribution and delivery. Management-training companies, for example, often have to deliver training programs to thousands of managers in dozens of locations — all at the same time. They can't deliver on their promises unless they have trainers available and in place when and where they need them.

Failing to plan for the method and cost of distribution or delivery can be a fatal business mistake. Consider the Internet grocery service that staked its reputation on the promise of free delivery on orders of any size. Customers accepted the offer — ordering a single frozen dinner, a bottle of wine, or even a candy bar. Delivery costs ran more than $10 on each order. It didn't take long for this particular business promise to fade away — along with the company.

Assess the importance of distribution and delivery to your business success by filling out the distribution and delivery survey in Form 6-7. Be as specific as you can. Flag areas where you need to track down more information, and then do the research.

As you complete the form, consider the following:

- ✔ Be aware of all costs involved with product distribution and delivery — including warehouse space, transportation, shelf space allocations, product returns, and other necessary expenses.

- ✔ Consider how you can use distribution and delivery to your competitive advantage. Look for ways that you can excel over competitors by offering home delivery, subscription delivery, or other means of distribution that fit the realities of your product and the desires of your customer.

- ✔ View distribution as an expansion strategy, looking for new *distribution channels* — new paths that your products can follow from your company into your customers' hands — as a way to expand into new markets. Offering your products online, for example, or through new distributor or retailer relationships are ways to open new distribution channels.

Use your responses to Form 6-7 to assess the importance of distribution to your business success. If you think it's an essential element, include a description of your distribution system in your written plans.

Management

The long-term success of many companies depends, above all, on the quality of the team providing the leadership, direction, and vision. In fact, in some cases, investors have funded start-up companies purely on the basis of the people who will run them.

Assemble background information on yourself and each of your senior team members to showcase in your business plan. Use Form 6-8 to compile a profile for each key person.

When describing team members, include everything that's relevant to the potential success of your business — but keep the descriptions brief and to the point, with biographical notes on each person filling a half page or less.

If yours is a single-person operation, you don't have to spend too much time describing yourself in your plan, although you should have a resume highlighting your education, experience, and accomplishments ready to hand out when the information is requested by a banker, supplier, or prospective customer.

DISTRIBUTION AND DELIVERY SURVEY
1. Outline the steps required in distributing and delivering your product or service:
2. Describe the extent of the geographic area you intend to cover, including any plans to expand:
3. Estimate the costs associated with the distribution and delivery of your product or service:
4. List the relationships and agreements you plan to forge with distribution or delivery companies in your industry:
5. Review any contingency plans you have in place in case your primary distribution or delivery services are interrupted:

Form 6-7: Use this form to survey your distribution and delivery systems and to assess the impact they have on your business success.

If you're running a larger business, feature biographies of up to five top managers in your business plan. Include background information on people filling senior posts, including all the big Cs, from CEO (Chief Executive Officer) and COO (Chief Operating Officer) to CFO (Chief Financial Officer) and CTO (Chief Technology Officer). Depending on the size of your company, you may also want to include brief descriptions of the members of your Board of Directors, Board of Advisors, or of consultants who play a major role in making your business a success.

Organization

Your company's success hinges on the quality of the people around you, but it also depends on having an organization in place that allows those people to work as effectively and efficiently as possible. A company's organization consists of the relationship of employees to one another — who reports to whom, for example. It also determines each employee's access to important company resources.

Organization is a pretty straightforward issue for small companies, but in large companies, organization is more complicated. And if you don't plan well, it can undermine the efforts of even the best staff.

Consider the saga of one of the biggest online health information and management companies. Part of the firm's early strategy was to gobble up smaller online information providers, acquiring their assets and eliminating competition. Trouble was, each of these small companies had its own organizational structure and editorial procedure. Before long, different groups within the larger organization were producing the same content, unnecessarily duplicating efforts. No one was sure who was supposed to report to whom, and the company lost editorial control over the site. What's more, content that should've taken only three weeks to produce began to require six and seven weeks. The result: The company bled money. The lesson: Organization matters.

Choosing an organizational model is hardly a slam-dunk experience. To make the task a bit easier, here are four basic organizational models to consider, each one most appropriate for a specific company size.

You won't find an absolute right or wrong way to organize your business, so use your instincts — along with the preceding suggestions — to come up with an organizational plan that allows everyone around you to work at their best. And remember: An organization is a living thing that grows and changes as business circumstances change. Reevaluate your organizational structure if your company experiences rapid sales or staff growth, adds divisions or product lines, or alters its production processes.

Your written plan needs to include a section on your company's organization. Use charts or diagrams to help make a complicated organization a little clearer. For example, use a flowchart to show who reports to whom or how the company's divisions relate to one another. Don't get hung up in the details; your goal is to present a coherent description of what your company's organization looks like — and why.

Read on for some examples of organizational structures used by varying companies.

MANAGEMENT TEAM MEMBER PROFILE ON: _____

1. **Title or position:**

2. **Describe duties and responsibilities (include the functions overseen and daily activities, where appropriate):**

   •

   •

   •

3. **List previous industry and related experience (include past employers, positions, duties, and responsibilities):**

   •

   •

   •

4. **List notable accomplishments (include successful projects, new product introductions, honors, awards, and so on):**

   •

   •

   •

5. **Education (certifications, degrees, and so on):**

Form 6-8: Use this form to complete profiles on each senior person in your company.

The pack

In this structure, one person holds the top position and everyone else in the company is an equal member of the pack. This organizational style works well in small companies — no more than 20 people — where everyone on staff has the training and the expertise to do almost any job required of them.

Advantages: A simple, flexible organizational structure allows the entire team to work together. A loose-knit arrangement is often effective when a small company needs to adjust quickly to changing business conditions.

Disadvantages: If the company gets too big, the top dog can no longer keep track of what the rest of the pack is up to. Also, people may end up doing jobs they've never done before, which can compromise both quality and efficiency.

Form follows function

In this type of organization, you divide people into groups depending on what functions they perform. For example, a company may have an engineering department, a marketing department, a production department, and a finance department. Each department has its own manager, and a general manager typically takes on the role of coordinating the activities of the various functional groups.

Advantages: You assign people to do the tasks that they do best, and each person knows his or her responsibility. If your business is medium sized and markets only one type of product or service, this structure is probably the one for you.

Disadvantages: Without good communication and oversight from above, functional hierarchies can break down into separate little boxes that work well on their own but aren't very good at carrying out the company's larger strategies and goals.

Divide and conquer

Companies that provide more than one product line or that operate in more than one business area often choose to organize around separate divisions. A firm that sells, installs, and services computer networks, for example, may separate those functions into independent divisions. In this organizational model, each of a company's divisions may be responsible for a particular product, service, market, or geographical area, and all the divisions may have to justify themselves as independent profit centers. In some of the largest companies, each division consists of a *strategic business unit* (SBU) — almost a company inside a company. For more details on SBUs, check out *Business Plans For Dummies,* 2nd Edition, by Paul Tiffany and Steven Peterson (Wiley).

Advantages: Companies that organize into divisions encourage each separate part of the company to focus on the real business at hand — selling computers, servicing them, or installing them, for example. Division managers can zero in on their own sets of customers, competitors, and strategic issues.

Disadvantages: Divisions may find themselves competing for the same customers. The company's divisions may unnecessarily duplicate overhead costs, and the company may end up becoming less efficient.

The matrix

In a matrix organization, everybody has multiple bosses and does more than one job. For example, an employee may be developing new content for the company Web site and also working with the marketing team on special projects designed to bring in new business.

> *Advantages:* This structure fosters flexibility by allowing different parts of a company to share talent, expertise, and experience. Companies using a matrix structure are often able to respond quickly to changing business conditions.

> *Disadvantages:* Managing employees can be tricky when each person wears several hats. Plus, employees can feel a tense tug of war as they try to respond to the demands of several bosses. This structure can also lead to confusion about business priorities unless a strong general manager sees that the company stays on track.

Focusing on What You Do Best

No company can be all things to all people. In fact, companies that try to please everyone all the time usually find themselves becoming less effective at almost everything they do. Business history chronicles a long and scary list of companies that tried to build on success by expanding in new directions — only to lose the focus that made them sharp and successful in the first place.

Whether you're starting or growing a business, think about what you do best and how you can build on that strong base. If you're having a hard time zeroing in on a description of what you do best, ask yourself this question: If your company closed down, what products, services, or attributes do you think customers would miss most or have the hardest time replacing? Your answer unveils what makes your company and its offerings unique — and what things your company does best.

After you pinpoint where you excel, ask yourself *how* you do it. Your answer leads you right back to the list of key business capabilities.

Is your success tied tightly to your R&D? Or to the efficiency of your operations? The flawless systems that back your distribution and delivery? The quality of your management? The effectiveness of your organization? The power of your marketing and customer service (see Chapter 7)? Or the strength of your financial condition (see Chapter 8)?

Make a list of your answers and as you pursue growth opportunities, be careful that your expansion plans do nothing to weaken your company's key capabilities or take your company away from the strengths that got you where you are.

In your written plan, give special attention to the business capabilities that contribute most to your success and also to the capabilities that provide the greatest value to your customers. These capabilities represent the heart and soul of your company. They're your strongest selling points as a company, and your business plan should include specific details about how you intend to make the most of each one.

Reevaluate how well you're doing in these key areas on at least an annual basis — more frequently if you sense opportunities to seize or threats to avert. And also take time to brainstorm new ways to build on your strengths and increase the overall value you provide to your customers.

Forms on the CD-ROM

The following forms on the CD-ROM help you come up with a clear and compelling description of your company and what your company does.

Form 6-1	**Product/Service Description Checklist**	A form to help you create your product or service description
Form 6-2	**Elevator Speech Planning Questionnaire**	Six questions to guide the development of your elevator speech
Form 6-3	**Operations Planning Survey (Location)**	Key factors to consider in planning the location of your operations
Form 6-4	**Operations Planning Survey (Equipment)**	Key factors to consider in planning your equipment needs
Form 6-5	**Operations Planning Survey (Labor)**	Key factors to consider in planning your labor needs
Form 6-6	**Operations Planning Survey (Process)**	Key factors to consider in planning the process requirements of your operations
Form 6-7	**Distribution and Delivery Survey**	Questions designed to help you get a handle on your distribution and delivery capabilities
Form 6-8	**Management Team Member Profile**	A form for collecting relevant background information on top management-team members

Chapter 7

Crafting Your Marketing Plan

. . . .

In This Chapter

▶ Getting a handle on your market situation

▶ Forming marketing objectives and goals

▶ Figuring out your positioning and branding strategies

▶ Devising your marketing strategies

▶ Setting your budget

. . . .

*B*usiness plans. Marketing plans. What's the difference, anyway?

Here's a quick-fix answer: Your business plan sells your company, whereas your marketing plan tells how you plan to sell your products. And because selling your products is key to your company's success, an outline of your marketing plan is at the heart of your business plan.

Marketing is a top concern of business CEOs, and it's the number-one issue on the minds of most entrepreneurs and small-business owners. Many business advisors and investors consider marketing the one area that can make or break a business plan, which is why the following pages are so important.

People reading your business plan want to know the potential buyers for your offering and whether your market is growing or shrinking. They want to know the extent of your competition and where your business fits in the competitive hierarchy. And they want details about how you'll present your product, including your plans for pricing, packaging, distribution, promotion, sales, and customer service.

In other words, anyone reading your business plan wants to know your marketing plan — the blueprint you'll follow to achieve sales success. That's why I devote an entire chapter exclusively to this topic.

Marketing at a Glance

The topic of marketing can fill a whole book, and it has! If you want to know plenty more about the subject, look through *Small Business Marketing For Dummies* (Wiley) by yours truly. I use excerpts of information from that book on the following pages to provide a broad-brush picture of marketing and to give you what you need to know to write the marketing section of your business plan.

The big marketing picture

Think of marketing as the never-ending process that you undertake to create and keep customers. Figure 7-1 shows a bird's-eye view of the marketing cycle, which includes

- **Customer, product, and competitive research:** The marketing process begins with research that enables you to understand your market environment.

- **Development of marketing strategies:** Marketing involves the development of strategies for building your product, pricing, packaging, and distribution to the meet the interests of your customers and the realities of your market environment.

- **Promotional efforts:** Promotion is a major component of the marketing process. Promotional efforts include advertising and public relations programs that grab attention, inspire interest, and invite product purchases.

- **Sales programs:** These programs convert the interest promotional efforts generate into purchases and are backed by flawless sales and delivery systems.

- **Customer service:** Customer service builds satisfaction, prompts repeat purchases and positive word of mouth, and inspires customer loyalty to your company.

The nuts and bolts of a marketing plan

A marketing plan includes the following components (which I detail in the following sections of this chapter):

- Your market situation, including your customer profile and descriptions of changes affecting your customers, competitors, and business climate

- Your marketing goals and objectives

- Your company's positioning and brand statements

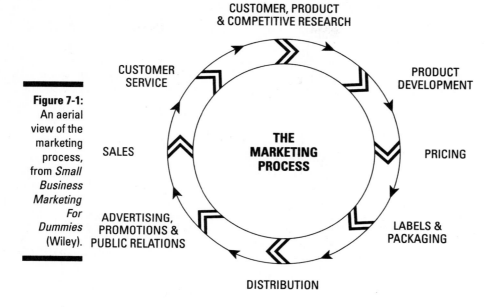

Figure 7-1: An aerial view of the marketing process, from *Small Business Marketing For Dummies* (Wiley).

(Diagram labels: CUSTOMER, PRODUCT & COMPETITIVE RESEARCH; PRODUCT DEVELOPMENT; PRICING; LABELS & PACKAGING; DISTRIBUTION; ADVERTISING, PROMOTIONS & PUBLIC RELATIONS; SALES; CUSTOMER SERVICE; THE MARKETING PROCESS)

✔ Your marketing strategies, including plans for your product, distribution, pricing, and promotions

✔ Your marketing budget

✔ Your tactical and action plans

✔ Your long-range plans

Detail all these essential topics in your marketing plan. In your business plan — in the part where you discuss your company strategy (see Chapter 1) — include a summarized version that provides the highlights.

Your business plan is mainly for external audiences — financial backers, business advisors, and key partners — so edit out details that people outside your business don't really need to know and that you may want to hold close to your vest. These include your tactical and action plans and details of how you plan to allocate your marketing budget.

Analyzing Your Market Situation

The first section of the marketing plan provides a snapshot view of your marketing arena. It presents what you know about the size and growth trends of your market, what you face in terms of competition, and what critical issues will affect your ability to sell your products — for better or worse.

MBA-types call this overview a *situation analysis* because, to sound like former baseball player Yogi Berra, it analyzes the situation you face as you launch your marketing plan.

Getting a handle on your market

Anyone who reads your marketing plan — or the summary of it in your business plan — wants to know that your ideas are grounded in reality. So start with a fact-packed summary of the market your business serves, including who will buy your offering and whether the number of prospects are growing, holding steady, or shrinking. Make sure to cover the following points:

✔ **Your customer description:** Define your customers in geographic terms (where they live), demographic terms (facts such as age, gender, race, education level, marital status, income level, and household size), and psychographic terms (lifestyle characteristics, including attitudes, beliefs, and behaviors that affect customer-purchasing patterns). If you don't have a ready description, turn to Chapter 4 to develop your customer profile.

✔ **How customers divide into market segments:** *Market segments* are comprised of unique groups of consumers that share similar characteristics. For example, women may buy from your company very differently than men do, and buyers from one geographic area may have different product interests than customers from another. Midweek customers may be decidedly different than weekend customers. (Chapter 4 includes a market segmentation framework and information to help you analyze who's buying what from your company.)

Here are a few ways that companies may divide their consumers into market segments:

- Companies selling to consumers may segment customers by gender, age, income, location, or buying pattern.

- Business-to-business companies may segment clients by size or type of company, nature of client relationship (contract business versus one-time purchase, for example), or product interest.

- Companies using a number of distribution channels (retail outlets, direct-mail catalogs, and e-commerce, for example) may find that customers arriving via each channel share similarities that make them very different — in terms of product interest and buying patterns — from customers that arrive via other channels.

A ski resort may segment its market into local area skiers, skiers who reside within a 150-mile radius and drive to the resort for two-day trips, and destination skiers who arrive by air and usually stay at least four days. The resort may further break down local skiers into occasional and frequent skiers. See how segmentation works? By knowing its market segments, the ski resort can promote specific offerings that appeal to each group.

✔ **The size of your market and the growth trends you see:** Indicate size and growth information for your overall market and for the various market segments your company serves. For example, if teenagers represent a sizeable segment of your clientele, include facts about the size and growth trends of the teenage population in your market area.

Don't base your projections on a hunch. Cite experts, refer to census data, excerpt industry analyses, present findings compiled by media organizations that serve your customers, or show a recap of your sales history to prove market momentum. Offering proof for what you say about market size and growth is important because this proof is the claim on which you stake your marketing plan — and budget.

Assessing your competition

To grow your business, you need to gain *market share* (commonly known as your slice of the market pie) by drawing customers and purchases away from competing companies. In this portion of your marketing plan, you summarize what kind of competition your company faces, including

✔ **Direct competitors:** These competitors are companies that your customers consider when they think about buying. Describe each one, along with what you know about the threats they pose to you. (Chapter 4 tells you how to use cloak-and-dagger methods in your intelligence mission.)

✔ **Indirect or stealth competitors:** These competitors are companies that go after your customers in different and unexpected ways. For example, cable television, satellite services, movie rentals, and low-priced DVD purchase offers are all indirect competitors to movie theaters. (See Chapter 4 for help identifying the stealth competitors that can blindside your company.)

Competition creates threats and provides opportunities, and how you handle both is a determining factor in the success of your company:

✔ **Competitive threats and opportunities:** Examples of threats include new competitors, improved or expanded offerings from old competitors, and new options that let prospects fill the need that your product addresses in a whole new way — such as online buying, do-it-yourself solutions, or new technologies that replace the need for your offering altogether. Opportunities include changes that weaken your competitors or the closure of longtime competitors.

✔ **How you plan to protect against threats and capitalize on opportunities:** Now you're conducting a strengths, weaknesses, opportunities, and threats (SWOT) analysis. (See Chapter 5 for the whole scoop.)

Winning a slice of the market pie

Sooner or later, some banker, advisor, or partner will ask you about your market share. Are you ready? These definitions and calculation approaches will help.

Market share is the portion of all the sales of products, like yours, taking place in your market area that your business captures. You can calculate your market share by units sold, customers served, or dollar volume. Following are examples of each approach:

✔ **Share of unit sales:** The manager of Open Fairways Golf Course discovers that all the courses in the market area together host 50,000 rounds of golf a year. Of those rounds, Open Fairways hosts 7,000, for a 14 percent market share. (7,000 ÷ 50,000 = 0.14)

✔ **Share of customers served:** The owners of Immaculate Carpet Cleaning serve homes within 15 miles of the business. That area includes 2,000 homes. However, the Immaculate owners estimate that only 1,000 homes are potential customers. The company currently cleans carpets in 125 homes a year, giving it a 12.5 percent market share. (125 ÷ 1,000 = 0.125)

✔ **Share of dollar volume:** The owners of Forever Green Landscaping operate in a market area where homeowners and businesses buy a million dollars worth of landscaping services annually. Forever Green has sales of $100,000, or 10 percent market share. (100,000 ÷ 1,000,000 = 0.10)

Some companies track their market shares with two or three of these calculation approaches. However, many companies have access to only one of the market size statistics, so they base their market-share assessments solely on that calculation approach.

Forecasting your business climate

The final step in your situation analysis involves looking at how outside forces may affect your company's success. For example, changing economic conditions can crimp or expand your customers' abilities to purchase your product or service (like rising fuel costs for companies in the travel industry). Consider some other factors:

✔ Increasing labor or supply costs that can impact your pricing

✔ New rules or regulations

✔ Emerging technologies that change how you or your competitors do business

✔ Social trends or shifting consumer preferences

✔ Scheduled construction that may affect your customers' ease of access

✔ Regional or industry events or promotions that can impact visibility for and interest in your offerings

In your written business plan, include highlights of your situation analysis, touching on the following key points:

✔ The market for your product or service, including facts about the number of prospective customers and whether that group is growing or shrinking

✔ Market segments that provide the best opportunities for growth and why

✔ Competitive threats and opportunities and how you plan to counter or take advantage of each.

✔ Market trends and business forces that will affect your company, along with your plans for overcoming threats and capitalizing on opportunities

Setting Marketing Goals and Objectives

Chapter 3 includes a great section on how to set business goals and objectives. Follow these steps as you set marketing goals and objectives:

1. **Review your business goals.**

   Some goals deal with operational, employee, management, and business-development issues. Others deal with marketing issues, including goals such as "Increase brand awareness" and "Find new markets for products and services." These business goals become goals of your marketing plan.

   When you adopt business goals as marketing goals, add clearly defined targets and timelines. For instance: You may expand "Find new markets for products and services" to "Find new markets to increase sales of Product X by 5 percent over the upcoming one-year period."

2. **Set objectives to define how you'll achieve your marketing goals.**

   Each objective should specify an action and a desired outcome. Table 7-1 shows an example.

Table 7-1	An Example of Marketing Goals and Objectives		
Goal/ Objective	Action	Timeline	Desired Outcome
Goal	To develop new markets	Over the upcoming one-year period	To increase sales of Product X by 5 percent

(continued)

Table 7-1 (continued)

Goal/ Objective	Action	Timeline	Desired Outcome
Objective	Establish a distributor relationship	During the first quarter	To achieve product placement in holiday gift catalogs
Objective	Place ads in geographically targeted tennis and golf publications	In early spring	To develop summer sales to Northwest outdoor enthusiasts
Objective	Enhance Web presence and launch permission-based e-mailings	Over the first quarter	To develop customers in distant market areas

Include your marketing goals and objectives in the marketing section of your written business plan.

Defining Your Position and Brand

Your *position* is the niche that your company — and only your company — fills in your customers' minds. To gain a market position, you first define how your company and its products and services are unique, and then you use marketing communications to convey that your company provides a meaningful and unique solution in your market area.

Your *brand* is the set of beliefs that consumers associate with your name. You build your brand by projecting a consistent look, tone, quality, and message in all your business communications. For example, instead of taking just any babysitting job, an 18-year old may *position* herself as the babysitter who's available to travel on vacations as a nanny. After parents rely on her services, they may *brand* her as the "best surrogate big sister our kids could've wished for."

Form 7-1 provides a formula to follow as you write positioning and brand statements for your company.

Include your brand and positioning statements in the marketing section of your business plan.

FORMULA FOR A POSITIONING STATEMENT		
Your business or product name	**+ What makes your business unique and different**	**+ Your market description**
Business Plans Kit For Dummies	is the easiest, most self-contained do-it-yourself resource	for brand-new or expanding businesses or any size
iPod	is the digital music player	for people who want 5,000 songs at their fingertips everywhere they go
TD Waterhouse	provides the best mix of products, prices and services	for customers who manage their own investments and personal finances
Now it's your turn...		

FORMULA FOR A BRAND STATEMENT	
A phrase that captures the promise your business makes to its customers.	
Yahoo!®	Search engine. Shopping engine. Life engine.
AOL®	The most valuable, convenient, relevant, and enjoyable online experience available.
Amazon.com	Earth's biggest selection.
Now it's your turn...	

Form 7-1: Use this form to develop positioning and brand statements to guide your marketing messages.

Designing Marketing Strategies

Creating a marketing success story is a little like baking a cake. You take a little bit of this, a little more of that, and you arrive at one result. If you change the mix, you get a different outcome.

In marketing, the ingredients you juggle are your *product, place (distribution), pricing,* and *promotions.* Together, these four elements are known as the *marketing mix* or the *four Ps.*

Every marketing action falls under one of the four Ps of the marketing mix, which is why you need a marketing strategy for each area. Use the following sections to guide your planning.

Your product strategy

You present your product development and production plans in other parts of your business plan. In the marketing section, you describe exactly how you plan to use your products to achieve marketing success. Use Form 7-2 as you set your product strategy.

Your distribution strategy

Chapter 6 helps you assess your company's distribution capabilities. Include the results of your assessment in the company description portion of your business plan. In your marketing plan — and briefly in the Marketing Strategy section of your business plan — describe how distribution supports your marketing goals and objectives. Use Form 7-3 to plan your strategy.

Your pricing strategy

One of the decisions most crucial to business success is how to price your products. Too many small businesses use a kind of flinch system — charging what they think the markets will bear, which may be too much for the value they deliver or too little to cover all costs plus a reasonable profit margin.

Get your pricing right by developing a strategy that addresses the nature of your clientele (you can't charge premium prices if you've established your business as a middle-of-the-road option), your production costs, and the operational costs that your sales revenue needs to cover.

Use Form 7-4 to arrive at a pricing strategy.

PRODUCT STRATEGY CHECKLIST
1. How will you present your products to develop customers and sales?
2. Which products or product features will you emphasize?
3. Will you introduce new product names, packaging, or labeling to re-inspire market interest?
4. Can you bundle products into packaged offers to increase sales?
5. Will you develop new products or add new design elements or functions to existing products to achieve market interest, meet competitive challenges, or address consumer demands?
6. Will you introduce or increase emphasis on quality assurances or service policies?
7. Other product considerations...

Form 7-2: Use this form as you make product decisions to support your marketing plans.

DISTRIBUTION STRATEGY CHECKLIST

1. Will you introduce new distribution or delivery systems to increase sales, serve customers, or gain advantage over competitors? Some examples of new distribution methods include home delivery, subscription delivery, free delivery to volume customers, and so on.

2. Can you increase sales by adding new distribution channels, such as online sales, distributor relationships, or new retail outlets?

3. Would your business benefit from business partnerships that allow you to achieve off-premise sales outlets in other retail settings?

4. If you use or are adding distributors or representatives, do you have adequate plans for recruiting, training, motivating, and compensating them, and do you have a clear plan for assignment of territories?

5. Other distribution strategy considerations...

Form 7-3: Use this form as you tailor distribution and delivery systems to fit your marketing objectives.

Your promotion strategy

Your promotion strategy is the heart of your marketing plan. It tells how you'll communicate your marketing message to prospective customers. For more information and advice on planning your promotional strategy, see *Small Business Marketing For Dummies,* by yours truly; *Marketing For Dummies,* 2nd Edition, by Alexander Hiam; or check out one of the other countless marketing books on the market.

Form 7-5 on the CD-ROM gets your promotional thinking started.

PRICING STRATEGY CHECKLIST
1. What is your pricing philosophy? Does your business want to be the high-end price choice? Middle-of-the-pack? Low end?
2. How do your current (or planned) prices compare with those of your competitors? If your prices are higher, do you offer extra value? If your prices are lower, what affects your lower price and can your pricing sustain profitability?
3. Do you plan to offer special initial pricing to gain trial and acceptance? If so, what is your plan for increasing prices later?
4. Do your prices cover all costs plus a profit margin?
5. Do your prices cover costs such as shrinkage, returns, bad debt, and allowance for employee errors?
6. Do you offer financing and does your offer affect profits for good or bad?
7. How often do you alter your prices or offer sale pricing?
8. Do you allow bargaining?
9. Do you — or can you — join a buying group, buy through an association, or establish bulk-buying agreements to reduce the costs of your product?
10. Do you offer a range of payment options, and do you know the impact of each choice on your financial condition?
11. Other pricing considerations...

Form 7-4: Use this form as you develop your company's pricing strategy.

PROMOTION STRATEGY WORKSHEET
1. To meet your marketing objectives, will you rely most heavily on advertising, personal presentations, sales promotions, or publicity?
2. Can you communicate with your prospects and customers one-to-one using direct mail, e-mail, and personal meetings or do you need to use mass media to reach your market?
3. For advertising or publicity, which media will best reach your prospect — local newspaper, radio, and TV; national/international media/ business-to-business publications; special-interest publications; Web presence; outdoor ads; or others?
4. Are trade shows important for meeting distributors or consumers?
5. Do you need promotional literature to attract prospects or to help move prospects to a buying decision?
6. What kind of message will you convey in your communications? (Remember: consistency is the key to strong branding and sales.)
7. Does your program require professional assistance from freelancers, Web site designers, advertising or public relations firms, or media buyers?
8. Name the three to five most effective ways to communicate with your consumers in order to meet your marketing objectives.

Form 7-5: Use this form to fill in the blanks of your promotion strategy.

Establishing Your Marketing Budget

Sorry, but I can't give you a magic formula for arriving at your marketing budget.

Some companies arrive at their budgets by dusting off last year's budgets and adding the cost of inflation. Some try to match their competitors' budgets. Others look in vain for some industry gauge that will tell them how much of their gross sales they should spend on marketing. But the best approach is to create what's called a *zero-based budget*. With a zero-based budget, you start with a clean slate and add in costs for every item in your promotion plan, including media buys, freelance or agency talent, trade-show registration fees, travel and entertainment for sales presentations, Web site development, hosting and promotion, and any other item on your list.

After you finalize your budget, get it approved, and then spend it. Spend it wisely, but spend it. Don't hoard it. Your marketing budget is the one business expenditure dedicated specifically to getting and keeping customers, so it isn't the place to cut back.

Summarize your promotion strategy in your written business plan. When appropriate, include samples of marketing materials (letterhead, business cards, brochures, and so on) in the appendix of your plan. Samples aren't necessary, but if you have professionally produced materials that contribute to a good, strong image of your company, their inclusion in your plan will contribute to the favorable impression that readers take away from your business plan.

Creating a customer-service environment

If you refer to the aerial view of the marketing process in Figure 7-1, you see that marketing doesn't end when you make the sale. After-the-sale service is the key to achieving customer satisfaction, earning repeat business, achieving good word of mouth, and building a valuable, loyal clientele. Use Form 7-6 on the CD-ROM to evaluate your customer service and to create a customer-service strategy that includes service standards, service objectives, and ways that you'll continuously monitor and enhance the service you provide customers.

(continued)

(continued)

CUSTOMER SERVICE CHECKLIST
☐ Does your company train and reward the staff for customer service?
☐ Does the staff promptly answer phone calls and e-mail?
☐ Does your company immediately follow orders with phone or e-mail acknowledgement?
☐ Does your company immediately follow orders, suggestions, and referrals?
☐ Does your company have a clear and generous return policy?
☐ Does your company offer warranties or service programs?
☐ Does your company have a hot line for questions, complaints, and concerns?
☐ Does your company resolve concerns quickly?
☐ Does your company bend rules and tailor service for customers?
☐ Do your company's services exceed those of your competitors?
☐ Does your staff communicate frequently with customers to find out their needs and how your company can serve them better?
☐ Does your company deliver quality products on time, on budget, and with friendly service?
☐ Does your company have programs that inspire loyalty?
☐ Does your staff make doing business with your company a highlight of your customer's day?

Forms on the CD-ROM

The following forms on the CD-ROM help you develop your marketing plan.

Form 7-1	**Positioning and Brand Statements Worksheet**	Formulas and real-world examples to help you write your marketing statements
Form 7-2	**Product Strategy Checklist**	Questions to answer as you develop a strategy for marketing your products
Form 7-3	**Distribution Strategy Checklist**	Issues to consider as you tailor your distribution and delivery systems to fit your marketing objectives
Form 7-4	**Pricing Strategy Checklist**	Questions to weigh as you develop a pricing strategy that takes into account the nature of your clientele and the production and operational costs your sales revenue need to cover
Form 7-5	**Promotion Strategy Checklist**	Issues to address as you select promotion approaches and determine the most effective ways to communicate with prospects
Form 7-6	**Customer Service Checklist**	Questions designed to generate new ideas for improving your customer service

Chapter 8

Deciphering and Presenting Your Financial Situation

In This Chapter

▶ Understanding income statements, balance sheets, and cash-flow statements

▶ Looking into your financial future

Some people love adding and subtracting columns of numbers. And then there are the rest of us. Although this chapter is for everyone, it's most of all for the vast group of people who are spreadsheet impaired and who wish that terms like income statement and balance sheet would just disappear — or that someone would at least take away the mystery. Well, you get half your wish.

The discussion in this chapter helps you understand your business finances and all the jargon they involve. This chapter also makes you better at keeping an eye on your money, plus it tells you how to examine your financial situation and gaze into the crystal ball to forecast your company's financial future.

If you love numbers, this chapter will be a breeze. If not, it'll be a little more work but all the more worthwhile — and necessary. Despite what you think, if you're in business, you're a numbers person, like it or not. So bring out the calculators and get ready to talk finance!

Decoding Financial Terminology

People hyperventilate when they hear the term *financial statements*, as if someone just told them that the rest of the conversation would take place in an arcane foreign language with no translation assistance.

Well, here's good news. You can master the language of business finance by understanding three key terms:

- **Income statement:** This report summarizes how much money your business earned and spent up until the minute the report was run. It reports your revenues over a given period of time and then subtracts all the costs of doing business over that same period to arrive at your *net profit*. Income statements are also called "earnings reports" or "profit-and-loss statements." Don't be confused; they're all one and the same.

- **Balance sheet:** This report captures a financial snapshot of your business at a particular moment in time, usually the very end of a month or year. The top half of the balance sheet tallies up your company's *assets* (the things your business owns that have monetary value). The bottom half combines your company's *liabilities* (the money your business owes) with your *equity* (the portion of your company's assets that you own as opposed to what you've borrowed and owe). The top and bottom portions of this report must balance each other out — in other words assets must equal the total of liabilities and owner equity — hence the name.

- **Cash-flow statement:** This financial report tracks money that flows in and out of your business over a given period of time (weekly, monthly, quarterly, or yearly.) The top half of your cash-flow statement details funds coming in and going out of your company over the statement period; the bottom half shows the resulting changes in your cash position. The top and bottom halves must match up in order to reconcile the net effect of the inflow and outflow of money with the difference in cash holdings over the report period.

Putting Together an Income Statement

Your company's income statement calculates your *net profit*, or bottom line, using this basic formula:

Net profit = Revenue – Costs

The outcome of this calculation gives a measurement of how your company performed financially over a certain time period. The IRS, of course, is interested in your income statement for the taxable year. Seasonal businesses — such as winter ski resorts or summer river-rafting operations as a few examples — view statements quarterly, and many other businesses run reports monthly to keep tabs on their bottom line.

Reviewing a sample income statement

Take a look at how a gift shop called Broad Street Emporium uses income statements to manage business finances. Figure 8-1 shows the company's annual revenues, costs, and profits for the most recent year as well as for the previous year. By comparing statements for two years in a row, the owners can see how their financial performance has changed over time.

BROAD STREET EMPORIUM				
INCOME STATEMENT				
INCOME STATEMENT AS OF DECEMBER 31				
			Last Year	Previous Year
1	Revenue on in-store sales		624,000.	595,000.
	Revenue on catalog sales	+	105,000.	+ 95,000.
	Gross Revenue	$	729,000.	$ 690,000.
2	Cost of goods sold	−	448,000.	− 445,000.
	Gross Profit	$	281,000.	$ 245,000.
3	Sales, general, and administration	−	126,000.	− 108,000.
	Depreciation expense	−	20,000.	− 20,000.
	Operating Profit	$	135,000.	$ 117,000.
4	Dividend and interest income	+	3,000.	+ 3,000.
	Interest expense	−	24,000.	− 25,000.
	Profit Before Taxes	$	114,000.	$ 95,000.
5	Taxes	−	22,000.	− 19,000.
	Net Profit	$	92,000.	$ 76,000.

Figure 8-1: An income statement summarizes your revenue and costs and shows your net profit.

The Broad Street Emporium income statement includes five sections. Each one provides important information about the company's financial condition.

Section 1: Gross revenue

The word "gross" has nothing to do with teenage jargon. In business finance, *gross revenue* refers to the total of all sales income collected by your business without subtracting any costs.

In the case of Broad Street Emporium, gross revenue comes from two major sources: money taken in via in-store retail sales and money collected through the store's catalog sales.

Depending on your business, your revenue may come from sales of a single product or product line or from a number of different products and services. If you have more than one revenue stream, itemize revenues from each source so that you can see at a glance where your revenue is really coming from and then add the categories to arrive at your gross revenue.

Section 2: Gross profit

In general, *profit* is the money that you get to keep after all the bills are paid.

Gross profit, also called "gross income," is the first stage of profit. It equals gross revenue minus the *costs of goods sold*, which covers the costs directly associated with producing, assembling, or purchasing what you have to sell.

To Broad Street Emporium, costs of goods sold include the wholesale costs of the merchandise displayed on the gift shop's shelves and in its catalog. To a service business, costs of goods sold include costs directly related to supplying or delivering the service. To a manufacturer, costs of goods sold include costs for raw materials and the labor, utilities, and facilities needed to put the product together.

You'll have to make judgment calls regarding which expenses count as costs of goods. After you decide, keep your definition consistent over time so that as you monitor gross profit, you're able to compare apples with apples.

Section 3: Operating profit

After you have subtracted your costs of goods from your gross revenue to arrive at your gross profit, the next step is calculate your operating profit, which involves several steps.

First you have to subtract from your gross profit your *operating expenses,* also known as general and administrative expenses or SG&A (sales, general, and administration) expenses. Under any name, these expenses include the costs involved in operating your business, including salaries, research and development costs, marketing expenses, travel and entertainment, utility bills, rent, office supplies, and other overhead expenses.

Next you need to account for something called *depreciation expenses.* When you purchase big-ticket items for your business — maybe a car to call on clients, a computer system, or even a building for offices, warehouse space, or other facilities — what you're really doing is exchanging one asset (cash in the bank) for another asset (the car, computer, or building). The business assets you acquire all have useful life spans, so one way to spread out the costs of these assets over the number of years they're actually in service is to calculate and deduct *depreciation expenses* each year.

To calculate your *operating profit* (you might also hear it called *operating income* or *EBIT,* which stands for earnings before interest and taxes), you subtract your operating and depreciation expenses from your gross profit.

> Operating profit = Gross profit – Operating expenses and Depreciation expenses

On the Broad Street Emporium income statement, operating expenses reflect staff salaries, advertising costs, and production and delivery of the store's catalog three times a year. In addition, the company takes depreciation expenses for its storefront building, computer system, and delivery van.

Watch your overhead expenses like a hawk. They're not tied directly to your products and services, so they don't contribute directly to your revenue. But if they get out of line, they can quickly eat away at your gross profits.

Section 4: Profit before taxes

Profit before taxes takes into account any income that your company made on investments of any sort and subtracts any interest expenses you paid over the statement period.

> Profit before taxes = Operating profit + Investment income – Interest expenses

The reason that you keep investment income and interest expenses outside your operating profit is because they result from money management and aren't really part of your business operations. For one thing, the amount of interest you pay depends on how you've structured your company financially, not on the business itself. For another thing, interest absolutely, positively has to be paid on a strict and unforgiving schedule.

Section 5: Net profit

Net profit (also called *net earnings, net income,* or *bottom line*) is what's left after you subtract your final expenses from your total business income. As you read that sentence, you're probably thinking, "Final expenses? We've already deducted every cost under the sun. What's left to subtract?" How about taxes?

Depending on how you structured your company, your business may or may not pay taxes directly on its profits. If you're a sole proprietor or if your business is a partnership, for example, your profits are funneled straight to the owners for tax purposes. But if your business pays taxes, you need to subtract those taxes before you state your final profit.

Figure 8-1 shows that after Broad Street Emporium paid its taxes for the year, the business was left with a net profit of $92,000. That's good news because it amounts to a 21 percent increase over the previous year.

Now it's your turn: Creating your income statement

To develop an income statement for your company, use the template provided on Form 8-1 (which looks just like Figure 8-1 except all the entries are blank and awaiting your input). If your business isn't up and running yet, use the template to project what you expect in terms of revenues and expenses. Doing so serves as a good basis when you prepare your new business budget.

If you use accounting or financial software to do much of the work for you, you can skip Form 8-1. If so, at least print your most recent income statement and look it over carefully. Make sure you understand each entry and are convinced that your overall financial picture makes sense.

Don't let your software program do all the number crunching for you. In the end, be sure you know what all the numbers mean and what they say about the financial health of your company.

Your income statement is an essential part of your written business plan. If your venture is up and running, include statements for the last year or two for comparison purposes. Also include income statement projections — whether yours is an existing business or a start-up. Show your income plans for a year or two, or even up to five years into the future. Jump to the "Forecasting and Budgeting" section near the end of this chapter for more information.

Creating Your Balance Sheet

Your balance sheet gives you a snapshot of what your business is worth at a particular moment in time. To make the calculation, tally up the monetary value of everything your company owns and then subtract the money you owe to others. What you own are your *assets* and what you owe are your *liabilities*.

The difference between the two is what your company is worth, usually referred to as the *equity* in your business.

You can represent your balance sheet in a really straightforward equation:

Equity = Assets – Liabilities

In a bizarre attempt to ensure job security, however, accountants rewrote the equation as follows:

Assets = Liabilities + Equity

This equation is the very same as the other — it's just harder to grasp. Go figure. Anyway, the layout of your company's balance sheet follows this second equation. The top half of the balance sheet lists your business assets, divided into a number of basic categories. The bottom half lists your liabilities by category and then tacks on your equity in the business.

The total value of assets must be equal to the value of liabilities plus equity. In other words, the top half has to balance out the bottom half. *How* they balance each other tells you a lot about your company's financial health. That's what the upcoming sections are all about.

At the very least, put together a balance sheet on the last day of each year. Include the numbers for the end of the previous year as well so you can compare how your assets, liabilities, and equity have changed over the year.

Reviewing a sample balance sheet

Figure 8-2 shows the balance sheet for the Broad Street Emporium gift shop as of December 31 of the most recent year. It also shows numbers for the end of the previous year for comparison purposes. Read on for explanations of each section.

Section 1: Current assets

Current assets represent all the items your business owns that are liquid enough to be converted into cash within a year. Anything with monetary value that your business owns is an asset. Your balance sheet shows not only how much your assets are worth but also how long it would take you to convert them into cold, hard cash. The length of time needed to dispose of an asset is often described in terms of *liquidity.* The more *liquid* an asset, the faster you can sell it off.

BROAD STREET EMPORIUM		
BALANCE SHEET		
BALANCE SHEET ON DECEMBER 31		
Assets	**Last Year**	**Previous Year**
1 **Current Assets**		
Cash	45,000.	36,000.
Investment portfolio	+ 20,000.	+ 17,000.
Accounts receivable	+ 15,000.	+ 18,000.
Inventories	+ 110,000.	+ 97,000.
Prepaid expenses	+ 1,000.	+ 1,000.
Total Current Assets	$ 191,000.	$ 169,000.
2 **Fixed Assets**		
Land	100,000.	100,000.
Buildings	+ 295,000.	+ 295,000.
Equipment	+ 15,000.	+ 10,000.
Accumulated depreciation	− 65,000.	− 45,000.
Total Fixed Assets	$ 345,000.	$ 360,000.
3 **Intangibles (goodwill, patents)**	$ 10,000.	$ 10,000.
4 **TOTAL ASSETS**	$ 546,000.	$ 539,000.
Liabilities and Owners' Equity	**Last Year**	**Previous Year**
5 **Current Liabilities**		
Accounts payable	4,000.	6,000.
Accrued expenses payable	+ 12,000.	+ 11,000.
Total Current Liabilities	$ 16,000.	$ 17,000.
6 **Long-term Liabilities**		
Building mortgage	210,000.	214,000.
Total Long-term Liabilities	$ 210,000.	$ 214,000.
7 **Owners' Equity**		
Invested capital	200,000.	195,000.
Accumulated retained earnings	+ 120,000.	+ 113,000.
Total Owners' Equity	$ 320,000.	$ 308,000.
8 **TOTAL LIABILITIES and EQUITY**	$ 546,000.	$ 539,000.

Figure 8-2:
Your
balance
sheet
shows your
company's
worth.

Current assets include

- **Cash:** You can't get more liquid than cash. Cash can be anything from the bills and change in the cash register or the petty cash drawer to the money you have in checking or savings accounts at the bank.

- **Investment portfolio:** Cash is nice, but it's even nicer to see your money put to work. Investments may include money market accounts, government bonds, or other reasonably safe securities.

- **Accounts receivable:** This asset consists of money customers owe you for products or services you've already delivered. If you provide products on credit, you may give customers 30, 60, or 90 days to pay. Watch your accounts receivable carefully. One deadbeat customer can throw your numbers for a loop.

- **Inventories:** This item reflects the equivalent cash value of products or supplies you have on hand. Coming up with a realistic estimate for the value of your inventories is often tricky. When in doubt, stay on the conservative side. Your balance sheet should reflect what you can reasonably expect to receive if you have to liquidate these assets.

- **Prepaid expenses:** Your company may have paid for services you haven't yet received — professional service retainers or insurance premiums, for example. List these payments as part of your current assets.

Current assets, especially the most liquid ones, are extremely important to your business. They represent reserves available to fund day-to-day operations or to draw on in case of a financial crunch. Figure 8-2 shows that Broad Street Emporium had a total of $191,000 in current assets as of the end of the most recent year, including $65,000 in cash or securities.

Section 2: Fixed assets

Fixed assets are usually big, expensive, and meant to last a long time, so they're not very liquid. Fixed assets include

- **Land:** If your company owns land — the ground under your office building, for example — you list it separately from your office building on the balance sheet. Unlike other fixed assets, land doesn't depreciate on your balance sheet because it's considered an asset that doesn't wear out over time. For that reason you leave the same land value on the books year after year.

- **Buildings:** As far as your balance sheet is concerned, the value of buildings is equal to the original price you paid for them plus the amounts you've spent on improvements over the years.

✔ **Equipment:** Equipment includes anything and everything you acquire for your business that's meant to last more than a year. Machinery, cars, office equipment, computers, telephones, and furniture all fall into this category. When you enter the value of each asset on your balance sheet, use the actual price you paid for it. If you didn't pay cash, assign a reasonable value to include on your balance sheet.

✔ **Accumulated depreciation:** Each big-ticket item that you acquire for your business has a useful lifespan. *Depreciation* measures the decline in useful value of each fixed asset over time. Don't worry, you don't have to come up with the numbers; the IRS provides standard depreciation schedules, depending on the kind of assets you own. *Accumulated depreciation* sums up the value loss of all your assets over your years of ownership and reduces the total value of your fixed assets accordingly.

On your balance sheet, the value of a fixed asset is based on the original price paid minus any accumulated depreciation according to the IRS's general depreciation schedule. The resulting number may have very little to do with the price you would receive if you sold the asset or the price you would pay if you replaced it.

Broad Street Emporium shows fixed assets valued at $345,000 after accumulated depreciation is taken into account, including $5,000 spent on new equipment during the most recent year. Also during the recent year, the book value of all assets was reduced by $20,000 because of depreciation. That same $20,000, by the way, shows up as a depreciation expense on the income statement illustrated in Figure 8-1.

Section 3: Intangibles

Intangibles are assets that, by definition, are hard to get your arms around. But these intangibles can turn out to be extremely important to your business. Intangible assets include things like an exclusive contract to supply services, a franchise ownership, or a hard-to-get license or permit to do business. An intangible asset can also be a patent that protects an invention, software technology, or a production process. Intangible assets are clearly valuable to the company that owns them, but the question is, what are they really worth?

Intangibles are usually not reflected as assets, although some companies allocate a symbolic $1 on the balance sheet to indicate that intangible assets are there and are valuable but aren't measurable. The exception is a purchased patent that may be amortized over the life of the patent.

As a business owner, one key intangible asset that you should be aware of is goodwill. *Goodwill* represents the positive value of a company's name, including its customer relations, its workforce, its reputation and other factors that

Sock puppet lives on

Sometimes a company's intangible assets prove to be worth a lot — in one case, more than the company itself. After a wild ride on the roller coaster of e-commerce, the pet-supply Web site called Pets.com closed down. But its mascot Sock Puppet lived on, spawning its own line of dolls and boasting its own licensing agent. The puppet turned out to be more valuable than the company's products or services. Who'd have guessed?

contribute to the company's ability to succeed in its marketplace. When a buyer purchases a company at a price above its fair market value, the buyer is probably paying extra to acquire the company's goodwill. Goodwill is only realized when a business is sold, and so it is not carried on a balance sheet unless it was acquired as part of a business purchase.

For example, Broad Street Emporium bought an existing gift shop a number of years ago and paid $10,000 more than the net value of the shop's assets at the time. The Broad Street Emporium's balance sheet lists that goodwill purchase as an intangible asset.

Section 4: Total assets

Total assets reflect the value of all the current assets, fixed assets, and intangibles that your company owns. Your assets include equipment, inventory, real property, and anything that is assigned a monetary value on your balance sheet. Your current assets are an indication of your company's liquidity or its ability to pay its current obligations. Your total assets minus total liabilities provide an indication of your company's solvency.

Figure 8-2 shows that Broad Street Emporium increased its total assets by $7,000 to $546,000 last year — the result of increases in current assets and fixed assets, as you see in the upcoming cash-flow statement section.

Section 5: Current liabilities

Liabilities are amounts of money you owe to creditors in the form of bills that are due, bank loans you've taken out, and bonds or warrants that you may have issued to raise money. The basic idea behind these so-called financial instruments is always the same: You receive money or something else of value in exchange for the promise to pay the debt back over a certain period of time (usually with interest). Sometimes an asset that you own secures the debts. (If you don't pay back what you owe as promised, the creditor can take the asset away from you.) Other times the debts are unsecured.

Current liabilities represent short-term debts that you have to repay within one year. These liabilities are closely tied to the current assets listed on the top half of your balance sheet because you have to pay them off with those assets. In most cases, current liabilities fall into two groups:

- ✔ **Accounts payable:** These liabilities come in the form of bills that haven't yet been paid for such things as utilities, telephone service, office supplies, professional services, raw materials, wholesale goods, or other invoices from providers or suppliers.

- ✔ **Accrued expenses payable:** In addition to outside accounts payable, your business continuously accrues liabilities related to salaries or wages (if you have employees), insurance premiums, interest on bank loans, and taxes you owe. Any obligations that are unpaid at the time you run your balance sheet get grouped together in this category.

To figure out the money available on a day-to-day basis to keep your business up and running — known as your *working capital* — subtract your current liabilities from your current assets.

Working capital = Current assets – Current liabilities

The Broad Street Emporium owners can do the math and see that they have $175,000 in working capital — a good, strong position that provides them with the financial flexibility to carry on their business activities and fund operations during fluctuations of revenue and expenditures.

Section 6: Long-term liabilities

Long-term liabilities are major financial obligations that you take on to get your company up and running or to expand your business operations. Perhaps you've taken a 10-year bank loan or issued bonds to a group of investors to be repaid in 15 years. Or maybe you've taken a mortgage to buy your business buildings. These liabilities are often at the very heart of your company's financial structure.

Broad Street Emporium has one long-term liability: A $210,000 building mortgage that the company will pay off in 26 years.

Section 7: Owner's equity

Equity is the part of a business that the owner or owners actually own. Think of equity this way: Lots of people who say they own their homes really own just a piece of their homes, and banks or mortgage companies own the rest. The same is true for business owners and their businesses.

What's more, the equity in your business might be distributed among a number of owners in all sorts of ways with various strings attached defining when equity can be sold or how it can be used. You may be the one-and-only owner of your company, or your company may be a publicly traded corporation owned by tens of thousands of investors. Under any ownership structure, though, when you strip away all the complexity, owner equity comes from two basic sources of equity: money coming from outside investors and money generated from profits that are kept inside the company. These two forms of equity are called

✔ **Invested capital:** Money invested in your company comes from various sources, including cash you put up as a principal owner of the business or cash you raise by selling small pieces of your company in the form of stock to outside investors. Outside equity may be privately held or, when your company is big enough, you may decide to go for an initial public offering (IPO) — making shares of your company available for sale on a public stock exchange. No matter how you exchange equity for cash, it's all lumped together as invested capital.

✔ **Accumulated retained earnings:** When your business turns a profit (meaning when revenues exceed all costs and expenses), you face the happy decision of what to do with the windfall. You may decide to give some of it back to the owners and investors in the form of *dividends*. Or you may plow some of the profits back into the business so that you can grow bigger and, as a result, create more equity for everyone who has a stake in your company. *Accumulated retained earnings* represent all the profits you've poured back into your business.

Total owner's equity is the sum of invested capital and accumulated retained earnings, which together equal the value of the part of the company that the owners actually own.

Total owner's equity = Invested capital + Accumulated retained earnings

The owners of Broad Street Emporium have a total equity of $320,000: $200,000 from owner investments and $120,000 from profits they've poured back into the company over the years.

Section 8: Total liabilities and equity

Total liabilities and equity sums up the value of a company's assets. It combines the current and long-term liabilities that your company is responsible for with the amount of owner's equity in the business. Basically, this means that your company assets are worth the sum of what you own plus what you owe.

Current Liabilities + Long-term Liabilities + Owner's Equity = Total Assets

As you can see, at the close of last year, the top and bottom halves of the Broad Street Emporium balance sheet were in balance at $546,000. In other words, the sum of the company's total liabilities and total owner's equity correctly equaled the total of the company's assets.

Now it's your turn: Building your balance sheet

You guessed it: You need to make a balance sheet of your own. If you're using accounting software, you can complete the task with the push of a button. However, your computer-generated balance sheet is only as good as the numbers you entered in the first place, so take the time to scrutinize them carefully.

If you're starting from scratch or just want to get a hands-on feel for what a balance sheet really means, get out a pencil and create your balance sheet the old-fashioned way — on a piece of paper, using the template provided on Form 8-2 (which looks just like Figure 8-2 but with blank spaces to enter figures showing your own assets, liabilities, and owner's equity).

Include your company's balance sheet in the Financial Review section of your written business plan to provide a snapshot of what you own, what you owe, and what your company is worth. If you're already in business, include year-end numbers for the most recent two years for easy comparison.

Constructing a Cash-Flow Statement

This report is important because it tells you how money flowed in and out of your business over a certain time period and how assets of your business changed as a result. Your balance sheet and income statements report revenues as they are earned and expenses as they are incurred, which is called "accrual basis accounting." The cash-flow statement converts the accrual basis of accounting to a cash basis. Instead of looking at what you have earned and what you owe, it looks at what you have collected and what you have spent and it lets you see at a glance whether more cash is going out than coming in, or vice versa.

In your business, you should review your cash flow at least monthly, using a report that presents side-by-side numbers for two periods so you can track changes in your cash position.

To see how a cash-flow statement measures financial activity and tracks the effects of changes in your cash position, look at Figure 8-3, which shows the cash-flow statement for the Broad Street Emporium gift store as of December 31 of the most recent year alongside cash-flow entries for the previous year for comparison purposes.

If you go to the bottom line you will see that after all the revenue was collected and all the bills were paid, $12,000 was left over, leaving the company in what is knows as a "positive cash position." The following sections explain how cash flowed before arriving at the final year-end position.

Section 1: Total funds in

The cash-flow statement tracks every single dollar as it comes into your company — and not a second before. You can't show the revenue on sales, for example, until you actually have the payment in hand. Following are the income sources that the cash-flow statement tracks:

- **Receipts on sales:** The money you take in from the sales of your products or services shows up in this section, but only after it's deposited in the bank. Billing a customer may be enough to generate a revenue entry on your income statement, but you can't include the amount on your cash-flow statement until you have a deposit slip to show for it.

- **Dividend and interest income:** Any interest you make on your business bank accounts or any earnings from your investment portfolio appear in this section — *if* the payments come in during the statement period.

- **Invested capital:** If your company receives funding from investors, on the date the money reaches your business, it's entered here on your cash-flow statement.

The Broad Street Emporium cash-flow statement shows that the gift store took in $740,000 cash last year. That number synchs with entries on the company's income statement (refer to Figure 8-1) and balance sheet (refer to Figure 8-2). Okay, to be honest, you have to do a little work before you can see how it synchs, but in a minute it'll all make sense.

Here's how it works: The income statement shows gross income of $729,000 and income from dividends and interest of $3,000. Plus, the balance sheet shows that the company also received $5,000 of investment capital from its owners (this money is reflected in the entry for invested capital, which went from $195,000 the previous year to $200,000 last year). Additionally, the company collected $3,000 in outstanding accounts receivable last year (shown on the balance sheet as a reduction in accounts receivable from $18,000 to $15,000). Together, these funds total $740,000, exactly as indicated by the cash-flow statement. Ta-da!

Section 2: Total funds out

This section of the cash-flow statement shows where the money went. You may notice a number of entries that don't appear as expenses on your income statement — such as buildings and equipment, long-term debt reduction, and distributions to owners. The reason is because these cash outlays don't result directly from to the cost of doing business and therefore they are not listed on the income statement, though they are tracked on the cash-flow statement.

- ✔ **Cost of goods acquired:** This line item includes all the products and materials that you paid for during the cash-flow statement period. It doesn't matter whether you sold the goods you acquired or whether they went into your inventory; if you paid to acquire them during this statement period, they show up here.

- ✔ **Sales, general, and administration:** This entry covers payments you made for so-called *overhead expenses*, including everything from paper clips to payroll. When the money actually leaves your hands, you enter those expenses here.

- ✔ **Interest expense:** This entry reflects interest you paid out during the cash-flow statement period, whether for short-term or long-term loans that your company has taken to finance anything from inventory purchases to buildings and equipment.

- ✔ **Taxes:** This line item reflects tax payments you made during the cash-flow statement period.

- ✔ **Buildings and equipment:** Big-ticket items that your business purchased show up as assets on your balance sheet and in the form of depreciation (described earlier in this chapter) on your income statement. At the time that you actually make the purchase, the amount of your purchase payment shows up here on your cash-flow statement.

- ✔ **Long-term debt reduction:** This entry includes the cash you paid to reduce any of your business debts.

- ✔ **Distributions to owners:** If your company makes a profit and your balance sheet is strong, you're probably in a position to give some of the financial rewards back to the owners of the business. If you do, enter distributions or dividend payments in this area of the cash-flow statement.

Figure 8-3 shows that Broad Street Emporium used $728,000 cash last year. Of that money

BROAD STREET EMPORIUM		
CASH FLOW STATEMENT		
CASH FLOW AS OF DECEMBER 31		
Inflow and Outflow	**Last Year**	**Previous Year**
1 **Funds Provided By:**		
Receipts on in-store sales	626,000.	596,000.
Receipts on catalog sales	+ 106,000.	+ 96,000.
Dividend and interest income	+ 3,000.	+ 3,000.
Invested capital	+ 5,000.	+ 10,000.
Total Funds In	$ 740,000.	$ 705,000.
2 **Funds Used For:**		
Cost of goods acquired	461,000.	442,000.
Sales, general, and administration	+ 127,000.	+ 109,000.
Interest expense	+ 24,000.	+ 25,000.
Taxes	+ 22,000.	+ 19,000.
Buildings and equipment	+ 5,000.	+ 1,000.
Long-term debt reduction	+ 4,000.	+ 3,000.
Distributions to owners	+ 85,000.	+ 65,000.
Total Funds Out	$ 728,000.	$ 664,000.
3 **NET CHANGE IN CASH POSITION**	$ + 12,000.	$ + 41,000.
Changes By Account	**Last Year**	**Previous Year**
4 **Changes in Liquid Assets:**		
Cash	+ 9,000.	+ 28,000.
Investment portfolio	+ 3,000.	+ 13,000.
Total Changes	$ 12,000.	$ 41,000.
5 **NET CHANGE IN CASH POSITION**	$ + 12,000.	$ + 41,000.

Figure 8-3:
Creating a cash-flow statement helps you monitor the cash that flows into and out of your company.

- $461,000 was expended for cost of goods acquired — a figure that matches up with the $448,000 entry for cost of goods sold shown on the company's income statement plus a balance sheet increase in company inventories of $13,000.

- Sales, general, and administration expenses took up $127,000, including $126,000 shown on the income statement and a pay down of $1,000 in current liabilities, shown on the balance sheet.

> ✔ The gift shop owners also spent $5,000 on equipment and $4,000 on long-term debt reduction, which you'll see reflected as an increase in equipment assets and a decrease in long-term liabilities on the balance sheet.
>
> ✔ The company distributed $85,000 back to the owners of the gift shop over the year.
>
> ✔ Finally, the company paid out $24,000 in interest expense and $22,000 in taxes, bringing the total funds out to $728,000.

Section 3: Net change in cash position

Your *net change in cash position* is the difference between the total amount of money your company brought in and the total amount that it expended over the reporting period. To find out the net change in your cash position over a certain period, subtract all the funds that left the company from all the funds that came in to the company.

Net change = Funds that came into the company – Funds that left the company

Broad Street Emporium increased its cash position by $12,000 during the most recent year, which means they brought in $12,000 more than they paid out.

Section 4: Changes in liquid assets

The bottom half of the cash-flow statement monitors where the money goes while it's inside your company:

> ✔ **Cash:** This entry tracks the total change in your cash reserves over the course of the statement period.
>
> ✔ **Investment portfolio:** This entry tracks changes in the value of your investment portfolio over the period.

Notice that the cash-flow statement only tracks the flow of cash. It does not reflect changes in the value of other company assets unless those changes delivered cash that was expended or invested.

Figure 8-3 shows that, last year, Broad Street Emporium increased its cash by $9,000 and its investment portfolio by $3,000 over the previous year. These increases add up to $12,000, which correctly matches up with positive change in total current asset entries ($191,000 - $169,000 = $12,000) shown on the company's balance sheet (refer to Figure 8-2).

Section 5: Net change in cash position

Because the top and the bottom halves of the cash-flow statement must balance, the total changes in liquid assets reflected in Section 5 should be identical to the net change in cash position shown in Section 3. In other words, you can determine a net change in cash position by subtracting money going out from money coming in or by monitoring changes to the accounts where the money is coming and going from.

Now it's your turn: Creating your cash-flow statement

Here's where all the pieces start to fit together. As you assemble your cash-flow statement, you'll probably notice that many of the entries are based on numbers from your income statement and your balance sheet. That's because your company's cash flow is tied closely to your revenues and costs, as well as to the assets you own and the debts you've taken on.

If you use accounting software to manage your finances, you can probably run a cash-flow statement by opening the menu and pressing a few keys.

But you may discover even more by using Form 8-3 (which looks just like Figure 8-3 only totally blank and ready for your numbers) to assemble a cash-flow statement from scratch.

Include a cash-flow statement in your written plan. If your business is up and running, include year-end numbers from the past few years for comparison. If you're just getting started, use a cash-flow projection to show exactly how you'll manage the start-up period.

Forecasting and Budgeting

Your financial statements capture how your company did over a certain period (that's what your income statement is about), where your finances stand (that's your balance sheet), and what happens along the way (your cash flow). But what tells you where your business is headed? That's where forecasting comes in.

COMPANY CASH FLOW STATEMENT		
CASH FLOW AS OF DECEMBER 31		
Inflow and Outflow	**Year:**	**Year:**
1 Funds Provided By:		
Receipts_____	+	+
Receipts_____	+	+
Dividend and interest income	+	+
Invested capital	+	+
Other_____	+	+
Total Funds In	=	=
2 Funds Used For:		
Cost of goods acquired	+	+
Sales, general, and administration	+	+
Interest expense	+	+
Taxes	+	+
Other_____	+	+
Buildings and equipment	+	+
Long-term debt reduction	+	+
Distributions to owners	+	+
Total Funds Out	=	=
3 NET CHANGE IN CASH POSITION (Total Funds In – Total Funds Out)	=	=
Changes By Account	**Year:**	**Year:**
4 Changes in Liquid Assets:		
Cash	+	+
Investment portfolio	+	+
Other_____	+	+
Total Changes	=	=
5 NET CHANGE IN CASH POSITION (Total Funds In – Total Funds Out)	=	=

Form 8-3: Create a cash-flow statement by using this form on the CD-ROM.

Lucky for you, financial forecasts are built around the same three financial statements covered in the preceding sections of this chapter. That means no new reports to master. But this time, you base your entries on what you see in your financial future. Then, using your projections, you develop a master budget summarizing your plans for sales, cost of goods sold, operating expenses, capital expenditures, and cash-flow projections that guide your allocation of anticipated resources toward investments and expenditures that are most likely to help your business succeed.

Your financial forecast

Your financial forecast includes your best guesses about the future based on a set of assumptions about what you expect to happen down the road.

Carefully consider every business assumption that goes into your financial forecast. Make sure you know what each one is based on. For example:

- ✔ If you're assuming that the economy will grow at a given rate, state the growth rate on which your plan is based.

- ✔ If you believe that you can raise the cash you need from at least three different funding sources, be specific.

- ✔ If you're almost certain that a new technology is going to completely change the way your industry does business, explain your reasoning.

- ✔ If you think competition will increase in a certain segment of your market, say so.

Spell out what's behind the numbers because the assumptions you make are just as important as the financial forecast itself.

See the following sections for descriptions of what three basic parts of your financial forecast should look like.

Pro forma income statement

Pro forma is one of those Latin phrases that sounds more complicated than it is. In this case, *pro forma* refers to anything you're going to estimate in advance. So your pro forma income statement estimates your revenue, expenses, and profit: one, three, or even five years in the future. You may even want to subdivide the first few years into quarterly projections to allow you to monitor progress in short-term increments during the early days of your company's life. To estimate your financial future, start with these steps:

✔ If you've been in business for a while, get together past income statements to serve as a starting point in making future projections.

✔ If you're just starting your business, you won't have a financial history to fall back on. Instead, search out people in similar businesses, go to trade shows, do online research, and find consultants who can give you guidance. It's work, but if your financial projections end up close to the mark, the results will definitely be worth it in the end.

To assemble your estimates, think about using the company income statement template in Form 8-1, following the income statement construction steps earlier in this chapter. When you're finished, your pro forma income statement should look quite similar in format to its real counterpart. That makes it easy to compare your projections for future performance with what really happens .

At the end of each quarter or year take time to go back to your pro forma income statements to compare actual financial performance with projected performance. Make notes indicating where you were right and wrong. After all, practice makes perfect.

Estimated balance sheet

The difference between an estimated balance sheet and the real thing is that the estimate projects what you will own, what you will owe, and what your company will be worth year by year — looking ahead four or five years. Projecting those numbers sounds tough, and it is. But do it anyway. Even if your projections prove to be less than perfect, they provide you with a financial road map to the future.

Start by listing the assets you think you'll need to support the growth you're looking forward to. Then think about how you'll pay for those assets and that means making major decisions about how much debt you're willing to take on, what company earnings you'll be able to plow back into the business, and how much equity you need to invest in the future.

The company balance sheet template in Form 8-2 provides a useful format that works just as well projecting the future as it does your current condition.

Projected cash flow

Want five good reasons to project your cash flow? Well, here they are. When you have a good sense of how cash will flow in and out of your business, you can

✔ Anticipate inventory purchases to meet seasonal business cycles.

✔ Take advantage of discount- and bulk-purchasing offers.

✔ Plan equipment and building purchases to meet your growth needs.

✔ Arrange financing if you're going to need it — whether that means recruiting investors, assuming long-term debt, making a personal loan, or establishing a short-term line of credit with your bank.

✔ Stay in control of your finances by anticipating cash needs before they arise and meeting obligations in an organized, timely way.

When you estimate your future cash needs and sources, use the company cash-flow statement template in Form 8-3. That way, later you'll be able to compare your projections with your actual cash-flow statements.

Without a financial forecast, your business plan is incomplete. In the financial review section of your plan include your pro forma income statement, estimated balance sheet, and projected cash-flow statement along with the business assumptions behind your projections. Then review and revise your forecasts on a regular basis. Your financial forecast just happens to be one of the most important — and fragile — parts of your business plan. Be able and willing to change it when the business circumstances around you change.

The master budget

The master budget you create for your company allows you to do two extremely important things:

✔ **Live within your means.** Your master budget summarizes your company's anticipated sales, cost of goods sold, operating expenses, capital expenditures and cash flow. By constructing your company's budget to align with your projected cash flow, you establish spending guidelines based on the most realistic financial picture you have. The budget, of course, fills in all the details.

✔ **Use your money wisely.** The master budget allows you to keep spending in line with your business plan. That way, you allocate funds in the most effective way possible to achieve company long-term goals.

To prepare a budget, start with copies of your projected cash-flow statements for the next year or two, paying particular attention to the section that lists where you expect to use cash (refer to Figure 8-3). Then take each of the broad categories (cost of goods acquired; sales, general, and administration expenses; buildings and equipment; and distributions to owners) and create detailed plans for each entry, defining, for example, exactly how much money your business should spend on a service or a piece of equipment.

If your company is large enough, you may want to get a few of your colleagues involved in the budgeting process. Creating a master budget is a big job. By working with the key people around you, you spread the effort while also upping the odds that your management team will buy into the master budget that you come up with.

Your master budget is a key part of your business-planning efforts, but you may or may not want to include it in your written business plan. For most of your audience, your pro forma income statement, estimated balance sheet, and projected cash-flow statement will provide enough information about your future finances.

Forms on the CD-ROM

The following forms on the CD-ROM are designed to help you examine your financial situation.

Form 8-1	**Company Income Statement**	A template that helps you determine your business profits
Form 8-2	**Company Balance Sheet**	A template for calculating your business worth
Form 8-3	**Company Cash-Flow Statement**	A template for tracking inflow and outgo of cash

Part III
Tailoring a Business Plan to Fit Your Needs

The 5th Wave   By Rich Tennant

"For 30 years I've put a hat and coat on to make sales calls and I'm not changing now just because I'm doing it on the Web from my living room."

In this part . . .

Different businesses pose different planning challenges, which is why this part has five chapters from which you can pick and choose.

Chapter 9 covers planning issues for the self-employed — especially those just striking out on their own. Chapter 10 takes on the challenge of small-business planning. Chapter 11 deals with growth issues unique to established businesses, whether those businesses are one-person shops or large enterprises. Chapter 12 looks at the unique planning issues faced by nonprofit organizations. Finally, Chapter 13 presents planning advice for online entrepreneurs and e-businesses as well as for companies adding e-commerce extensions to their brick-and-mortar operations.

If you can, take time to browse through all five chapters. Chances are good that several contain advice that will help you tailor a plan to fit your one-of-a-kind business situation.

Chapter 9

Planning for a One-Person Business

"**B**e Your Own Boss!" the advertisements beckon. What could sound better? No more punching a time clock. No more answering to supervisors. No more having someone else tell you what to do.

Almost everyone who's ever felt stuck on the corporate treadmill (or in a long commute) has dreamed of pitching the rat race, printing up business cards, hanging a shingle, and opening the smallest of small businesses — a SOHO or, spelled out, a small office/home office one-person shop.

The Internet, cellphones, and ever-evolving technologies that let you work from almost anywhere make the idea even more enticing. But, are you ready to take the plunge? Can you make a living? Can you keep yourself disciplined and focused?

This chapter helps you plot your strategy and build a bridge between your dream and the success story you intend to live. It makes the case for why a business plan is important even if you'll be the only one who ever reads it. It directs your attention to the parts of business planning that matter most to those who are self-employed. It helps you figure out what to charge and how to get paid for your product or services. Plus, as proof that going it alone doesn't mean you're out there all by yourself, it directs you toward resources that make your job a whole lot easier.

Confronting the Biggest Self-Employment Obstacles

Deciding to quit your "real" job sounds like the hard part, and starting a business of your own sounds like the reward. But to succeed, you need to overcome a few obstacles that confront nearly every small business and derail the plans of more than a few:

- **Commit to doing one thing well:** How many self-employed people have you met who shuffle through a stack of business cards as they explain the many ventures they're into, personifying the old line "jack of all trades, master of none." See Chapter 3 as you focus on the purpose and focus of your business.

- **Establish pricing, billing, and collection policies:** From the get-go you need to know what you will charge and how you will collect. Whether you're selling time or products, your pricing must be competitive, an accurate reflection of the value of your offering, and high enough to cover your production costs plus an adequate amount of profit to your business.

- **Run your business like a business, not like an adjunct of your personal checkbook or a hobby that you pursue in your spare time:** Small business start-ups are born in back bedrooms and on kitchen counters. But to succeed, you need to turn your idea into a formal business structure — complete with a designated work space, a dedicated business bank account, and a written business plan that includes financial projections and reporting systems to keep your business on track.

Getting your one-person business off to a strong start is hardly like rocket science. *If*, and this is a big if, you plan in advance and stick to your decisions. That's what the upcoming section is about.

Planning for success

After you've weighed the pluses and minuses of working for yourself and decided that the self-employed life is for you, you're at the precarious point where too many businesses take a giant misstep. You guessed it: They dive in without a formal plan to guide their efforts.

Maybe they get hung up on the word *formal*. When you're planning for a one- or two-person enterprise, formal doesn't mean long or complicated. It just means putting a plan in writing to explain your business, your product, your market, your expertise, your goals, your growth plans, and what it will take to be successful.

Pros and cons of a solo career

Here's the upside: When you work for yourself, no one else tells you when to start or when to knock off for the day. You have no salary cap, no performance reviews, no corporate politics, and no supervisors.

But here's the rest of the story: Solo careerists usually work longer and harder than salaried employees and require more self-discipline. And, although they don't answer to bosses per se, they do deal with clients, who sometimes make tough bosses look easy in comparison.

If you work for yourself, you get to

✔ Be your own boss

✔ Determine your own schedule

✔ Control your own economic fate

✔ Choose the kinds of work you want to do

But you don't get

✔ A regular paycheck

✔ Employer-provided benefits

✔ Unemployment insurance and workers' compensation

✔ Protection under labor laws

If you're not quite sure whether you're ready to go it alone, fill out the survey in Form 9-1 on the CD-ROM. If you answer yes to five or more of the statements, you probably have the discipline to be self-employed. If not, you may want to spend more time mulling over your options.

Naturally, as a one-person business you're the primary audience for your plan. But after you have your plan down on paper, you'll find many reasons to be glad that you wrote it in the first place. Here are just a few:

✔ **To seek business financing:** If you want help financing your business, bankers and potential investors will ask to see your business plan, and especially your financial projections, for proof that that you're serious about starting and running a successful business.

✔ **To create marketing materials:** Your business plan, with its description of your products and services, your target markets, and your customer benefits, will guide what you say to potential customers.

✔ **To hire an employee or outsource work:** When you want to describe what you do, what kinds of customers you serve, and how you run your business, your business plan is available as reference material.

Don't try to keep your business plan in your head. Putting it in writing is important for the following reasons:

✔ It establishes a contract with yourself by stating what you intend to do and how you plan to accomplish it.

✔ It lists the resources you'll need to get your business underway.

✔ It formalizes your goals and objectives.

✔ It provides a road map that will direct your efforts and boost your confidence, two important keys to making a solo career work.

✔ It helps you anticipate and address funding needs before they turn into funding crises.

Chapter 1 provides more detail about the benefits of a business plan. Read it, and you'll convince yourself yet!

Putting a price on what you do

Pricing is a balancing act that takes into account

✔ The costs involved to provide your service or to make your product

✔ The prices competitors charge for similar products or services

✔ The pricing level that best reflects the value you offer and that your customers seek

✔ What you need to deliver an adequate profit to your business

What's in a price?

Here's the dilemma you face:

✔ If you charge too much, your customers won't buy — or they will buy but won't feel they received good value and they'll share their discontent with others.

✔ If you charge too little, customers may interpret your low price as an indication of low quality and choose to buy elsewhere. Or maybe they will make the purchase and reap the bargain, walking away with your unrealized profit in their billfolds.

So, what to charge? When determining your price tag, think about

✔ How customers perceive the value of your product or service. Flip back to Chapter 7 for information on establishing the position your company holds in the competitive marketplace. If customers believe that your business is the most convenient or most reliable or that you offer the greatest expertise, the highest quality, the best features, or the most certain support, they'll think you offer high value and will be willing to pay well above the lowest price in the marketplace. On the other end of the spectrum, if customers choose you because you offer the lowest-cost solution, you'd better offer the lowest pricing as well.

✔ **How you can offer customer-responsive pricing.** If your customers seek a wide range of solutions from your business, consider charging a base price and adding costs for extra features and benefits, thereby tailoring prices to your customers' choices.

✔ **How often you can adjust your pricing.** Retailers can shift pricing as they bring in new lines or offer new promotions, giving them great pricing flexibility. Service businesses that announce hourly rates are less able to change pricing policies without a formal announcement. To build in flexibility, many service companies provide project estimates based upon their current rates without actually stating hourly fees. This allows the service provider to maintain pricing flexibility

Knowing how to charge

Most self-employed service providers charge in one of the following ways:

✔ **By the hour:** You establish an hourly rate, keep track of your time, and bill clients for hours spent on their behalf. This is the standard pricing approach for service businesses handling small-project jobs.

✔ **By the project:** You and your client agree in advance on a fixed price for a defined amount of work. This is the standard pricing approach for service businesses handling large-project jobs.

✔ **A combined approach:** A building contractor, for example, may bid on a set of plans and establish a fee for the project. But he may also stipulate that additional client-requested work over and above that covered by the estimate is to be paid at an established hourly rate.

Other businesses follow other billing approaches. For example, authors often receive a *royalty,* or a percentage of the cover price, for each book sold. A photographer might sell rights to photos based on the way the purchaser will use them. And some professionals are paid *retainers,* or upfront payments, in return for their availability to work on an as-needed basis.

A computer network expert might charge clients a monthly retainer. In return, he agrees to keep their computer systems updated and up and running. If a client needs him, he's available 24/7. If not, he enjoys his free time. The monthly fees provide him a steady month-by-month income, and his clients couldn't be happier because they view the monthly fee as a computer insurance policy that's always in effect.

Figuring out how much to charge

Whatever payment arrangement you settle on, you still have to figure out exactly how much to charge.

If you provide a service of some sort, begin by establishing an hourly rate. Even if you end up charging by the project or product, when you know your hourly rate, you can estimate the number of hours a job will take and multiply that number by your hourly rate to arrive at your project or product cost.

So how should you establish an hourly rate? Simple: Find out what other people doing similar work charge for their services. If you're a freelance editor, for example, find out the rates of other freelance editors in your market area. To be competitive, set your rates within a similar price range. If you're just starting out, you may want to begin at the lower end of the scale. If you have a long list of credentials and have earned rave reviews from clients, you can shoot for the upper end.

Another way to arrive at your pricing is to consider the following:

- ✔ How much you personally want to earn each year
- ✔ How many hours a year you think you can spend on billable activities
- ✔ How many hours a year you need to devote to running your business
- ✔ How much it costs you to run your business
- ✔ How much profit you want your business to make

Say that you're a consultant who wants to personally make $80,000 a year. Further, assume that your overhead costs total $22,000 a year, plus you want to earn at least $8,000 profit annually to fund future growth. That means your consulting business needs to bring in at least $110,000 each year.

Next, say that out of each 40-hour workweek you'll spend 12 hours running your business (doing the banking, networking, making new business calls, working with accountants, and on and on). That leaves 28 hours a week 50 weeks a year (assuming that you give yourself two weeks off for a well-earned annual getaway) for billable activities — or a total of 1,400 billable hours a year.

With all that information in hand, you can divide $110,000 by 1,400 hours to arrive at an hourly billing rate of $78.50.

If that's more than you think clients will be willing to pay, you have a few choices: You can reduce your overhead costs, you can reduce your earnings and profit expectations, or you can spend more hours on billable activities, which probably means working longer weeks.

To get a good idea of how you spend your working days, use the survey in Form 9-2. This information will be useful as you work to set your hourly rate.

TASKS AND TIME SURVEY		
Activity	**Estimated Hours Spent**	
	(Week)	**(Month)**
Developing new products and services		
Producing your product or service		
Marketing and business development		
Distribution or delivery		
Customer service or client management		
Office management		
Bookkeeping and accounting		
Other:		
Other:		

Form 9-2: Complete this form on the CD-ROM to assess where you spend your business time so you can plan your hourly billing rates accordingly.

Here's another pricing example, using a slightly different approach to the calculations.

Say a custom jeweler wants to earn $42,000 a year. Working 40 hours a week 50 weeks a year, she'll put in 2,000 hours a year. Some of those hours, though, she'll spend on marketing, billing, and business chores not directly related to making jewelry, including an occasional sunny afternoon spent enjoying the great outdoors. That leaves her with about 1,500 hours a year to actually make jewelry.

To earn $42,000 in 1,500 hours, she needs to charge $28 an hour. On top of that, she needs her pricing to cover about $9,000 in costs involved to run the business — from overhead to the costs of raw materials that go into the jewelry. This adds $6 to her hourly rate ($9,000 divided by 1,500), bringing her total to $34 an hour.

But she still has more to consider, like profit — or extra money she can use to buy better equipment or expand to a bigger studio. To earn $4,500 of profit a year to support her long-term business goals, she needs to add $3 to her rates. That brings the grand total to $37 an hour if she wants to cover her salary, expenses, and profit in 1,500 hours of billable time a year.

Of course, a jeweler usually charges by the finished piece rather than by the hour. But by knowing her hourly rate, she can estimate the number of hours that go into a piece of jewelry and multiply to set its price. For instance, a set of gold earrings that require ten hours of work will cost $370. Knowing that figure, she can do a reality check: Given her market and her competition, is this price reasonable? If it is, great. If not, she's going to have to think a little harder about her business model. (For more information on business models and other strategies, flip to Chapter 5.)

Even if you're self-employed, plan to make and set aside a profit above and beyond what you pay yourself. Doing so allows you to expand and develop your business when times are good. It also provides an important safety net, should your business experience an unforeseen setback.

Take time to figure the hourly rate you need to charge to cover your salary, overhead, and profit projections. You may want to use Form 9-3 to make sure that your rate covers all your business expenses. Check all categories that apply to your business and enter the rough amounts you expect to spend.

In your business plan, include information on how and what you intend to charge for your service or product. Show the calculations behind your pricing decisions. (Turn to Chapter 8 for information on managing the financial end of your business.)

SELF-EMPLOYED EXPENSE CHECKLIST	
Expense Category	**Estimated Cost (week, month, year)**
☐ Rent	
☐ Utilities	
☐ Equipment costs	
☐ Maintenance costs	
☐ Office supplies	
☐ Postage and delivery costs	
☐ Automobile expenses	
☐ Travel expenses	
☐ Business-related meals	
☐ Advertising and marketing	
☐ Clerical or office help	
☐ Accounting and tax fees	
☐ Legal expenses	
☐ Other	
☐	
☐	

Form 9-3: Use this form to get a handle on your overhead expenses before setting your business pricing.

Stay home and get rich fast 'n easy

You've seen ads: Earn $5,000 to $10,000 a month working at home. *In your spare time*, no less. Most of these get-rich-quick schemes are bogus and even fraudulent. They seem to be cooked up by the same people who promise a 25-pound weight loss in a week with no dieting.

But that doesn't mean you can't make money working by yourself and from your own home or small office. In fact, according to *The Wall Street Journal*, independent contractors are typically paid 20 to 40 percent more per hour than employees doing the very same job. Why? Because the hiring firms don't have to pay them additional benefits, including health insurance, sick leave, workers' compensation, and so on. The companies also have absolutely no obligation to their outside contractors. It's no wonder they can afford to pay higher hourly rates. The only drawback to this plan is that if you're in

business for yourself, you need to think seriously about providing yourself with the most important of these benefits, including a good health plan.

The ranks of the self-employed can also come out ahead by taking advantage of various business-related tax deductions. These deductions include necessary expenses related to your work — as long as the expenses are both reasonable and typical for the type of business you're in. You can even deduct the expenses of running a home office. Check out Form 9-4 on the CD-ROM to help you decide whether working out of your home is right for you, and then take a look at IRS *Publication 587 (Business Use of Your Home)*, which you can get from the IRS Web site at www.irs.gov. If you're self-employed, you can also establish your own retirement plan, which can offer significant tax advantages.

Establishing billing policies

Employees have the luxury of picking up a paycheck every week or two. Not so for the self-employed. When you're in business for yourself, you typically send out a bill and then wait — 30 to 60 days isn't uncommon — for your clients to hold up their end of the bargain and actually pay you. Most do. But sometimes things go wrong, and a company (or an individual) may be slow to pay. Worse yet, they may be unable or even unwilling to pay, so you have no surefire way to avoid trouble. But the following tips may help:

- ✔ **Discuss costs before you perform the work.** Put your cost estimate in writing and present it and answer any client questions about the costs involved. Discussing fees can be uncomfortable, but it's way, way better to discuss them upfront rather than after the fact.

- ✔ **Get signatures on your cost estimate or contract.** Doing so helps you later if you have trouble collecting what you're owed.

- ✔ **Establish and explain billing policies:** Also include how you bill for work outside the scope of service covered by your estimate or contract and how you charge for client-requested changes.

✔ **Put your billing and payment policies in writing, even if they just appear as fine print on the back of your estimate or contract:** By presenting them as established policies, clients are less apt to feel singled out when extra charges apply.

✔ **Avoid billing surprises that don't show up until the client opens the bill.** Get additional costs approved, in writing, along the way.

✔ **Send bills out on time.** The more promptly you bill, the more quickly you get paid.

Getting paid

Here's an irrefutable fact: The longer an account goes unpaid, the more difficult it is to collect. In the field of accounts receivable, time *is* money.

As an independent businessperson, you're your own collection agency unless a bill goes really delinquent, which you can try to avoid by using the following steps:

✔ **Get personal.** When a bill is past due, don't rely on e-mail or letters; pick up the telephone. Ask to speak to your contact for the project. Get the names of the people in accounts payable or purchasing and call them. Make appointments to visit in person.

✔ **Be persistent.** The squeaky wheel gets the grease, as the saying goes. If other creditors are trying to get money, the more persistent you are, the closer you'll get to the front of the line.

✔ **Be pleasant.** Ask whether there is a problem with the bill. Perhaps it's held up awaiting approval or maybe a line item is being questioned; you won't know if you don't ask. Your queries may uncover customer service issues or may even generate additional sales. Ask and then listen.

✔ **Don't wait longer than 60 or 90 days.** If all else fails, take your case to court. Small claims courts resolve disputes involving small amounts of money — usually under $10,000. You can represent yourself, and the process is relatively quick and inexpensive. (If it's any comfort, you aren't alone. Debt collection is the most common case heard in small claims court.)

Get proactive by establishing credit policies before the need even arises. Local collection or credit bureaus often provide free planning advice plus they stand by to serve as collection agents for delinquent accounts.

Treating your business like a business

Owning your business isn't a hobby. If you quit your job and started your own business, it's your means of livelihood. Follow these steps to form a strong business foundation and to separate your work and personal lives:

- ✔ **Pay yourself.** The previous section on pricing your services will help you focus on how much you want to earn and how to price your services to achieve your income objective.

- ✔ **Reward yourself with praise, raises, bonuses, and retirement savings.** Some self-employed businesspeople tie their rewards to their business goals and objectives. If, say, you reach one of your more ambitious goals, give yourself a cash bonus out of the business profits. This strategy may sound a little silly — it's your own money, after all, but many freelancers and independent contractors say that these kinds of incentives are key to staying focused and on track.

- ✔ **Review your performance.** Judge your performance against business goals and objectives. Make sure you involve your clients. That is, following major projects, discuss their satisfaction levels as a way to monitor how you and your business are performing.

- ✔ **Implement your business plan.** Getting absorbed by day-to-day business needs — whether collecting an unpaid bill or addressing a looming client issue — is easy to do. If you're not careful, you'll be so busy serving clients that you'll forget to run your own business. That's where your business plan can rescue you, keeping you focused on your goals and objectives and the deadlines of your action plan.

- ✔ **Separate your business life from your personal life.** Set up a designated workspace with professional surroundings. Establish working hours that ensure personal time where business issues don't encroach on free time and family time. And, by all means, separate your home and business finances by establishing bank accounts to handle your business funds.

- ✔ **Set money aside in case work slows down or a client doesn't pay on time.** Decide how much money is enough to carry you through a month, two months, six months, or whatever. Then build up a cash reserve — not in a personal bank account but in a business savings account where you're not likely to raid the money around the holidays or vacation time.

Tailoring a Business Plan to Fit Your One-Person Enterprise

Chapter 1 describes each component of a business plan. Lucky for you, though, when you're self-employed, you can skip a few of the parts because they simply don't apply to your business or your business plan:

✔ You can ditch the executive summary completely. Your plan is probably concise enough to read quickly and won't require a summary version.

✔ You won't have much to say about your company's organization. It's hardly necessary to explain the chain of command when you're running a company with a staff of one.

✔ Your company description can be short, so long as it's clear. Larger businesses include management team descriptions and information on technology and product attributes in their descriptions, but yours will probably describe your abilities, the advantages you offer, and the market potential you will tap into.

✔ The financial review can be basic, as long as it provides thorough explanations of your projected revenues and expenses and how cash will flow in and out of your business.

When writing your business plan, don't worry about polishing your prose until it's perfect. The important thing is to get the key points down on paper.

What your business plan *does* need to include is

✔ An overview of your company

✔ An analysis of your business environment

✔ Your business strategy

✔ Your financial review

✔ A copy of your action plan

Together these five sections cover the nuts and bolts of self-employment planning. See Chapter 14 for how the pieces of the plan come together in a finished business plan. But first go through the following sections for tips on tailoring your business contents to the needs of your one-person operation.

Company overview

Before you wave off this section with the personal assurance that you know what business you're in and what you intend to do, realize that if your direction is even slightly fuzzy at the launch of your business, you'll pay the price for your lack of focus ever after. So don't skip these two steps:

1. **Write vision and mission statements.**

   These statements describe the purpose of your business and what you hope to achieve.

2. **Set goals and objectives.**

   Your goals and objectives define exactly what you want to accomplish and how you will go about achieving your aims. For most people, becoming self-employed is a venture into uncharted waters. For the first time, you're the captain, first mate, and crew all rolled into one with no boss calling the shots or evaluating your performance. Goals and objectives are essential because they serve as an important yardstick to measure your progress.

Chapter 3 offers help as you take both these steps.

Business environment

You can find out everything you need to know about assessing your business environment in Chapter 4. It helps you analyze your industry, your clientele, your competitive environment, and the economic and business trends on the horizon that can affect your success. As a one-person business, you can take some of the advice with a grain of salt, but you can't ignore it all together.

For instance, you've probably looked around to see whether your regional economy has room for a number of construction contractors, self-employed accountants, freelance designers, or whatever other independent service you're offering. Even so, you want to look more closely to find out how many others are out there doing the same kind of work you do and decide what makes you a different and better choice — and whether there is, in fact, enough business to go around.

Just as important as assessing your competitive environment is the need to track key trends in your industry. If growth is booming in your area, business might be ripe for the picking. But if economic trends don't look so hot, you may need to dedicate time and energy devising strategies to attract new business in a slowing market.

As you study industry trends, be sure you read the indicators not just for the moment, but for the future as well.

A tax accountant moved into a great new office space at a time when there was more work around than she could possibly take on. What she failed to pick up on, though, was that the local economy was actually slowing. What's more, many individuals and small businesses — the accountant's traditional clients — were beginning to rely on tax software programs rather than accounting services. Between higher office rent and a declining client base, she found herself in a financial crunch that she could have averted if she'd taken time to evaluate her business environment beforehand.

Company description and strategy

You're self-employed, so obviously you don't need much space to describe your company's organization. Instead, devote the effort to an explanation of

IN THE PLAN

Developing a business network

When you're self-employed, business relationships you establish outside your company can be like lifelines. Your one-person company won't have a business team to bounce ideas off of, or to share concerns, ideas, or dreams. Instead, you'll want to develop a network of associates that you can count on for business contacts, ideas, and advice. So include in your business plan a discussion of how you will establish and maintain a business network. You can

✔ **Keep track of your business contacts.** Use contact management software or keep lists manually but, one way or another, record names, numbers, and personal and business interests.

✔ **Stay in touch.** Call associates from time to time just to say hello, see how business is going, and share insights. Send or forward useful news articles and call to congratulate them when appropriate. The bottom line is that you want to maintain contact, but also realize that friendly calls often yield new business.

✔ **Make contact with your competitors.** Chances are good that you have more to gain by networking with people in your industry than you have to lose. Minimally, you get to know each other, and the contact may well benefit your business. Competitors often refer clients to others when they can't or don't have time to handle a piece of business themselves.

✔ **Join a business group to create an instant network.** Think rotary clubs, chambers of commerce, and industry associations. You can find groups full of people involved in the same kind of business as yours or loose alliances of businesspeople working in the same geographic area. Some groups represent specific interest groups, such as women, minorities, or gay businesspeople. Your local chamber or economic development office may have lists, or you can look up "associations" in the Yellow Pages. The checklist included in Form 9-5 on the CD-ROM will jump-start your thinking.

---

how your company will operate — how you'll work with customers, deliver products and services, get new business, outsource work, and so on.

In this section of your business plan, also describe your strengths and weaknesses, both personal and professional. You *are* the entire management team and staff, so defining your own capabilities and how you'll compensate for shortcomings is an essential element of your business planning. For guidance, check out the section on company strengths and weaknesses in Chapter 5.

Financial review

The financial review section of your business plan doesn't have to be long, but it does have to be complete. Show how much you plan to make, how much you need to spend to get started, and how much you need on an ongoing basis to keep yourself in business. The earlier section titled "Putting a price on what you do" will help as you define your pricing and billing policies. To create financial statements, forecasts, and budgets, check out Chapter 8.

Action plan

Your action plan is just what the name suggests — a nuts and bolts plan of action, broken down step by step, to move your business ahead. Don't go forward without one.

Start by carefully looking at your personal strengths and weaknesses. If you know you're a strong service provider but a bit thin in the marketing area, for example, your action plan may include enrollment in a marketing class or arrangements for freelance marketing or agency assistance. If you're a little wobbly when in accounting, your action plan may be as simple as hiring an outside accountant.

The reason the action plan is so important to a one-person business is because no supervisor or boss is telling you what to do next. You're the one who has to set the direction, steer a course, and measure your progress. Ultimately, your action plan is a good device for making sure your company stays on track.

Forms on the CD-ROM

If you're self-employed, check out the following forms on the CD-ROM to help you plan.

Form 9-1	**Is Self-employment Right For You?**	A survey that helps you identify the traits needed to be successfully self-employed
Form 9-2	**Tasks and Time Survey**	A survey to help you estimate how much time you spend on each area of your business
Form 9-3	**Self-employed Expense Checklist**	A checklist to help you get a handle on your business expenses
Form 9-4	**Evaluating Your Home Office Options**	A questionnaire to help you evaluate your home office options
Form 9-5	**Checklist of Business Networking Resources**	Resources you can turn to in order to track down business networking groups in your own industry

Chapter 10

Planning for a Small Business

*T*he big guys like IBM, Ford, General Electric, Microsoft, and AT&T make the business headlines. But the powerhouses driving the nation's economy are — you guessed it — small businesses. Places like Giovanni's Pizza, Main Street Marketing, Woody's Custom Furniture, and Eye of the Needle Tailoring. Small businesses like these employ more than half of the U.S. private sector workforce and create the majority of the nation's new jobs.

What qualifies as a small business? The official definition of a small business, direct from the Small Business Administration (SBA), is any business that is "independently owned and operated and that is not dominant in its field of operation." If your company employs fewer than 100 people and has only a few locations, it probably fits the definition.

For the purposes of business planning, if your company's big enough to be publicly traded on the NASDAQ or the NYSE, you're too big to be called a small business. On the other hand, if your business consists of you and you alone, you're self-employed — and you get your very own chapter (see Chapter 9).

This chapter focuses on the aspects of business planning that matter most to small businesses — especially those that are just starting up or ones that are playing catch-up and writing business plans for the first time. If your business is already in full motion, supplement the information in this chapter by turning to Chapter 11 to find out about planning for an established business and to Chapter 16 to gain advice for when and how to overhaul and update your business plan.

Recognizing the Importance of a Plan

Business planning is critical to the success of a small business. In fact, according to the SBA, planning ability is one of the keys to small business success. (The others are sound management, industry experience, and technical support; you can find more details at the SBA Web site at www.sba.gov.)

Chapter 1 offers a complete description of the value of business planning. For small businesses, three benefits of business planning are particularly important.

- ✔ **Analyze your resource needs before you commit to a business idea.** One of the major reasons small companies go under is because they lack adequate resources from the get-go. By writing a business plan, you detail your requirements for time, cash, and people and establish your equipment needs, location requirements, and the staff you'll have to hire. Together, these elements determine how much money you'll need upfront and how long you'll have to fund your enterprise while you wait for it to start turning a profit.

- ✔ **Develop the information necessary to make the case for a business loan.** Unless you have a deep-pocketed relative waiting in the wings with a check to underwrite your business, you'll probably need to get a loan or attract the support of one or several small-business investors. And that means you'll need a convincing business plan. According to the SBA, a good business plan is a crucial part of any loan package, and business advisors second that statement.

- ✔ **Shape a successful business strategy.** The business-planning process requires you to think clearly about your potential customers and your competitors. It also prompts you to assess your own strengths and weaknesses and the opportunities and threats that you face in your industry and marketplace. Your findings will lead to a business strategy that fits your market environment, builds on your business capabilities, and lays the foundation for your success.

Preparing Your Small Business Plan

You've probably already put together some of the pieces of a business plan, and about now, you're probably wondering whether you really need to put together a full plan, and if it really has to be a big deal.

Yes, you need a full plan, and no, it doesn't have to be a big deal. But if your business plan is going to help you be successful, it needs to cover all the bases, including the resources you need, your financial situation, and the strategy you'll employ to make it all work.

Your business plan contains the following five parts:

✔ A summary of your business environment

✔ A description of your company

✔ An outline of your business strategy

✔ A summary of your financial statements and forecasts

✔ Your action plan

The following sections cover these parts and the issues that deserve the most attention — and why.

Analyzing your business location and the surrounding environment

The very first section of your business plan summarizes how the environment around your business will affect your company's success. It examines the industry you're in, your customers, and your competition. For a thorough look at your business environment, go to Chapter 4, which leads you through such an assessment.

The first factor that affects the success of most small businesses is location, because it often determines who your customers are and what businesses you compete against. When you are clear about the geographic scope of your market area, you can evaluate the composition of the population, economic conditions, and competing businesses. If your business serves multiple market areas, you need to assess these same issues in each area to arrive at a useful analysis upon which to plan your business.

Especially if your business relies on foot traffic and spontaneous buying decisions, where you place your shop or office — on a busy thoroughfare or on a less-traveled alleyway — can mean the difference between success and failure to attract adequate visibility and activity. So make sure you spend serious business-planning time weighing the pros and cons of your location and make an equal effort evaluating the business environment of your market area.

Location can be critical even for businesses that don't rely on store traffic or drop-in customers. Suppose you're starting a small software company that will depend on highly trained software engineers. You have to locate your company in a place where these kinds of people live — or at least are willing to move.

Complete the business environment section of your business plan in three parts. Chapter 4 helps you arrive at your answers:

- ✔ Describe your business or industry arena, including the trends you're seeing. Note whether the market is growing or receding; what it takes to enter the arena; and any technological, regulatory, or other changes you see on the horizon.

- ✔ Describe your customers by stating where they live or are located; facts about their age, gender, income, marital status, and so on; and anything you know about why and how they buy products like yours.

- ✔ Describe your competitive environment, including the strengths, capabilities, and growth plans of major competing businesses and how you plan to differentiate your business.

Defining your business and its purpose

Your *company description* is the component of your business plan that states what kind of business you're in and what you look like as a company. The company description tells exactly what your business intends to do, how it intends to do it, and what is going to make it unique and successful.

The reason this description is so important usually boils down to one word: Money. Most small companies have to take out business loans, enlist the help of outside investors, or arrange for lines of credit to cover bills that need to be paid before revenues roll in. The first thing investors want to know is what your business does, and the best way to persuade them that your business idea is sound is to describe it concisely and convincingly.

As you describe your company, communicate the most important aspects of your business, including the kinds of customers you serve, the products and services you offer, and the capabilities that will underpin your success. Chapter 6 provides descriptions and forms to help you write your company description.

Plotting your business strategy

The *strategy section* of your business plan describes exactly how you intend to accomplish your business goals.

- ✔ **If your goal is to get your business off the ground,** you need to outline your strategy for obtaining financing and launching your operation. See Chapter 18 for information on approaches for funding your business.

- ✔ **If your goal is to expand your business,** you need to describe your growth strategy. Chapter 5 presents growth options and planning advice, and Chapter 11 helps set a plan for growing an established business.

✔ **If your goal is to introduce a new product,** you need to detail strategies for research and development, production, and product introduction. Chapter 6 can help as you define and present your capabilities in each of these areas.

In addition to all other strategies, this section of your plan needs to outline your marketing strategy, showing how you plan to reach customers and persuade them to buy what you sell. Your marketing plan is the blueprint you'll follow to achieve sales success. For that reason, those reading your business plan are keenly interested in what you have to say. For more information on writing this section of your plan, see Chapter 7, and for complete guidance on developing a plan scaled to your business size and needs, take a look at my other book, *Small Business Marketing For Dummies* (Wiley).

In the strategy part of your business plan, list your business goals and objectives and accompany each one with the strategy you'll follow to achieve success.

Clarifying your financial situation

Your business plan absolutely has to include a complete financial picture of your company — including planned income, estimated balance sheet, and cash-flow projections. No ifs, ands, or buts. Your financial reports provide the navigational tools that you need to keep your business on track, plus they provide the essential information that bankers and other supporters need to see and monitor.

Whether you've run a business before or not or whether you're starting a brand-new venture or are expanding an existing enterprise, when you're estimating how much money you need in the bank, unknowns are everywhere, and the guesswork is tough. But estimating how much you need gets a little easier if you focus on two kinds of spending:

✔ **One-time start-up costs:** Every small business faces a long list of items that you have to spend money on only once just to get up and running — everything from a business license, start-up furnishings and equipment, and introductory marketing materials to that Grand Opening promotion you've planned.

✔ **Regular monthly expenses:** After you're open for business, you have all sorts of ongoing expenses to deal with, from paying salaries to buying supplies. Over time, of course, you expect your sales revenue to cover these expenses. But that situation doesn't happen overnight, so you have to set aside funds with which to pay the bills in the early tough-sledding period. Having a three- to six-month cushion is a good place to start, but how long you'll need a cushion depends on what business you're in.

Uncle Sam's helping hand

The SBA has a mandate from Congress to help small businesses with their financial needs. In other words, the SBA exists to help small companies just like yours. The administration does its good deeds through the following four programs:

✔ **The 7(A) program:** This program provides financing for a variety of general purposes and is the most flexible loan program the government offers to start-up and existing small businesses. Small businesses can use the loans for working capital or to purchase machinery and equipment; furniture and fixtures; land and buildings; leasehold improvements; or, under special conditions, for debt refinancing. Funds are available through commercial lending institutions.

✔ **The 504 program:** Also known as the Certified Development Company, this program offers long-term, fixed-rate financing to small businesses acquiring big-ticket items for expansion or modernization.

✔ **The microloan 7(m) program:** This program offers short-term loans of up to $35,000 to small businesses to use for working capital or business purchases, but businesses can't use the money to pay off existing debts. The government makes this type of loan to a *microlender,* an intermediary who then makes the actual loan to your business.

✔ **The Small Business Investment Company (SBIC):** The SBIC program supports the creation of independent investment companies that provide equity capital to invest in small businesses as well as long-term loan financing when required.

To find out more about SBA programs, visit www.sba.gov.

For a good idea of what size bankroll you'll need to finance your small business start-up, use Form 10-1 on the CD-ROM. Fill in the blanks to detail your estimated start-up costs. Next, estimate the ongoing monthly expenses you expect to incur and multiply by the number of months you think will pass before your business is bringing in sales revenue sufficient to cover its overhead. Add the two totals together, and the resulting number is the financial cushion you need to start out with in order to have cash available when you need it.

Use the figures you come up with in Form 10-1 as a starting point for developing the financial statements that you include in your written business plan. (For a step-by-step guide on how to put together your financial picture, flip to Chapter 8.) Be sure that you accompany your financial forecasts with descriptions of the assumptions you made as you put the numbers down on paper.

For the IRS's view on financial and tax matters, go to the horse's mouth. Check out *Business Expenses (IRS Publication 535), Tax Guide for Small Business (IRS Publication 334),* and *Small Business Tax Workshop Workbook (IRS Publication 1066).* All three publications are available on the IRS Web site at www.irs.gov.

Establishing your action plan

Your business plan should include an action plan that outlines the sequence of all the steps you intend to take to implement your business plan, focusing first on the most immediate and pressing tasks you face.

A good way to approach your action plan is to look back at the strategies you selected to meet each of your goals and objectives. Break each strategy into steps and then prioritize which ones need to happen first, second, third, and so on. Put the steps in order, and you have an action plan.

First, you probably want to detail steps to get your financial house in order. Shortly thereafter, you most likely want your action plan to address the process of putting together a top-notch staff. Then you want to define the actions you'll take to establish your business, gain name familiarity, and build and polish your reputation. No doubt your business will face some degree of change over the time period covered by your business plan, so you want to detail actions that will help you manage the change your business will inevitably encounter. And finally, you want to define steps you'll take to grow your business if, in fact, growth is among your goals.

The upcoming sections help you think through a few of the major issues you want to consider as you prepare your action plan.

Keeping an Eye Out for Changes on Your Business Horizon

Change is an inevitable part of the economic landscape, whether you're in a big city or a small town. And change is coming faster than it used to, especially for small businesses. For an analogy, imagine a luxury ocean liner. When it encounters a little squall, the passengers barely feel it. The same is true for large companies: They can weather economic downturns or changes in the marketplace. However, small businesses are like small boats — and small towns; the winds of change can bounce them around pretty hard and, sometimes, capsize them completely.

To succeed over the long haul, you have to navigate your small business through all the changes that are bound to happen. How? First, keep an eye on the horizon, watching out for what may be coming along. Second, be ready to change course or shift position to avoid trouble or to take advantage of good winds and strong currents.

Now shift from the nautical metaphors to the real world of business, where change is most likely to happen in one of these five main areas:

- ✔ **The economy:** Economic change is usually measured in terms of the ups or downs of interest rates or inflation, or changes in the value of one currency in relation to another.

- ✔ **Technology:** Changes in technology may mean the introduction of a brand-new technology or new ways of using an old technology. It may also lead to process improvements — better ways of manufacturing a product or delivering a service or new ways to better serve customers.

- ✔ **Business trends:** Changes in the business climate may result from new competitors coming into an industry or area or companies getting out. Business trends may open new markets and close off others.

- ✔ **Cultural change:** Everything from changes in the *demographics* of an area — changes in the age, income, marital status, education level, or other factual characteristics of people — to social and lifestyle changes can affect industries and markets. Although these changes are often gradual, they can be extremely powerful and almost impossible for your company to escape.

- ✔ **Government affairs:** The government's influence over business often takes the form of new regulations, legislation, or court rulings that may reflect longer-term shifts in federal, state, or local political agendas.

In the first section of your business plan, where you describe your business environment, make sure that you address looming changes that may affect how your company operates. Identify the trends and changes that are most likely to affect your business and describe how you will watch and respond to each of the specific issues and events that could play a significant role in the future of your small business. Such trends and changes may include a pending legal case, an emerging technology, or an upcoming regulatory decision.

Growing — or Not Growing — Your Small Business

Many small businesses want to and always will remain small. Other businesses start small with the dream of growing big — sometimes very big. Take Starbucks, which began as a local Seattle coffee shop, and Apple Computers, which was first headquartered in a garage. When small businesses grow into giant corporations, it's not by accident. Behind that growth is a well-thought-out business plan along with the drive and the resources to get there. But becoming a big business isn't for everybody.

An entrepreneur who started a stereo shop in a small Illinois town a few years back created just the kind of friendly, cluttered, slightly disorganized place you'd expect to see in a college town. But the salespeople who worked there really knew and loved audio equipment, and the business was stocked with great components at very competitive prices, thanks to the fact that overhead was so low. The unbeatable combination of quality, service, and price soon made the store a huge success — and the owner began to dream about expanding into a chain of stores throughout the Midwest.

We'd like to say that this idea sounded good on paper, but the owner never even put his business plan in writing. He launched right into action, building inventory and leasing storefronts without once thinking about how he would find knowledgeable sales teams, promote the new stores, or create an organization that could manage the jump from one shop to half a dozen. The laid-back, disorganized style worked fine for a single store with a garage-worth of inventory, but it turned out to be a disaster for the small chain. The losses from the new outlets soon eroded the original store's profits. Six months later, the owner closed up and went back to school, even though he'd already been through the school of hard knocks.

A well-crafted business plan may have helped avoid disaster. But even before the planning, the owner should have asked one simple question: *Do I really want to grow my business?*

Some small businesses are meant to remain small, and some business owners are meant to run small companies. In this case, an entrepreneur loved audio equipment, worked well with his sales team, and had a great rapport with the customers who came through his door. But he wasn't particularly well organized or good at delegating — the two main characteristics he needed to run a larger operation.

Before you make plans to grow your own small business into something bigger, take time to ask yourself whether you really want to manage a larger company:

✔ How will the day-to-day operations of the company have to change?

✔ How will my own duties and responsibilities be different?

✔ What additional skills will I need to make the growing business work?

✔ What weak points or limitations do I have that may get in the way?

Don't be discouraged if your answers make you think twice about growing your business into something bigger. Not every business is suited to expansion — and not every small-business owner really wants to manage a big organization. Many business owners are perfectly happy and successful staying small.

On the other hand, if your answers give you confidence that growth is a smart move, buckle down and really start planning. Turn to Chapter 5 for more details on the ways that companies typically grow and for a checklist of critical resources that you'll need as your company begins to grow. Then turn to Chapter 11 for information on how to write a business plan when you're working to grow an established business.

Forms on the CD-ROM

If you're part of a small business, check out the following forms on the CD-ROM to help you plan.

Form 10-1	**Start-up Costs Worksheet for Small Business**	A worksheet designed to give you an idea of how much cash you need upfront to get a small business off the ground
Form 10-2	**Job Description Profile**	A template designed to capture all the relevant information that a job description should include
Form 10-3	**Job Recruiting Checklist**	Places small businesses can go to find qualified employees
Form 10-4	**Employee Retention Checklist**	Approaches to help you improve overall employee job satisfaction
Form 10-5	**Tips on Promoting Teamwork**	A list of ways you can promote a sense of team spirit and teamwork in your own company

Chapter 11

Planning for an Established Business

*O*wners of established businesses sometimes need a little (or even not so little) push to get into business planning. Back when you were starting up, creating a business plan felt essential. You knew that you needed all the answers to the questions that bankers or others asked you right at your fingertips, so you wrote a plan — or at least felt pangs of guilt if you didn't.

But after your company is up and running, you tend to shove business planning toward the back burner. Putting out daily fires trumps all other activities, and the thought of setting aside time to update or write a business plan begins to seem like an optional luxury. And even when you have time, you may embrace the tenet, "If it ain't broke, don't fix it." If business is going okay, why plan to change what's working at the moment?

Here's why: If you're not fine-tuning your business to meet the realities of today and the forecasts for tomorrow, you're apt to get overtaken — by technology, by competition, by market conditions, and by the changing world around you.

Hopefully, these reasons motivate you to spend time planning for the future of your company. Whether you want to grow, seek financing, prepare for a sale, or plot a business turnaround, the following pages help you take stock of your business situation today so that you can develop a plan that steers you clear of trouble and toward opportunity in the days and years ahead.

Purpose-Driven Planning

If your established business doesn't have a business plan, you're on a trip without a road map, and that's reason enough to start writing one today. Maybe writing a business plan is the reason you're holding this book and reading this chapter. Or maybe you already have a plan, but you're wise enough to know that change is constant and that your plan is only good if it's up-to-date. For this reason, you're on a mission to review your business situation, set your sights on ever-loftier goals, and write an up-to-date plan for getting where you want to go.

But if your business is like most established businesses, you're getting ready to write or rewrite your business plan to address one of the following, pressing situations:

- ✔ You're raising capital or seeking new rounds of financing
- ✔ You're posturing for a sale or merger
- ✔ You're preparing for business expansion
- ✔ You're working to overcome business downturns or disruptions

The upcoming sections deal with what's involved in planning for each of these purposes.

Planning to Raise Capital

Entrepreneurs in need of money to get their businesses started or to fund expansion plans can finance their business plans in many different ways. (Chapter 18 outlines 10 places to turn for business funding). Of the alternatives, most established businesses focus on two options: bank financing and investor capital.

Bank financing

If a primary purpose of your plan is to obtain bank financing, bankers are your primary audience, and the bank where you have established relationships is likely your best starting point.

Bankers need to see your complete business plan, for sure, but be aware that your executive summary — the part they'll flip to first — is where they expect to find a good, comprehensive, and succinct overview of your business purpose, situation, finances, goals, and the strategies you'll follow to achieve success. (Refer to Chapter 1 to see what all goes into an executive summary.)

Plus, bankers want to see the specifics of your loan request:

✔ How much do you want to borrow?

✔ How will you use the loan funding? In reviewing a loan request from an established company, a banker will want to see how the funds will be used for positive purposes that will contribute to business growth and profitability, and thus to the certainty of loan repayment. Will you use the funds to hire new employees, to fund a major marketing effort, to purchase equipment or a business building, or to pay off debts? Be specific.

✔ What positive impact do you expect the loan funding to have on your business? What goals or objectives will it help you achieve?

✔ What repayment terms are you requesting?

✔ How can you demonstrate your ability to meet the payment terms? Show financial statements, forecasts, and cash-flow projections to prove that you'll be able to repay the loan on the schedule that you're proposing. See Chapter 8 for help assembling your financial statements.

✔ What collateral or assets will you pledge to secure the loan? As you seek loans, refer to Chapter 10 to review different types of loans and visit the Small Business Administration Web site at `www.sba.gov` for information on government-backed loan programs.

Investor capital

Major capital investors fall into two categories: Venture capitalists and angel investors. Venture capitalists are professional investor groups whose major motivation is return on investment. Angels are successful and wealthy entrepreneurs who invest in up-and-coming companies with their money and also with their expertise and guidance. Both types invest in established companies with proven products, markets, and business models, but angel investors are more willing than venture capitalists to entertain smaller investment requests and to invest at an earlier stage in a company's life cycle.

For information on approaching venture capitalists, see Chapter 19.

To find out more about angel investors, visit the site of the SBA-initiated Angel Investor Network at `www.angel-investor-network.com`. Also, find out about angel-matching programs in your area by asking your banker or financial advisor or by inquiring at your chamber of commerce, regional economic development, or commerce offices.

Whichever approach you decide to pursue, when you're trying to raise capital through investors, you need to present much of the same information that bankers require — and then some.

Whereas bankers want to know how you'll repay them, investors want to know when and how they'll see not only a repayment, but also a sizeable return on their investments.

How does being an established business influence investors when you're asking for money? Both types will ONLY fund existing businesses with established plans. As you make a proposal to investors, be sure to cover the following points:

✔ The amount of funding you're seeking

✔ How you'll use the funds and what impact the investment will have on your success

✔ What return on investment the investors can expect to receive

✔ When the investors will get their money back

Will the investors get paid back when you go public? When you receive the next round of financing? When you achieve a certain sales level? The way that investors recoup and realize a return on their loaned capital is called the *exit strategy*, which is an important part of your investment proposal.

✔ What the investors will receive for their backing

Typically, investors seek equity in your company and a role on your board.

✔ What reporting you will provide

Investors usually demand detailed reports and accountability for how you spend their money.

Venture capitalists and angel investors want to see that your idea will provide a return on their investment. Don't waste your time or theirs unless you're certain that your executive summary and business plan can convince them that your business idea is unique and timely with a large and growing market; that you have proven personal leadership abilities; that your management team has strong and relevant expertise; and that your strategy is capable of delivering impressive sales and profit margins.

Planning for a Merger or Sale

The time will come when you're ready to hang up the reins and call an end to your involvement in your company. To allow for a positive conclusion, your business plan needs to include an exit strategy that defines how you'll reap the value of your business upon your departure. Chapter 5 includes a section on how to outline your exit strategy.

If your exit strategy involves selling your business or merging it with another company, as the time for action nears, business planning takes on a whole new urgency. Before contacting a business broker or approaching likely buyers, use Form 11-1 to ready your business for presentation.

SELLING YOUR BUSINESS WORKSHEET	
Consideration	**Improvement Plans**
Personal Issues	
Do you have a good idea of what you will do with your time if you sell your business?	
Do you know what you want to realize from a sale? Revenue to fund retirement? An ongoing role in the business?	
Are you prepared to share details about your business and its finances?	
Operational Issues	
Can you dedicate time to selling your business without compromising its strength?	
Is your business plan current? Does it detail growth potential and strategies?	
Does your business have strong accounts and account contracts?	
Does your business rely on a few accounts or suppliers who might defect after a sale?	
Does the success of your business rely on you personally?	
Do you have a good management team? Do key employees have incentives to stay with the company?	
Are your systems (employment, information management, and so on) current or compliant?	

Form 11-1: If you're thinking of selling your business, use this form to address the issues that are of greatest interest to potential buyers.

Does your business have weak areas that you can improve or eliminate?	
Is your place of business ready to show? Is it neat, clean, and impressive?	
Legal Issues	
Is your business incorporated? Is it a distinctly separate, saleable entity?	
Does your business have multiple owners? Is there a clear agreement regarding who will remain with the business and who will get paid off?	
Do you have or foresee any legal issues troubling your business?	
Are trademarks and patents in order?	
Are all leases and contracts current?	
Financial Issues	
Have you established a means of putting a value on your business?	
Can you accept a portion of the sale price in cash and carry the remainder as a loan to the new buyer?	
Are your finances in good order? Do you have good control of costs, receivables, and debt levels?	
Do you have financial statements for at least the past three years?	
Are your sales and profits increasing?	
Does the financial condition of your business match your sales price expectation?	

Page 2 of Form 11-1.

Planning to Grow Your Business

Chances are good that you want to see your business grow — a little or a lot. And to do that, you probably want to ring up more sales, which means winning new customers or winning more business from existing customers. To achieve your goal, you may need to

✔ Open new market areas

✔ Introduce new products

✔ Initiate new customer-service programs

✔ Enhance your competitive position so that more customers choose your business offerings over those of your major competitors

If you want to grow, your business plan needs to set and describe such growth strategies. See Chapter 5 for information on the major ways that companies plan for growth and then complete Form 11-2 to consider approaches you may want to pursue.

Planning in Times of Trouble

As the saying goes, stuff happens. The economy tanks. A big client takes its business elsewhere. A product that looked really good on paper doesn't appear nearly as attractive in real life. Some regulatory ruling abruptly alters your business landscape. A competitive assault blindsides your business. Key employees stage a mutiny.

Stop! you're probably yelling. You hardly need more examples to get the drift. In business, sometimes the going gets tough, and your strategic plan is reduced to tatters as a result. That's when you need to get out your business plan — in a hurry — to begin a dust-off.

Maybe your business model — your plan for how you make money — isn't quite what it was cracked up to be (see Chapter 5 for information on business models). Maybe your financial projections were a little too rosy. Maybe your analysis of your strengths, weaknesses, opportunities, and threats (see Chapter 5 for the lowdown) missed some key points. Instead of throwing up your hands in despair, use this moment to pinpoint what went wrong and to begin planning a way to turn the situation around.

GROWTH STRATEGIES WORKSHEET
Product Strategies
☐ Introduce new uses for existing products
☐ Introduce new products
☐ Introduce new product features, functions, or benefits
☐ Introduce new product names, packaging, or labeling
☐ Bundle products into packaged offers
☐ Introduce new quality assurances or service policies
☐ Other...
Pricing Strategies
☐ Introduce trial offers
☐ Introduce financing or new payment options
☐ Reduce cost of production to lower prices or increase margins
☐ Introduce preferential pricing for bulk purchases, contract customers, or other preferred buyers
Distribution Strategies
☐ Introduce new distribution or delivery systems
☐ Add distribution channels (online sales, catalogs, dealers)
☐ Open new locations or establish off-premise outlets
☐ Enhance distributor relationships and incentives
☐ Other...
Promotion Strategies
☐ Attract new customers by marketing in new geographic market areas

Form 11-2: Use this form on the CD-ROM if you want to grow your business.

☐	Attract new customers by marketing to new demographic groups in current geographic market areas
☐	Increase sales to established customers by introducing new products or features, new product packages, new promotions, and other incentives
☐	Heighten awareness with increased marketing communications
☐	Create promotional materials to pave the way for or to help close sales
☐	Other...
	Customer-service Strategies
☐	Institute programs to reward frequent or large purchases
☐	Introduce or enhance service guarantees
☐	Institute customer-service analysis programs followed by employee training and incentives
☐	Develop customer-loyalty programs (buy-ahead discounts, rewards for attaining purchase levels, services, and recognition)
☐	Other...
☐	Other...

Page 2 of Form 11-2.

Diagnosing your problems

Most companies don't land in hot water overnight. Usually some warning signs present themselves, even if they're slight and build slowly over months or years before someone at the top finally says, "Uh-oh."

So how do you know if your company is headed for trouble? Use Form 11-3 to scan some of the early warning signs. If you see items that hit close to home, check out those issues as they relate to your company. If your company passes the test, keep the list handy and return to it from time to time, just to be on the safe side.

CHECKLIST OF COMMON WARNING SIGNS
☐ Key goals and objectives have gone unmet
☐ Sales are lagging in a growing market
☐ Key customers have gone over to the competition
☐ Quality and service complaints are on the increase
☐ Employees are coming in late and leaving early
☐ An unusual number of employees have left for good
☐ Morale and motivation are down across the company
☐ Personality conflicts are on the rise among the staff
☐ Relationships between employees and managers are strained
☐ Revenues are down, expenses are up
☐ Projects are coming in over budget
☐ Payments to vendors are falling behind
☐ Customers aren't paying on time
☐ Cash reserves continue to fall
☐ Management meetings are cancelled at the last minute

Form 11-3: This checklist presents warning signs that your business may be headed for trouble.

If you check three or more items on Form 11-3, definitely revisit your business plan and the assumptions behind it.

Suppose that customers aren't flocking to your new location the way you thought they would. Go back to your original market analysis to see what assumptions you made at the outset. Next, look at how the current situation differs from the way you envisioned it to be. Do you face unanticipated competition? Have your customers' wants and needs changed? Was your promotion inadequate? Pinpoint the problems and redraft your business plan to accurately address your business situation.

Don't launch into the blame game or look for scapegoats. Even if you ultimately decide that you need to make personnel changes, the first step isn't to place blame; you need to figure out what went wrong and how to get your business back on track.

Getting a second opinion

Sometimes getting an outside opinion about a difficult business situation can be very beneficial. When your company faces a crisis or near crisis, you can bring in *turnaround professionals* to help determine what's wrong and how you can revise your business plan to address the situation. To find consultants, start at the Turnaround Management Association Web site (`www.turnaround.org`).

Before you enlist outside help, you may want to bring your own management team together to assess the damage and to attempt to find a solution. Done right, this meeting of minds will create a stronger sense of teamwork and inspire the troops. And, with any luck, you'll come up with good creative and strategic solutions.

Your own management team may not see critical issues objectively. Vested interests, assumptions, and emotions can get in the way. Outside consultants such as turnaround professionals don't carry the excess baggage. They can take a clear-eyed and unemotional look, pinpoint what's wrong, and help arrive at a solution — even if it's a painful one. Most are available to guide the redirection of your business plan and to help steer the turnaround process.

Analyzing your current situation

If your company is in trouble, chances are your business isn't where you expected it to be six months or a year ago. If you want to begin shaping a plan to get your business back on course, you first have to know exactly where you stand — with an emphasis on the word *exactly*. You won't do yourself any favors whitewashing your situation or clinging to overly optimistic projections. The time has come to get real.

When your company is in trouble, focus on three parts of business planning:

- **Financial review:** Business troubles usually boil down to a simple, painful fact: Money is flowing out faster than it's coming in. Maybe revenues are too low, expenses are too high, or your money in the bank just isn't enough to cover what you planned to do. Now you have to assess your current financial picture, focusing on cash flow and revised financial projections. (Check out Chapter 8 for details.)

- **SWOT analysis:** The opportunities and threats your business faces today may have changed since you last analyzed your business situation. Even your relative strengths and weaknesses may be different. Take time to revisit your last SWOT analysis, and direct your attention to the strategic issues that are most likely to have an immediate positive impact on your situation. (Refer to Chapter 5 for assistance.)

- **Business model:** Your *business plan* describes how you plan to build your business. Your *business model* defines how your business will make money. If your business plan isn't working, or if your finances are askew, a shaky business model is very likely to be, at least, part of your problem. Look at the assumptions you built into your model in the first place and revisit your notions about how your company expected to make money. Spend some time thinking about ways to revise or expand your model to bring in more revenue as you work to turn your business around. (Again, Chapter 5 helps out.)

Back to basics

For years, Moe's Music did modestly well renting and selling musical instruments. But in the early 1990s, the California music shop decided to expand into music education. The plan made sense on paper because many junior high and high schools were dropping music education programs, and Moe's Music hoped to pick up the slack.

The company's plans hit a sour note, however. It had trouble recruiting and retaining qualified music teachers, and it struggled to find ways to control the quality of music instruction. On top of those problems, expanding its facilities to accommodate practice and rehearsal rooms proved more costly than projected. Within two years, the company was singing the blues.

Fortunately, the management team moved quickly to refocus the company's strategy back onto its core business of renting and selling musical instruments. Music education rooms became customer audition rooms as well as spaces to hold an expanded inventory of instruments. It took a full year for Moe's, by returning to its core business, to return to profitability.

The moral of Moe's: When trouble hits, companies often find their way back by returning to what they do best. They refocus on their core businesses — the essential things that they do above everything else that offer real value to their customers.

Charting a Turnaround

If your company is facing a business downturn or even a crisis, create a revised business plan that reflects your new realities and sets out a step-by-step action plan to address them.

Chances are good that you won't have to start the whole process of business planning from scratch. Far from it. Your mission and vision statements are likely still intact. Your company overview probably hasn't changed all that much. In fact, you can probably focus your immediate attention on the following four areas of your plan (the rest you can tend to later, after the heat is off):

✔ Modify your goals and objectives.

✔ Revise your company strategy.

✔ Update your financial review.

✔ Revise your action plan.

The steps you take are pretty much the same as those involved in assembling any other business plan (see Chapter 14 for information on putting a plan together). The big difference when you're trying to orchestrate a turnaround is to keep the most urgent issues front and center. Focus your goals and objectives on resolving your direct threats and getting your company back on an even keel. The same goes for your revised strategies and action plan: Make sure that they specifically address the immediate problems you face and that they can achieve the solutions you propose within the time frames you set.

Desperate times sometimes call for desperate measures. If you're awash in red ink or burning through resources faster than you can say venture capital, you have to take bold action like slashing expenses, letting people go, or shaking up your management team. Doing so isn't easy or pleasant, but remember: If you can't do it, your investors will find someone who can. In fact, when turnaround professionals are brought in from the outside, one of the first steps they take is to order a change at the top.

Keeping an eye on the clock

When you're creating a turnaround plan, time is critical — and not just because your money may be running out. When times get rough, employees grow restless, morale slides, and your company's reputation — both inside and out — begins to suffer. Over time, your relationships with suppliers, distributors, bankers, and even clients can deteriorate.

The faster you turn things around, the smaller the impact this rocky period will have on your business and its future. As you draft your revised goals and objectives, keep one eye on the clock. Set precise deadlines by which to complete steps, and make sure that everyone takes those deadlines to heart.

You want to set aggressive but not unreasonable time frames. Meet with the people who will actually be doing the work to discuss exactly what it's going to take and to agree on the quickest deadlines that make sense. Get ironclad commitments all around. Your number-one goal must be to reassure everyone around you that your company can make good on its word — and that means making promises that you can keep.

Focusing on what's doable

When your company is in trouble, you're looking for bare bones, no-nonsense planning. You have to focus on what you *can* do, not what you *want* to do. Don't make the mistake of turning your goals and objectives into a wish list. Sure, developing a new technology to streamline your manufacturing or expanding into international markets would be nice — and maybe someday you will — but, when times are tough, focus on what you can afford to undertake with your strained budgets and time frame.

Getting the right people in the loop

If your business is in trouble, you'll hear from plenty of unhappy people: unhappy investors, unhappy vendors, unhappy employees, and unhappy customers. You can't order smiles back onto their faces (they will come when the company's back in the black again), but you can follow this good advice: Whatever you do, keep on talking. Keep everybody continuously informed about exactly what's going on.

Turnaround professionals advise that you

- Meet with your management team
- Meet with your senior advisors
- Meet with your employees
- Meet with your customers
- Meet with your suppliers
- Contact the tax authorities
- Contact your bank

In other words, stay in close communication with everyone who has any stake in your company and the turnaround you're working to accomplish. Don't pretend that business is better than it is. Be honest about what people can expect and when they can expect it. The more straightforward you are, the better the odds are that you'll keep people on your side. Remember, people are often your biggest asset, especially when your company experiences hard times.

Using your plan to communicate

You won't find a better way to convince people that you can change the fortunes of your company than by putting together a solid turnaround plan. In fact, make your revised plan the basis for communicating with all your stakeholders. Your investors and lenders will probably insist on seeing the plan. (In some cases, they may even play a role in shaping it.) Your suppliers aren't likely to clamor for it, but fill them in on the details anyway, especially if you can't pay them on time. At least you can give them the confidence that your good intentions are supported by a solid plan.

Make sure that you also share your turnaround plan with employees — every last one. Teamwork is always important, but never more so than when a company is in trouble. If your whole staff is in on the plan, you enlist everyone's support along with their loyalty, plus you make it clear that everyone is on the same team. Sharing your plan boosts morale at a time when people must work harder, often under difficult circumstances.

Forms on the CD-ROM

To help your established business meet new goals, check out the following forms on the CD-ROM to help you write or revise a business plan:

Form 11-1	**Selling Your Business Worksheet**	Issues to address as you prepare your business for sale
Form 11-2	**Growth Strategies Worksheet**	Approaches to consider as you chart a growth strategy for your business
Form 11-3	**Checklist of Common Warning Signs**	Common danger signals that may mean your company is headed for trouble

Chapter 12

Planning for a Nonprofit Organization

In This Chapter

▶ Being a businessperson — even in the nonprofit world

▶ Using your plan to explain and pursue your purpose

*Y*ou may have heard the joke about the company that lost money year after year until it finally decided to become a nonprofit organization. It offers a good punch line, but people in the world of philanthropy know it's a long way from the real reason that organizations become nonprofits.

To nonprofits (also known as not-for-profits and NPOs), the bottom line isn't and never was about making money. Sure, fundraising is essential to underwrite programs, but to nonprofits, the ultimate motivation isn't the dollar but the good deed. To industry associations and business groups, doing well means helping others succeed. To charitable organizations, it means making the world a better place by aiding disaster victims, protecting the environment, offering childhood vaccinations, enhancing the arts, preserving history, protecting individual rights . . . the list goes on and on.

Because nonprofits don't seek to make a profit, however, you may be wondering why they even need a business plan — especially when, by its very definition, a business is a profit-generating enterprise. Here's why: Business planning makes nonprofits more businesslike in how they operate and how they achieve success. When you develop a business plan, you develop a clear mission and vision, and you zero in on the people you plan to serve and what you aim to accomplish. You establish a plan of action, a strong organization, and increased efficiency. And by doing all that, you put your organization in a position to raise more funds to devote to your good work. This chapter leads you down the nonprofit business-planning road.

Nonprofit-speak

In the world of nonprofit organizations, you're likely to hear a different language than the one spoken in the hallways of for-profit companies. Here's a quick translation guide:

For-Profit Jargon	Nonprofit Lingo
Balance sheet	Statement of financial position
Profit-and-loss statement	Statement of financial activities
Customer	Client
Investor	Funder, contributor, donor
Product or service	Programs or services
Market analysis	Needs assessment

Running a Nonprofit Like a Business

Every organization, whether for-profit or nonprofit, needs to manage its staff, set goals, market, deliver products and services, maintain budgets, and measure progress. In fact, the business rules are pretty much the same whether you're providing meals to shut-ins or turning your mother's cookie recipe into a million-dollar enterprise. Regardless of your profit or nonprofit status, ignore the business fundamentals at your own risk — no matter how lofty your mission.

Ditto for business planning. The same steps apply whether your venture is big or small, service or retail, online or brick-and-mortar, for-profit or nonprofit. But to nonprofit organizations, certain steps require special attention. The following sections show you where to focus your efforts when writing your business plan.

Fine tuning your mission and vision

Be sure that your business plan describes exactly what kind of a future you're working to create (your organization's *vision*), backed by a description of the purpose of your organization, what you do, who you serve, and how you intend to achieve your vision (your organization's *mission*). Although mission and vision statements are important to all business planners, they're absolutely essential to the people running nonprofits. Here's why:

✔ The vision and mission statements define your organization's entire reason for being. Look at these two examples:

- A pharmaceutical company may work to find cures for diseases, but the real reason it's in business is to make money. In contrast, a nonprofit organization that's dedicated to providing breast cancer treatment to uninsured patients follows its mission to assist women in need.

- Bookshop owners do what they do because they love books, but they also sell books to earn income. A lending library, on the other hand, exists solely to encourage reading and promote knowledge.

✔ They describe reasons why others should believe in and support your efforts.

✔ They convey a compelling sense of what your organization is and what it does.

✔ They communicate the value your organization delivers and why its work is important.

✔ They appear in every grant proposal and fundraising request, and they need to be compelling enough to attract and persuade contributors — who make all your good works possible.

In addition to your vision and mission, you may want your business plan to include your organization's *values* by listing the underlying beliefs and principles that guide all your business decisions. Chapter 3 outlines all the steps involved in creating mission, vision, and values statements. It also features 12 mission statements from both the for-profit and nonprofit worlds.

For more examples of mission statements from a variety of nonprofit organizations, go to Form 12-2 on the CD-ROM. Evaluate what you like and don't like about each one as you work on your mission statement.

Work with your board of trustees to review your organization's mission statement on a regular basis to see that it accurately reflects the current situation. If the profile of the clients you serve or the causes you champion change over time, revise your mission statement accordingly.

Creating the appropriate structure

The United States alone has more than 1.5 million nonprofit organizations, ranging from small groups like the Walk on the Wild Side hiking club to the largest charitable foundation of them all, the Bill and Melinda Gates Foundation, endowed with approximately $27 billion.

Follow your beliefs

Before launching a nonprofit organization, test your idea by asking these questions:

✔ **Is this idea something you really believe in?** A driving passion isn't the only qualification for success, but it sure helps. For one thing, having that passion helps balance the fact that most people who start, run, or work with nonprofit organizations earn less money than they would working in the private sector. What motivates them isn't the money but doing something that they really care about.

✔ **Does the nonprofit fill a need?** The process of planning is to make sure your venture — for-profit or nonprofit — is likely to succeed. One indicator is whether it addresses a real market need.

To test your idea, fill out the nonprofit planning worksheet in Form 12-1 on the CD-ROM. Don't agonize about how you word your answers; just give your responses serious consideration. Your findings will be useful when you write your mission, goals, and business plan.

As you organize your nonprofit venture, you want to choose a legal structure appropriate for your situation. The following represent your basic options:

✔ **Informal nonprofits:** As the name implies, these organizations are loose-knit groups of like-minded people who get together for activities or to be of service to the community. Examples include local book clubs, self-help support groups, or graffiti cleanup patrols. Informal nonprofits have no legal structure and typically raise and manage only small sums of money. They aren't big enough to fall under the watchful eye of the IRS.

✔ **Nonprofit corporations:** Incorporation allows a nonprofit organization to protect its directors and staff from certain types of liability, similar to the protective shield offered to for-profit companies. Incorporation also ensures that the organization will be able to continue its activities even when the founding members are no longer around. To get the details on incorporation in your state, check with the office of your Secretary of State, Division of Corporations, or Attorney General.

✔ **Tax-exempt nonprofits:** Nonprofit corporations with charitable, educational, scientific, religious, or cultural purposes can file for tax-exempt status under section 501 of the Internal Revenue Service Code. The major types of tax-exempt organizations include

- Charitable organizations (religious, educational, scientific, and literary organizations, for example)

- Social welfare organizations (civic leagues and community groups)

- Labor and agricultural organizations (labor unions and farm bureaus)

- Business leagues (trade associations and chambers of commerce)

- Social clubs (country clubs, fraternities, and sororities)

- Fraternal organizations (lodges and other clubs)

- Veterans' organizations (armed forces groups)

- Employees' associations (employee-benefit groups)

- Political organizations (campaign committees, political parties, and political action committees [PACs])

✔ **Qualified nonprofits:** Donations to qualified nonprofits may be tax deductible — a distinction that can matter a great deal to contributors. Qualified organizations include religious, educational, scientific, and literary groups, as well as child and animal welfare organizations, certain veterans' organizations, fraternal societies, and more.

For information on whether your organization qualifies for tax-exempt status, check out *IRS Publication 557*. For a current list of qualified nonprofits, look at *IRS Publication 78*. Both publications are available on the IRS Web site at www.irs.gov.

Setting goals and objectives

How do you spell success? That's really what a discussion of goals and objectives is all about. To for-profit companies, the answer is easy: M-O-N-E-Y. To nonprofit organizations, however, the answer is far less tangible. You measure success not in dollars, but in how well your organization serves those in need or how well it advances the causes it champions.

Goals and objectives provide a road map that helps keep your organization on track; they keep your efforts focused on providing the greatest possible value to the clients you serve; and they help convince contributors that you're making a real difference in the world by stating in measurable terms the outcomes you deliver.

Think of it this way: Because your goals and objectives define the real bottom line of your nonprofit organization, they're the keys to unlocking support from donors and foundations. Without gifts and grants, you can't achieve your purpose. It's that simple.

Make sure your written plan includes your organization's goals and objectives. If you don't already have them down on paper, turn to Chapter 3 for some easy-to-follow goal-setting tips. Also, be sure to think about your goals from the standpoint of your clients and your contributors by considering these questions:

✔ What goals are most meaningful to the people you serve or the cause you're fighting for? How can you best meet those goals through a series of specific objectives?

✔ What goals would best persuade your contributors that the work you do is important and makes a difference? What specific objectives would help convince them that you're meeting those goals?

Even the highest ideals don't substitute for clearly stated goals and measurable objectives. Funders need more than an assurance that you're working to make the world a better place. They want to know for whom, in what way, and exactly how you'll measure your impact.

Sample goals and objectives

Take the example of a nonprofit group, Jobs For All, that matches unemployed people with employers who have entry-level positions to fill. One way to gauge its effectiveness would be to count the number of clients served each year or, better yet, the number of clients who were actually placed in jobs. If the organization's mission involves preparing people to work by teaching them job skills and helping them deal with issues like childcare, an even better measure of success would be to track how many people were placed in jobs that they kept for a reasonable length of time.

Measuring the nonprofit's results may lead the organization to set a goal to increase the number of clients successfully placed in long-term job situations. Another goal may be to increase funding in order to expand services.

Knowing their goals, the staff's next step is to write objectives that detail the measures they'll take in order to achieve each goal. For example, to increase the number of clients successfully served each year, objectives may include the following:

✔ Enlisting 10 new employers into the job-placement program over the next six months

✔ Finding jobs for an additional 75 unemployed people in the coming year

✔ Increasing the percentage of clients who actually remain employed for at least six months from 60 percent to 85 percent

A sample solicitation based on goals and objectives

After you establish your goals and objectives, use them as powerful motivators in fundraising campaigns. Take a look at this funding solicitation letter from the job-placement organization featured in the previous section:

Last year, Jobs For All placed 350 unemployed people in productive and meaningful positions in our community. This year, with your help, we plan to make that number 425. What's more, we're committed to increasing the percentage of our clients who remain on the job for at least six months from 60 percent to 85 percent.

How will we do it? First, we plan to expand our job-placement program. But that's only the beginning. We're working with the community college to offer basic computer-skills classes. And we're creating a job-assistance hotline to provide immediate help to our clients when they encounter problems at home or on the job.

But to do any of this, we need your help. This year's fundraising goal of $500,000 represents a 20 percent increase over last year's target. We know that's ambitious. But we also know that with your generosity, we can change lives for the better.

Organizing to Do Good Work

By their very name, nonprofits don't have a profit motive, but that doesn't mean they don't have to be efficient and accountable. If your organization relies on charitable contributions, donors will weigh your organizational capabilities in much the same way they weigh the capabilities of a for-profit company. That's because whether they're directing charitable funds or nest-egg dollars, investors want to ensure that their money goes into ventures that will succeed.

Before investors and charitable donors pledge their support, they want to know that an organization has the capabilities to turn ideals into reality. We describe the qualities they look in detail in Chapter 6, and you need to summarize them in the company description section of the business plan. As you write the plan for your nonprofit organization, pay special attention to these four qualities:

✔ Strong and streamlined operations

✔ Efficient organization

✔ Experienced management

✔ Innovative ideas based on R&D expertise that's capable of designing, developing, and enhancing distinctive products, services, and technologies

The following sections take a look at the aspects of these four qualities that are particularly important to nonprofit organizations.

Operations

The term *operations* typically refers to how companies carry out their business; that is, how they handle day-to-day activities and how they produce products and provide services efficiently and cost-effectively in order to maximize profits.

To nonprofit organizations, efficient operations are just as important, but for different reasons. In your world, efficiency means that your organization does more with less. It means that you leverage maximum value out of every donor dollar by spending as little as possible to deliver quality services and support for your causes. And that means you end up reaching more people, doing more good, and, as a bonus, having an easier time raising funds in the future.

See that your business plan includes a discussion of how you'll address the following four areas that comprise your operations:

- **Location:** As an example, an organization providing food to homeless people needs a location close to homeless shelters and social services.

- **Equipment:** For instance, if you plan to enhance online donor communications, you may need to acquire computers, a server, modems, software, and other equipment.

- **Labor:** No matter what your mission, you need a plan for recruiting and training paid staff and volunteers.

- **Process:** You need to describe how you'll operate your organization. A food bank, for example, needs a process for gathering food contributions, sorting them in a central location, and delivering them to those in need.

As a nonprofit, your operations are important for another reason, too: Your organization will likely apply for grants, and grant applications require a detailed description of operational procedures in order to assess your ability to serve your constituents, recruit and keep necessary staff, and do your good work efficiently and effectively. Successfully managing these areas allows you to achieve a positive return on the grant dollars being invested in your organization. The good news is that you can probably cut and paste directly from your business plan — or at least borrow from the main points.

Organization

Some nonprofit groups manage to do their work entirely through the services of unpaid volunteers. When the groups reach a certain size, however, most organizations add a core staff of paid employees who work closely with the volunteer corps.

Often, the person who heads the professional staff is called a Chief Executive Officer (CEO) or sometimes a Chief Professional Officer (CPO). Some nonprofits also appoint a senior volunteer to the position of Chief Volunteer Officer (CVO). The CEO or CPO manages paid staff, and the CVO oversees volunteer activities.

In your business plan, include your organizational chart, indicating which positions are paid and which are opportunities for volunteer assistance. Assign titles — director of programs, for example, or director of fundraising — and include a summary of key job descriptions and responsibilities.

Because the overriding purpose of most nonprofits is to promote worthy causes or serve people in need, salaries and compensation can be delicate issues. It's easy but inaccurate to view money spent on staff salaries as money not available for investment in your mission. Well-selected professionals make your organization efficient and effective and make achieving your mission possible. Although most people who choose to work for nonprofits are in it for reasons other than money, they still want to be compensated fairly for what they do.

If you're not certain how much to pay staff members, start by finding out what professionals in similar positions in for-profit and nonprofit organizations in your market area get paid.

Management

Most states require incorporated nonprofit groups to have a *board of trustees,* or a group of people who serve as the organization's official governing body, providing oversight and direction while also helping to raise funds, guide the organization, and shape its programs. (Contact your attorney or the office of your state's Attorney General for details.)

Even if your organization isn't incorporated, consider creating an informal advisory board to help steer your organization. As you select nominees for your board, look for people who are

  ✔ Passionate about your nonprofit's mission

  ✔ Ready, willing, and able to raise money

  ✔ Experienced in the for-profit world of business

Form 12-4 on the CD-ROM provides a checklist of major duties that nonprofit boards of trustees often assume. Check the ones that are relevant to your organization and its requirements. Filling out this worksheet provides an idea about the kinds of capabilities you seek in board members, and it helps as you evaluate the overall makeup of your board.

In your written plan, list the members of your board of trustees along with their affiliations. If you don't yet have a board, describe the kinds of people you hope to recruit and how you plan to go about approaching them.

Opening hearts, minds, and wallets

Fundraising will probably play a starring role in your business plan for the simple reason that it's crucial to the health and well-being of most nonprofit organizations.

In your plan, be sure to describe who will head your fundraising effort and how you will organize activities. Include your strategy for targeting and communicating with likely donors, who most often come from one or more of the following sources:

✔ Individuals

✔ Corporations

✔ Private foundations

✔ Community foundations

✔ Government agencies

Individuals represent by far the largest contributor group. In fact, most nonprofit fundraising campaigns receive 70 to 80 percent of their money from individuals:

✔ People who have given in the past are the most likely candidates to give again — so long as they have a sense that their money is being well spent.

✔ People who somehow benefit from your programs are usually receptive contributors.

✔ People who know firsthand of your good works are likely to support your work by writing checks. For example, a person who knows someone with Parkinson's disease is more likely to support related medical research than someone who knows very little about the illness.

What's the best way to reach individual donors? The answer depends on the nature of your organization and the kinds of contributors you plan to target. Door-to-door solicitations are great for local nonprofits or for large organizations with strong grassroots networks. If you can tell your story clearly and compellingly in print, a direct-mail campaign can be a cost-effective way to generate results.

As you craft your fundraising plans, use the questionnaire in Form 12-3 on the CD-ROM to gather information about your ideal individual donor.

Research and development (R&D)

In the nonprofit arena, R&D rarely involves technological breakthroughs or science and engineering feats. For nonprofits, R&D usually means researching issues that affect the clients and funders of your organization and developing programs that fit the changing realities of the world around you.

In the for-profit marketplace, changes are pretty hard to miss. When customers stop buying a company's products, the firm adapts or goes bye-bye. Nonprofits, on the other hand, are a bit more insulated from competition, and that's precisely why research is so important: It helps your organization stay a step ahead of change, which, in turn, helps ensure that your services are responsive to real and current needs.

Snare that grant

Literally thousands of foundations and government agencies have money earmarked to fund work by nonprofit organizations. To unlock their largesse, though, you need to persuade them that yours is the best organization to turn their dollars into good deeds. And that takes a strong *grant proposal* — a written description of your organization, your programs, your financial request, and exactly how you plan to spend the money and carry out your plans.

Writing a grant proposal may not be anyone's idea of a good time, but it doesn't have to be agony. In fact, as long as you have a good, solid business plan in place, you're already well on your way to writing a grant proposal because a lot of the information that goes into your grant proposal comes right out of your business plan, such as your mission statement, your philosophy and vision, and a description of how your organization is set up and how you operate. If you've done your business-planning homework, the information is ready to go — or at least waiting to serve as useful background material.

Form 12-5 on the CD-ROM outlines the parts of most grant proposals along with estimates of how much space you should allocate to each section. As you write your next proposal, include the information highlighted in each of the major sections on the form.

Large nonprofits hire outside specialists to conduct studies and write reports on the key issues they address, but you can take steps on your own, too. For instance, you may conduct a survey of your client groups, obtain and pore over government reports, or analyze statistics that apply to your organization's work (like the regional rate of domestic abuse, the continuing loss of regional open space, or the changing face of local homelessness).

Whatever the focus of your research and whoever carries it out, the goals of your research should probably include the following:

✔ Understanding basic issues and root problems

✔ Tracking major trends and external changes

✔ Identifying unmet program and service needs

✔ Weighing the pros and cons of alternative solutions

✔ Evaluating the effectiveness of existing programs

In the Company Description of your business plan, include key research to underscore the importance of the work you do. Also, describe how you plan to conduct ongoing research in order to stay abreast of the changing needs of your clients, your causes, and your organization.

Keeping the Books

Nonprofits aren't in business for the money, but if they don't keep track of the money they handle in a businesslike way, they may find themselves in hot water — or even out of operation entirely. You can find everything you need to know about the basics of business accounting in Chapter 8, and the same rules pretty much apply to for-profits and nonprofits alike. However, a few special financial considerations apply specifically to nonprofits, and that's what this section is all about.

Finding funding

Because fundraising is so crucial to many nonprofit organizations, your written plan needs to explain exactly where you intend to get the money to support your efforts and how much you expect to raise.

Typically, nonprofits take in the money they need to operate from the following sources:

- Donations from companies and individuals
- Government or private foundation grants
- Income from endowments and trusts
- Income from products and services, such as proceeds from the museum shop, concert tickets, and door-to-door cookie sales

Most nonprofits rely on a combination of these funding sources. National Public Radio, for example, is made possible by donations from listeners like you, corporate sponsors, and a little bit of help from Uncle Sam.

Wherever your dollars come from, be sure you establish a detailed record-keeping system. If your nonprofit is incorporated, official corporate documents, board-meeting minutes, financial reports, and other records must be preserved over the life of the organization. For more information, check with the office of your Secretary of State or state Attorney General.

Managing overhead

Imagine if a nonprofit organization spent 80 percent of its revenue on fundraising events and 20 percent of its revenue on supporting its causes and clients. Donors would quickly question whether they were contributing to a charitable group or to a fundraising engine.

The bottom line is that you want to keep your expenses in line. Whether you're talking about office rent, supplies, advertising and promotions, or the budget for your next fundraising event, watch your costs like a hawk:

 ✔ Be sure your overhead matches the standards that donors expect from charitable organizations.

 ✔ Keep your spending to the lowest possible percentage of your organization's income, aiming for a number under 25 percent.

 ✔ Let your expenses climb at your own peril. Organizations like the Wise Giving Alliance (formed when the National Charities Information Bureau merged with the Council of Better Business Bureaus Foundation) provide donors with reports on the charitable performance of soliciting organizations. Their guidelines stipulate that member organizations spend at least 65 percent of funds raised on program activities, keeping overhead to less than 35 percent. Even small organizations are wise to adopt similar ratios. For more information on the Wise Giving Alliance, visit www.give.org.

Putting working cash to work

Just like for-profit companies, nonprofits need a cushion of cash or other liquid assets on hand. The question is, how much? The answer depends largely on the nature of your nonprofit's mission. For example, a relief agency that responds to unforeseen disasters needs a large bank balance ready to draw upon when the unforeseen need occurs. A nonprofit that runs a community food bank, however, probably doesn't need anywhere near as great a reserve.

You can imagine why cash reserves are a touchy subject: People donate money to further a good cause, not to see their money sitting around in a bank account somewhere. (The exception is endowment funds, which are set up specifically to generate interest income to fund nonprofit programs.)

The Wise Giving Alliance offers the following guideline: "A charity's unrestricted net assets available for use should not be more than three times the size of the past year's expenses or three times the size of the current year's budget, whichever is greater."

If you do keep a sizeable reserve fund, be sure your donors understand why the reserve is necessary. Also be sure that your organization has a procedure in place to protect the funds for the appropriate programs and against erosion from administrative or operational expenses.

Staying accountable

Nonprofit organizations are founded on trust. Donors trust that you'll use the money they give wisely, and grant makers trust (and usually verify) that you use the funds they provide for the purposes described in the grant application. The members of the board of trustees are responsible for making sure that the organization lives up to its pledges, and that means maintaining accountability by keeping track of where, when, and how the organization spends each dollar.

In your business plan, include provisions for an annual audit of your organization's finances.

Many nonprofits hire professional accounting firms to conduct an audit in order to make sure it's independent and objective. But if your nonprofit is small or relatively new, you may opt to create a volunteer committee of people with experience in accounting to review the records, verify bank balances, and produce a written report of their findings. In order to ensure that the committee has no conflict of interest, it should operate completely independently of the board of trustees.

Forms on the CD-ROM

If you're part of a nonprofit organization, take a look at the following forms on the CD-ROM to help you plan:

Form 12-1	**Nonprofit Planning Worksheet**	A worksheet that helps you develop your nonprofit idea
Form 12-2	**Examples of Real-World Nonprofit Mission Statements**	A selection of nonprofit mission statements along with space to record your impressions
Form 12-3	**Ideal Individual Donor Questionnaire**	Questions that help you gather information about your ideal individual donor
Form 12-4	**Checklist of Responsibilities for a Nonprofit Board**	A list that helps you determine the capabilities you seek on your board of trustees
Form 12-5	**Checklist of Typical Grant Proposal Sections**	The typical sections you should think about including in your grant proposal

Chapter 13

Planning for an E-Business

In This Chapter

▶ Looking at lessons from the recent past

▶ Building an e-commerce business model

▶ Adding e-business to your brick-and-mortar establishment

*W*hen the first edition of this book came out in 2001, lessons from the April 2000 dot-com crash were works in progress. Hundreds of Internet-based businesses had folded, 100,000 jobs had evaporated, and the economy was still quaking.

Surviving Web-based enterprises faced dueling realities: The technology-based economy was devastated, but interest in information technology in general and in the Internet specifically was at an all-time high. Despite the dramatic failures of Internet-based businesses, online sales soared to $66 billion in 2001 (and they kept climbing; a widely cited study by the Boston Consulting Group projects sales of $168 billion in 2005). As e-businesses plotted their next steps, debate raged regarding how much the old business-planning concepts — mission statements, business models, goals and objectives, financial forecasts, profit projections, exit strategies, and everything in between — really mattered.

Well, that was then and this is now. As this 2nd Edition of *Business Plans Kit For Dummies* goes to press, the lessons learned from the dot-com crash are clearer. The luster has worn off the phrase "new economy," and with it went the idea of brand-new rules and revolutionary ways of doing business. If anything, the aftermath of the late 1990s polished the appeal of traditional business basics.

Web-based ventures no longer get a pass from bankers, investors, or business advisors when it comes to writing, presenting, and implementing good old-fashioned business plans.

The jury is no longer out: Whether you're launching or running an Internet business or adding a Web-based component to your brick-and-mortar establishment, you need a business plan. Use this chapter as your guide in tailoring your plan to the rapid pace of the e-business world.

Dot-com lessons learned

Following the crash-and-burn of the dot-coms in April 2000, armchair quarterbacking netted some worthwhile reflections and advice. Here's a roundup of what business gurus have to say:

✔ **Profits matter:** A few years ago, investors evaluated businesses based on how many "eyeballs" or "clicks" they would attract — the 1990s terminology for how many people visited and took action at a Web site. Today, the measurement is back to basics. What are you selling? How much revenue will you generate? What costs will you incur? How many dollars will make it to your bottom line in the form of profit? (See Chapter 8 for a crash course in business finance.)

✔ **Costs matter:** So much for the posh offices, new cars, and office spaces stuffed with expensive toys. Business owners are once again spending money as if it were their own — because more often than not, it is. The phrase "return on investment" now has an all-new ring to it.

✔ **Your value proposition matters:** Your *value proposition* is also called your core-marketing message or your unique selling proposition. When figuring out your company's value proposition, ask yourself the following questions:

- Who's your ideal customer?

- What problems or challenges does your product solve for your customer?

- What results or benefits can your customers count on?

- What makes your product a better and more valuable solution than any other offering on the market?

- How does your offering deliver value beyond the time and money customers will spend to obtain it?

✔ **Service matters:** This is one of the big lessons of the technologically centered 1990s. Today's customers demand double doses of customer service, which means you have to know your customers. Here are some tips for knowing your customers and anticipating their needs:

- Know what they want from your Web site.

- Know what kind of equipment they use so your site is compatible.

- Watch for user responses and reply immediately.

- Set up 24-hour, toll-free phone lines for live help.

- Send customer comment cards with product deliveries.

- Send thank-you notes or gifts.

- Remember that online customers are like all other customers: They value prompt service, clear communication, and proof that you appreciate their business.

✔ **Expertise matters:** As business gurus aptly put it, if you plan to run a billion-dollar enterprise, be sure you have people with billion-dollar expertise onboard.

✔ **Your business model matters:** The lessons don't get more basic than this: To stay in business, you need a business model designed to bring in more money than the combined total of your costs and expenses. The 1990s proved that business models built around the word "free" rarely survive. "Give it away now and profit later" is basically a formula for bankruptcy. If you open a Web site that gives away consulting advice with the hope of later enrolling site visitors into your seminars, for example, at the very least, you have to admit that your Web site isn't an e-consulting business but a channel for selling your seminar business.

✔ **Patience matters:** The newer your new business concept, the longer it takes to win market acceptance, so you need to factor the time lapse into your business plan. (See Chapter 1 for information regarding business-planning time frames.)

Avoiding the Well-Traveled Bumps on the Cyber Highway

No question about it: The Internet is fundamental to today's lifestyles and business dealings, and online communication has transformed the way people worldwide live, work, shop, and buy.

Getting to this point took brave exploration by businesses that dared to forge the path into the world of e-business. Along the way, they hit some pitfalls and weathered some scrapes that all who follow can gratefully avoid, starting with the four revelations in the following sections.

Web presence isn't an all-or-nothing proposition

Web presence is a *strategy* for doing business. The closer your e-business strategy aligns with the rest of your business plan, the more it will strengthen your ability to build relationships with suppliers, distributors, customers, and employees. The most successful online retailers today integrate the Internet as a vital selling and communication channel in their overall business models. However, they view the Net as *a* channel, not *the* channel.

E-business planning is a continuous process

The online world is constantly developing with new opportunities and new competitive threats arising almost daily. You can't rely on once-a-year planning to scan your business environment and monitor your company's performance. On an ongoing basis, watch for the following:

✔ **New technologies and their impact on your marketplace:** Luckily, many of the same technologies that drive e-business also make easy work of tracking all sorts of information, from the keywords that online prospects use to find businesses like yours to the paths they follow to reach your site.

✔ **Changing customer preferences and shopping patterns:** Web site activity reports can tell you the nature and number of visitors arriving at your site, as well as what they did while in your Web space. Monitor the pages viewed, files downloaded, dates and times of visits, referral sources, session length, navigation path, and most certainly the keywords entered to find your site in the first place. This information reveals who looks at what and who buys what. Incorporate this data into the ongoing business-planning process.

✔ **Changes to your business environment:** Chapter 5 offers step-by-step instructions for conducting a SWOT analysis to assess your business strengths and weaknesses so you can seize market opportunities and avoid threats. Put the process to work on a regular basis. Don't wait until year-end; by then, your business could be blindsided by new technologies, competitors, or customer preferences.

Stay ready and willing to adjust components of your business plan as the need or a new strategic opportunity arises.

Know and stick to your mission

The opportunities of the online world can easily blow an e-business way off its course. The antidote is a strong mission and a compelling vision for how you plan to reach your business goals. Sure, you need to be flexible and ready to adapt as conditions change. But you have to remain true to your mission and to the goals you plan to reach as a company. Chapter 3 provides good information on writing your mission and vision statements.

Know where the money is coming from

Having a hand on the source of money flow comes right back to the revitalized term "business model," which, in the simplest terms, is how your business will generate revenue and profit. To develop your business model, you need to know

✔ What you plan to sell and the value your product delivers to customers

✔ The profile of your prospective customer

✔ How you plan to reach, acquire, and keep customers

✔ How you define and differentiate your offerings

✔ That your product pricing covers all costs plus some profit

Chapter 5 has more information on business models and what it takes to keep your business on the right side of the profit margin.

Ironing Out Pressing Planning Issues

Whether you're starting, revamping, or expanding an e-business, the same checklist of important planning issues applies:

- ✔ **Evaluate your business environment.** So much for the pie-in-the-sky days of "If you build it, they will come." When the topic is Web sites, that approach just doesn't work. Tens of millions of Web sites are up and running. Getting customers to land on yours takes planning, promotion, and investment, and getting them to buy when they arrive is even trickier. Be prepared: Chapter 4 helps you assess your competitive environment and your customer profiles and preferences.

- ✔ **Estimate your upfront costs.** One of the biggest mistakes e-businesses make is underestimating the software, hardware, and development costs involved in getting a Web site up and running — not to mention what's involved in maintaining the site after it opens for business. To create a realistic budget that doesn't leave anything out, flip to Chapter 8.

- ✔ **Fine-tune your business model.** You can't expect your e-business to succeed if you're not absolutely sure about where the money's going to come from. Take a look at Chapter 5 for an overview of business models.

- ✔ **Create a realistic business timeline.** Face it, you don't have all the time in the world to get your business up and running, find customers, generate revenues, and make a profit. But at the same time, it won't happen overnight. In between, you need start-up cash to hold you over until your business can turn a profit. Set a realistic timeline so that everyone from investors to employees knows what to expect. Chapter 1 has more information on business time frames.

- ✔ **Build flexibility into your plan.** Most business plans include contingencies — "what if" scenarios that provide alternatives in case something goes wrong. Contingency planning is especially important for an e-business. If your business plan depends on Web site ad revenue, for example, include a contingency in case those dollars don't roll in as anticipated. Or if your business plan counts on return business from previous customers, you need to have an alternative plan in place in case customers are more fickle than you expect.

- ✔ **Plan for the people you need.** A strong staff of highly committed and experienced employees is essential to the success of any business but doubly so for e-businesses. Make sure your business plan addresses exactly how you intend to find top-flight software engineers or skilled content providers and how you'll recruit them and keep them on board.

Form 13-1 on the CD-ROM lists the previous issues in a single checklist. Use it as you seriously consider the opportunities and hurdles your business faces. Fill in your responses to each of these key areas, and then return to the form on a regular basis to monitor your situation and fine-tune your responses.

Creating an Online Customer Profile

Whether you're opening a Web-based company or adding an Internet extension to an existing company, your business plan needs to describe the customers you intend to attract — and how you expect them to behave when they get to your Web site. This step is *essential*.

After you know who you're planning to attract and what visitors you expect from your site, you can configure your online offerings to match expectations and trigger desired consumer responses.

This task sounds straightforward, but it isn't as easy as it seems. Even the 1,000-pound e-gorillas like Amazon constantly monitor what makes their online customers tick (or click), and they adjust their offerings accordingly.

Use the questionnaire in Form 13-2 on the CD-ROM to capture the key characteristics of your most likely online customers. As you answer the questions, you begin to define your online customer profile. For additional details on how to size up your customers, flip to Chapter 4.

Building an Internet Business

Remember when futurists predicted that we would spend our lives in cyber cafes and cyber boutiques doing cyber shopping and cyber chatting and being entertained by cyber sports and cyber music? Well, very few e-businesses (or e-customers) operate entirely in cyberspace, conducting all operations and business over the Internet.

Amazon.com is perhaps the most famous e-business in the world, yet even it relies on operations grounded in tradition — stocking warehouses, for example, or filling orders and seeing to it that the goods get delivered to customers by truck or plane. In fact, Amazon.com even offers in-store pickup options so that online shoppers can go to participating brick-and-mortar outlets to pick up books, DVDs, CDs, office products, electronics, or other items ordered on the Amazon site.

Contrary to all the tradition-shattering predictions, most online businesses consider Web presence as a business strategy that integrates with traditional operations. They move business functions online when and if that's the most efficient and effective way to build relationships with suppliers, distributors, customers, and employees.

Establishing your value proposition

To increase your odds of e-business success, step back and consider your company from your customers' point of view:

- What benefits and solutions are you providing your customers?
- What problems or needs do they have that your offering addresses?
- How's your solution better than the solution offered by any competitor?
- What's the value of your offering from your customers' perspectives?

The answers to these questions combine to form what's called your *value proposition* — fancy jargon for a simple statement of the value that your product, service, or process delivers to your customers. Sometimes a company's value proposition seems pretty obvious:

- Wal-Mart offers low everyday prices on a wide range of merchandise.
- Rolls-Royce offers unparalleled luxury and the ultimate in snob appeal.
- Travelocity.com offers cheap airline tickets to anywhere in the world.

However, a company's value proposition may include offerings far beyond those that first come to mind. Think about Amazon again. It sells books and other merchandise at a discount, so part of its value proposition is clearly based on low prices. But Amazon also stocks one of the largest inventories of books anywhere in the world. Thus, having a wide selection is also part of its value proposition. Amazon's appeal to book lovers doesn't stop there. The online bookseller invites readers to review and rate books — a feature that many customers like so much that they wouldn't dream of shopping for books anywhere else. In addition, customers can read recent book reviews from magazines, newspapers, and other media with the click of a mouse. They can read the first sentence of the book right on the book's Web page or click to read the first chapter of many of the books on sale. The offerings go on, with each feature representing additional customer value.

The more that customers value your product, the more likely they are to remain loyal to your business.

Use Form 13-3 on the CD-ROM as you assess your company's value proposition. By understanding the needs of your customers and the value that your e-business offers, you can communicate to your customers that you have what they want to buy — and what they're willing to pay for.

Figure 13-1 shows how a travel-related site called Cultural Escapes completed the form. The company's responses uncover the following points:

✔ **Challenges faced by the company:** The company's responses show that customized information is a hallmark of the business. But to be useful — and to keep customers coming back — the site's information absolutely, positively must be right on the mark. If a customer has one bad meal at a favorably reviewed restaurant, in other words, the site loses one of its principal values to customers. This realization may lead to a quality control division that monitors reviews on an ongoing basis.

✔ **Features that offer revenue-generating potential:** By realizing the unique value Cultural Escapes offers to customers, the company may develop some of its features into revenue-generating products. For instance, a traveler who's planning a trip to Barcelona and happens to be passionate about great food and culinary culture may be willing to pay a small fee for a customized package of information that includes hot new restaurants in the city, cooking school courses, and background on the city's culinary history. This same customer may also be willing to pay for a subscription to a monthly newsletter that highlights upcoming culinary events in major cities around the world. In addition, because the Web site attracts visitors interested in food, travel, and culture, it may be attractive to businesses that want to advertise cooking schools or culinary events — even cookbook publishers or gourmet magazines.

By developing its value proposition, the travel site can build a promising business model that includes a number of revenue streams: fees for personalized travel-information packages; subscription fees for special interest travel newsletters; and revenues for site ads placed by companies with related products or services.

Constructing a workable e-business model

Coming up with a business model is one thing. Coming up with a model that actually works can be quite another.

The only business model that works is one that delivers enough revenue to cover all your costs plus some profit. Answer the following no-nonsense question:

> *What value do you offer to site users or site advertisers, and how can you convert that value into cold, hard cash (or at least plastic)?*

Where will your sales revenue come from? That's your business model in a nutshell.

E-BUSINESS VALUE PROPOSITION WORKSHEET

1. Write a one-sentence description of your e-business:

Cultural Escapes offers visitors to its Web site personalized travel information packages tailored to their specific cultural interests, from arts and music to language studies and culinary adventures.

2. Describe three or four of the most important features on your Web site:

- A personal profile that allows visitors to describe the kinds of information they want to see presented about travel destinations under consideration

- A customer feedback feature that allows users to give their own reviews of restaurants, hotels, museums, performances, tours, cruises, cities, and countries

- An online "classified lodging" section that allows travelers to arrange short-term rentals or house-swaps with people in other parts of the world

- E-mail alerts and travel reminders highlighting special events, exhibits, performances, and limited-time travel offers

3. List three or four benefits customers receive when they visit your Web site:

- The most comprehensive and up-to-date cultural information about travel destinations available anywhere

- The ability to tailor information to meet personal interests, such as concert schedules, gallery openings, and well-reviewed restaurants in a given destination

- The chance to hear what other like-minded travelers are saying about popular and undiscovered travel destinations

4. Looking back at #3, describe the essential value that customers take away:

- Access to timely, reliable, personalized travel information

- Time-savings when it comes to the travel planning process

- Peace of mind about major travel-related decisions

5. Think about your ideal customers. What's the best thing they can say about your e-business?

They can count on us to provide them complete, reliable, and up-to-date information about travel destinations that's tailored to their own personal needs and interests.

Figure 13-1:
Use this form to determine why customers come to your Web site and what value they receive.

As you think through your answer, use the e-business model construction worksheet in Form 13-4 on the CD-ROM. Answer the questions as part of a brainstorming exercise that helps uncover sources of site revenue. Look at Figure 13-2 to see how Cultural Escapes, an online travel information Web site, built its business model.

Feature a discussion of your business model prominently in the company strategy section of your business plan.

Getting funded

A written business plan is an absolute must for an Internet venture. In fact, if you're seeking funding, you'll have a hard time finding a serious investor who will even let you past the receptionist without a detailed plan down on paper (but not too detailed). Chapter 19 offers 10 things you should know about venture capital, but one phrase to remember is "short and sweet." Some old hands in the game swear that 10 pages is the absolute limit.

Consider a few other tips when tailoring your plan for investors:

- ✔ Avoid technical jargon in favor of plain, everyday language.
- ✔ Emphasize the expertise of your management team.
- ✔ Include a complete analysis of the marketplace — not only the obvious markets, but also the tougher markets to break into.
- ✔ Describe your competitors and how you plan to distinguish your company from the rest of the pack.
- ✔ Include a thorough overview of your financials and a summary of what they mean.
- ✔ Define your company's growth potential.

Present your condensed business plan, but keep the full-blown version close at hand. If all goes well, investor prospects will want to see and find out more.

With the lessons of the dot-com bust came new scrutiny of the business plans of Internet ventures by everyone from bankers to venture capitalists (VCs). Don't be discouraged. Yes, you have to spend more time and effort hammering out a rock-solid plan, but the investment will pay off for you and for people who sign on to support your dream.

A serious business plan can provide the momentum you need to keep on going when the going gets tough. Truth is, successful entrepreneurs return to their written business plans time and again to recapture the inspiration, the spirit, and the direction that started them out planning a business in the first place. Don't go online without one!

E-BUSINESS MODEL CONSTRUCTION WORKSHEET
1. List three key value-added features that your Web site offers: • Personalized travel information packages • Monthly newsletters focused on specific interest areas • Customized email alerts and travel reminders
2. Given your key Web site features, identify potential sources of revenue: • Sale of travel information packages • Subscriptions to special interest newsletters • Merchandising of select travel products
3. Is your Web site attractive to advertisers? If so, list at least three examples: • Tour companies • Travel industry (airlines, hotels, cruise lines) • City and institutional sponsors • Publishers
4. Will you capture useful demographic information on your Web site? Are there additional ways to leverage your customer database? • Merchandise tie-ins • Event ticketing opportunities • Direct market travel offers
5. Identify at least one up-and-running e-business with a similar business model: 2AHealthyU.com is a Web site that provides customized disease prevention and health maintenance information based on an online questionnaire format.
6. How does your business model resemble the one above? How does it differ? Both Web sites offer customized information to consumers. But our model allows us to learn more about our customers and offer more personalized products and services. We are also in a better position to match up our clients with targeted advertisers.
7. Describe what you see as the key strengths of your business model: • Strong and growing market for travel services • Information with high value-added content • Multiple revenue sources
8. Describe major concerns or uncertainties inherent in your business model: • Strong competition among online travel resource Web sites • Challenges of maintaining reliable, up-to-date information • Internet advertising rates and demand still quite uncertain

Figure 13-2:
Develop your business model to keep a firm hand on your revenue pulse.

Talking the talk

People in the world of business financing talk a language all their own. Use this sidebar as your translation guide.

Venture capitalists (VCs) range from small, independent operators to large firms that evaluate thousands of new business-funding proposals every year. *Angel investors* are high net-worth individuals (that is, rich people) who are interested in getting richer by investing in promising new companies. When you enter the world of VCs and angels, you need a glossary of jargon to know how to talk the talk:

✔ **Seed financing:** The initial investment in a start-up business. This funding may go toward testing and proving your business concept, developing your product prototype, or conducting market research.

✔ **Start-up financing:** The initial level of investment required to get your company off the ground. The funds are used for everything from assembling your business team to developing your product or service, testing it, and bringing it to market.

✔ **First-stage financing:** Additional money that comes in after your initial start-up funds run out. These funds are often used to support further growth by ramping up new product development, production, marketing, or your sales efforts.

✔ **Second-stage financing:** Money raised down the road after your business has initially proven itself. The funds are typically used to allow the company to expand quickly by supporting growth in all areas of the company's operations.

✔ **Mezzanine financing:** We're not talking about theater tickets here. *Mezzanine* means in between, and this financing falls in between an equity investment and a standard bank loan. This money allows your company to expand in a particular direction without having to give up additional ownership in the business.

✔ **Bridge financing:** Like a bridge over troubled waters, this kind of financing can help your company through temporary rough spots. For example, companies sometimes get bridge loans before an Initial Public Offering (IPO) to smooth out any cash shortfalls that may occur before the IPO is completed.

Adding an Internet Extension to Your Brick-and-Mortar Business

Thinking of a company that doesn't already have at least some level of online presence is difficult, even if it's just a company contact Web site — which is like an online Yellow Pages ad — or the ability to send e-mail to customers, suppliers, and colleagues. But maybe you're ready to expand your online presence. Maybe you want to reach prospects outside your current market area or enhance customer service with online communications. Or maybe you're ready to dive in to the realm of online sales. Before jumping in, ask yourself these questions:

✔ **Who will use your site?** Will your customers, prospects, suppliers, job applicants, employees, or a combination of users use this site?

✔ **How will people use your site?** Will they want general information (for instance, your open hours, address, or product lines)? Will they want answers to frequently asked questions? Do they want to do business with you online (to request quotes, submit job applications, or make purchases)?

✔ **What do you expect from your site?** Is your goal to generate leads and make sales? Provide customer support? Cultivate customer relations?

✔ **How much are you willing to invest in your site?** The more complicated your site and the more aggressive your online goals, the more you need to invest to achieve success.

The following sections help you think through your answers to these questions.

Retailing online

E-commerce is an ever-expanding economic engine, but it isn't the answer for all businesses. See *Small Business Marketing For Dummies,* 2nd Edition (Wiley), by Barbara Findlay Schenck, for a full chapter on tapping the Internet's marketing power. Weigh these questions from that book as you consider opening an online sales channel:

✔ **Is your product easy to explain in words and pictures?** If an online customer needs to feel the fabric or test-drive your product, for example, your online presentation will be more complicated and costly.

✔ **Is your product perishable, hard to package, or difficult to ship?** Can you ship it over international borders? Remember, the Internet serves a global market.

✔ **Can you absorb shipping costs, or will customers willingly pay the freight?** If your product is unique or hard to find, customers will likely pay for delivery. Otherwise, the cost will likely come out of your profits.

✔ **Do customers need much after-purchase support?** If so, you need 24-hour help lines and online service support at the very least.

- ✔ **Are returns easy and inexpensive to handle?** If your company pulls product from inventory and ships it out, absorbing a return is fairly easy for you. But if your company customizes each product, you need a means to verify all specifications on online orders.

- ✔ **Is your product highly unique?** If not, you need killer pricing — and high volume — to succeed with online sales.

- ✔ **Are you ready to build and support an e-commerce operation?** To do so, you need aggressive site marketing; online systems for ordering, paying, and customer data entry; prompt processing and shipping; and ongoing customer service and support.

Budgeting for your online presence

Estimating costs for Web-site presence is notoriously difficult because every site is different, with its own features and unique challenges.

Creating an online presence is a lot like remodeling your kitchen: The costs depend on the features you want to install, and they nearly always mount up to more than you anticipate. To give you an example — of an online presence, not a kitchen — consider the outdoor equipment retailer Recreational Equipment, Incorporated (REI). In 1996, the company spent $500,000 to get its Web site up and running. By 2001, it had tallied up more than $15 million in additional costs related to online upgrades and redesigns. Although the total outlay was far greater than the company or its Internet-business director ever anticipated, REI still considers all the money well spent.

To estimate your Web-development bill, ballpark development, and mainte-nance costs, factor in the following list of typical expenses:

- ✔ **Development costs,** including computer hardware, communications equipment, systems installation, Web-site design, Web-site content development, and testing and launch.

- ✔ **Maintenance costs,** including Web-site administration, Web-site content updating, communications services, hardware servicing and upgrades, and software upgrades and support.

To establish an online presence, you need what's called an *Internet server,* along with all the associated network communications links. Before you invest in this stuff, think about having an outside company host your Web site for you. Web-management companies can provide you with the entire hardware and software infrastructure you need and guarantee that your site is up and running 24/7, often at a very competitive price.

Ain't no mountain high enough

So, you think putting up a Web site for an existing business is easy? Well, according to Matt Hyde, an avid mountain climber and vice president of Internet sales at the outdoor outfitter Recreational Equipment, Inc. (REI), it's about as easy as climbing a 23,000-foot mountain. "Do it because it's a challenge," he told *The New York Times*, "not because it's fun."

REI.com is one of the real e-commerce success stories. The company's Web site turns a tidy profit — proof that an e-business can actually make money. But on the way to profitability, REI had to climb across more than a few of the pitfalls. Here's what the company discovered:

Myth #1: Running a retail Web site is cheaper than running a physical store. Not true. The start-up costs may be less, but the need to continuously upgrade equipment and technical staff sends operating costs on a consistent climb; plus, frequent computer overhauls run more than half a million dollars a pop.

Myth #2: Internet retailers can save a bundle on personnel costs. Forget it. Automation may allow an e-business to hire fewer sales people than is required by a brick-and-mortar store, but the technical people needed to maintain a Web site are harder to find and are more expensive to hire and retain than retail sales people.

Myth #3: Online retail companies can maintain a more extensive selection than a catalog business or a storefront. Well, maybe. But REI.com discovered that creating digital images of the many items it carries is unexpectedly expensive, and maintaining the online catalog is also costly. In addition, the more items an Internet retailer carries, the more complex the job of filling orders becomes, especially when some of the vendors — the people who actually make the products — don't have the state-of-the-art distribution systems that Internet shoppers have come to expect.

So how did REI succeed where so many other retail e-businesses failed? Part of its success hinges on the reputation that the company's brick-and-mortar outlets had already established with customers. Although Internet-related costs are high, the company, which is privately held, keeps a watchful eye on its bottom-line results. Finally, REI works closely with its many vendors to continuously improve and expedite the order-fulfillment process, thus avoiding delivery problems that have brought some high-flying online retailers down.

After you've estimated the tab for your new or expanded Web presence, list the business benefits you hope to gain from your presence on the Internet. If some of the benefits add revenue, include the sales in your financial projections. Don't be surprised, however, if you have a tough time attaching revenues to some or many of the benefits you expect your site to deliver. If you do, consider how the investment will enhance your business efficiency, heighten customer service, or add other attributes that may help justify the cost of your Internet-development plans.

Forms on the CD-ROM

If you're planning or expanding your company's Internet presence, take a look at the following forms on the CD-ROM to help you plan your business:

Form 13-1	**Checklist of Key Steps in Planning an E-Business**	Key steps that help you streamline your planning process
Form 13-2	**Online Customer Profile**	A questionnaire that captures the key characteristics of your most likely online customers
Form 13-3	**E-Business Value Proposition Worksheet**	Questions that capture the key benefits your Web site offers and the value it delivers to customers
Form 13-4	**E-Business Model Construction Worksheet**	Questions to help you create a workable e-business model

Part IV
Making the Most of Your Plan

The 5th Wave   By Rich Tennant

OUT OF BUSINESS

Main Street CHINA SH

"What made you think you were the
one to own and operate a china shop,
I'll never know."

In this part . . .

Part IV is where your planning efforts come together. This is the point where the hard work you've put into shaping a business idea, analyzing the business environment, creating a strategy, and putting together a plan of action gets distilled into a written business plan. The result is likely to be the most powerful single document you'll create for your company: It can help you gain funding, grow, make money, and stay on track — which is why the next few chapters are so important.

Chapter 14 is full of ideas for organizing the business-plan assembly process, bringing your planning team together, addressing various business audiences with your plan, and accessing more resources to make the job easy and successful. Chapter 15 is all about putting your business plan to work — using it to organize your staff, structure your systems, develop a strong sense of teamwork, operate your business effectively, and troubleshoot problems if and when they arise. In the best sense of the phrase, this is where the rubber meets the road. You're on your way to finalizing and using your plan!

Chapter 14

Putting Your Plan Together

. . . .

In This Chapter

▶ Assembling your business-planning team

▶ Addressing important audiences

▶ Writing, reviewing, and finalizing your plan

. . . .

*R*eady, set, go! You've reached the point where you actually *write* your business plan. If you're arriving at this chapter sequentially (every author's dream!), the business-planning spadework is behind you. By now, you've defined your business purpose (Chapter 3), assessed your business environment (Chapter 4), charted your strategy (Chapter 5), detailed your company capabilities (Chapter 6), designed your marketing plan (Chapter 7), and untangled your finances (Chapter 8). The next step is to assemble the raw materials to formulate your plan.

Here's a note for people who rank the idea of writing right up there with paying taxes or for people who find putting one word in front of another as excruciating as rolling boulders up a hill: The following pages keep the process easy. Plus, you can expect some good payoffs for your literary efforts:

 ✔ **The cream rises to the top.** Putting your plan into writing makes it easy to see which ideas don't hold water and which ones look even better when you formalize them in black and white.

 ✔ **The parts become a whole.** Like many entrepreneurs, you may have dozens of ideas rattling around in your head. Organizing them into a written plan forces you to think about how they fit together and which ideas should receive priority status in your action plan.

 ✔ **Mistakes get circumvented.** Your written plan is the first serious test of your business venture. If your business doesn't make sense on paper, what are the odds that it will pass muster in the fiercely competitive world of business?

Count on the upcoming pages to help you review the components of your plan, put together your planning team, target your audience, and assemble a plan that creates a cohesive sense of who you are and what you plan to do.

Making a List and Checking It Twice

Putting together your written business plan is a bit like preparing for a final exam: You want to make sure that you're well prepared and that you have all the resources you need at your fingertips.

As you organize your effort, use the checklist in Form 14-1. It lists all the items you may want to include in each of the major components of your business plan. Check off the items that you already have in hand, at least in a rough form. (Don't worry about the table of contents and the executive summary at this point. You put these two pieces in place last, and I cover them in the "Addressing more than one audience" section later in this chapter.)

Not every business plan will contain every item on this list. Still, take a good look at the items you *haven't* checked. Make sure that the omission is intentional and that you're not leaving out important information.

If you discover that you still have some homework to do before sitting down to write your plan, here are the main topics and where to turn for help:

- ✔ Company overview: Chapters 3, 5, and 6
- ✔ Business environment: Chapter 4
- ✔ Company strategy: Chapter 5
- ✔ Company description: Chapter 6
- ✔ Marketing plan: Chapter 7
- ✔ Financial review: Chapter 8
- ✔ Action plan: Chapters 1, 3, and 5

In addition, you can use the chapters in Part III to tailor your plan to your business. Make use of Chapter 9 if you're self-employed, Chapter 10 if you're planning for a small business, Chapter 11 if you're growing or revamping an established business, Chapter 12 if you're involved with a nonprofit organization, or Chapter 13 if you're starting or expanding an e-business.

Locating Additional Resources

As you begin to put your business plan together, you may discover that you need some additional tools — a book devoted to marketing, for example, or business-planning software that can help you create and maintain your written document. The following sections give you some advice on where to go and what to look for when you need some additional resources.

BUSINESS PLAN COMPONENTS CHECKLIST

☐ **Table of contents**

☐ **Executive summary**

☐ **Company overview**
- ○ Mission statement
- ○ Vision statement
- ○ Values statement
- ○ Listing of key products and/or services
- ○ Business model summary
- ○ Major business goals
- ○

☐ **Business environment**
- ○ Industry overview
- ○ Barriers to entry
- ○ Market segmentation
- ○ Ideal customer profile
- ○ Competitor analysis
- ○

☐ **Company strategy**
- ○ SWOT analysis
- ○ Business model
- ○ Business goals
- ○ Marketing plan
- ○ Plans for growth
- ○ Exit strategy
- ○

☐ **Company description**
- ○ Introductory highlights
- ○ Products and/or services offered
- ○ Research and development
- ○ Operations
- ○ Sales and marketing
- ○ Distribution and delivery
- ○ Customer service
- ○ Management
- ○ Organization
- ○

Form 14-1: Use the checklist on the CD-ROM as you prepare the pieces of your business plan.

The bookstore

Okay, we're partial to the book you're holding, but you can find dozens of other useful titles in the marketplace — particularly ones that concentrate on specific areas, such as marketing or financial planning, or ones that focus on particular kinds of businesses, such as nonprofits or sole proprietorships.

For additional background on general business-planning issues, you may want to pick up a copy of *Business Plans For Dummies,* 2nd Edition, by Paul Tiffany and Steven Peterson (Wiley). For help preparing your marketing plan, consider *Small Business Marketing For Dummies,* by Barbara Findlay Schenck (Wiley).

If you're not sure what book to pick up, scan the contents to see which one has the answers you seek. Booksellers like Amazon.com invite you to click and read a detailed table of contents and the entire first chapter online. They also post reader reviews and ratings, which can steer you toward other useful books.

Although the basic principles of business planning may be timeless, certain subjects — Internet marketing, for example — change rapidly, and a book that's more than a few years old may reflect ancient history. If you want timely information — details about tax considerations for a small business, for example — be sure to check when the book was published.

Magazines, newspapers, and journals offer another way to track what's happening in the world of business in general and your industry in particular. Identify several titles of interest and become a subscriber so you can routinely scan the business environment for trends or new developments that may affect your business plan.

The Web

The Internet hosts an ever-growing number of Web sites offering information on business planning. Most are free; others tease you with samples of what they have to offer and then charge you for more details. Check first to see what's free for the asking. In particular, the federal government offers heaps of solid information on planning, starting, and operating your own company through its Small Business Administration site (www.sba.gov). Even the IRS presents helpful planning tips in its handbooks, which are also available on the Web (www.irs.gov).

Hot lists of top business-related Web sites have a way of going out of date as quickly as today's newspaper. Your best bet is to spend a couple of hours online looking for useful resources on your own. Enter the keywords *business plan* in a search engine and get ready for millions of results, ranging from the sites of leading business-planning experts to generic planning information to — unavoidably — an awful lot of junk. You can refine your search by adding keywords specific to your business area (*nonprofit, retail, travel, financial services,* and so on).

You can also use the Internet to uncover information about competitors, markets, business trends, and new technologies — all the factors you need to account for to put together a complete picture of your business environment. Going to the home pages of your competitors is a good starting point. From there, you can enter online pressrooms with current news announcements, executive bios, recent publicity, and other information.

Fishing the Net for business links

The Internet is a goldmine of business-planning information and resources. As you delve into the riches, begin with this list of popular sites where you can find useful and reliable tips, tools, and examples — including samples of real-life business plans:

✔ **www.sba.gov:** The Small Business Administration (SBA) site is far and away the best source of information on planning, funding, starting, and running a small business. You can find useful answers to frequently asked questions as well as business counseling help and shareware software programs.

✔ **www.irs.gov/smallbiz:** This site is great if you run a small business or are self-employed. The IRS provides all kinds of useful industry and profession-specific information. The site also includes links to other helpful non-IRS business resources on the Web.

✔ **www.nfib.com:** The National Federation of Independent Business (NFIB) calls itself the largest advocacy organization to represent small and independent businesses in the United States. Its Web site features a frequently updated set of tools and tips that small business owners may find useful.

✔ **www.nonprofits.org:** The Internet Nonprofit Center is a great online resource for information about every aspect of planning, starting, and operating a nonprofit organization. Go to the FAQs area to access information on dozens of topics.

✔ **www.score.org:** The Web site of the Service Corps of Retired Executives (SCORE) offers start-up businesses free counseling via e-mail. The site also includes a learning center, business toolbox, updated success stories from a variety of small- and medium-size companies, and a valuable list of business-related links.

✔ **www.nolo.com:** You can't find a better place to turn for basic information on the legal aspects of virtually any kind of business than Nolo. This Web site also offers free advice, including information on insuring your home business, independent contractor arrangements, trademarks and copyrights, debts, bankruptcies, and employment law.

✔ **www.bplans.com:** This Palo Alto Software site includes more than 60 sample business plans, an extensive article library, an archive of expert advice summaries, business calculators, a business-planning product catalog, and a Web directory.

✔ **www.toolkit.cch.com:** The Business Owner's Toolkit Web site includes a small business guide and ready-to-use business tools, templates, and checklists. On the home page, click on Business Tools, scroll to Marketing, and click Business Plan Components: Sample Plans.

Beware that amidst the treasures, the Internet also presents some fool's gold. Unlike magazine articles, which are typically checked and rechecked for accuracy, online content isn't always validated or confirmed by anyone beyond the person who posts it, so follow three simple rules when you use the Web for business research:

✔ **Check the date.** Many Web documents aren't dated, so you may not know whether you're reading the latest scoop or dated material. Look for a publishing or posting date. If you can't find one, dig a little deeper to see whether or not the information is still relevant.

✔ **Verify the source.** Be suspicious of information that a credible source doesn't back. For instance, if you read a rave review of a new software program that's an excerpt from a respected business magazine, you can attach a different level of faith in that information than you can give to information that appears without a source.

✔ **Double-check key facts and statistics.** If you use specific pieces of information — about business trends, markets, competitors, technology, or whatever — as the central building blocks of your business plan, make darn sure that the facts you gather from the Internet are correct. If your financial projections are built on the fact that the market for online lingerie is growing at 40 percent a year, for example, verify that you're dealing with a fact and not some online entrepreneur's fantasy.

Business software

Software programs allow you to automatically assemble all the components of a business plan, turning them into a polished, ready-to-print document. The best programs also make easier work of the financial parts of business planning — creating income statements and cash-flow statements, for example, or making financial projections (see Chapter 8). Most software programs also allow you to add graphics, such as tables and charts, into your plan, providing an easy way for your audience to see at a glance what you're describing in the written document.

To review the latest software offerings, enter Business Plan Software into the window of a search engine, and then browse through the offerings of leading software providers. You can often find sample business plans that you can review to get a sense of the product you can produce with each software tool.

Business-planning software programs can make the job of business planning seem a bit too easy. With all the software bells and whistles, newcomers can inadvertently skip the serious (that is, difficult) work of creating and writing an effective plan. Remember, the best software-planning tools guide you through the important aspects of business planning and then keep track of your words, sentences, and paragraphs — they don't think for you. You still have to do the serious mental work yourself.

Investors and bankers who make a living reviewing and funding business plans are all too familiar with the look and feel of the most popular software-generated business-planning documents. When using one of these programs, customize your plan to make it unique. The last thing you want is for your business plan to look exactly like the others that cross a venture capitalist's desk.

Expert advice

No one knows the ins and outs of planning and running a business better than someone who has done it before. If have questions you can't answer, or if you run out of ideas on ways to get your company off the ground, turn to someone with tried-and-true expertise for advice.

The first place to look for expert advice is in your address book. You'll probably have an easier time getting a "yes" from someone you know on a personal or professional basis. If that tactic doesn't pan out, ask friends and colleagues for suggestions. Other good places to look for help are the chamber of commerce and the business section of your local newspaper. You may end up paying for some of this advice, but when you really need help, it's worth the investment.

When looking for an expert who can guide you, you want to choose someone with experience in a company that's similar to the one you're planning. After you identify such a person, decide exactly what kind of assistance you need. After all, you can't ask someone to plan your whole business for you, but you can ask for help fine-tuning your marketing strategy, for example, or reviewing and critiquing your financial projections.

Consider contacting the Service Corps of Retired Executives, or SCORE, a nationwide organization that works with the Small Business Administration (SBA) to provide help to business owners. SCORE has a free online newsletter and provides free e-mail counseling. The group also has local chapters around the country, with retired business people ready and willing to help. For more information, check out www.score.org.

A retired schoolteacher came up with a business idea that promised to keep her busy while helping out some of the hardest-working people in town. She wanted to start an agency to represent the dozens of women who were cleaning houses in the area. She wanted to help these women find more work than they could get on their own. She also planned to help them organize their schedules, communicate with clients, and do the bookkeeping. Over time, she hoped to offer them benefits such as health insurance. In return, she would take a small percentage of the money they earned. But how much of a percentage? And how much money would she need to get her business going?

She tried to put together a plan on her own, but she felt overwhelmed by questions and uncertainty. She happened to read about a local businessman who was retiring from a high-tech business he started. On a whim, she wrote to him, describing her idea and asking whether he had time to help her put together a plan. He called her immediately; they met a few times, and within a month, she had a solid business plan in place. She was also able to get a small business loan for the start-up money she needed. Her business continues to grow, and the retired businessman continues to serve as her advisor.

Self help

Many local communities have organizations of businesspeople who get together to share ideas, exchange contacts, help each other out, and just plain socialize. Some of these groups are comprised of people with like interests or needs, whereas others are made up of local people from across the business spectrum. Thanks to the Internet, you can also find virtual business groups that regularly schedule online meetings to support one another.

For more than three years, the Lakeland Area Chamber of Commerce has been running a small-business mentoring program in Lakeland, Florida. Companies that have asked the program for guidance include a day-care center, a software company, and a professional cleaning firm. Most of the program's mentors are senior or retired executives who review the problems faced by these small businesses and then work with their protégés to find solutions. For example, the owner of a small day-care center asked for help when her company began to experience serious cash-flow problems. Her mentor, the retired chief financial officer (CFO) of a local tile company, helped her develop a business plan along with a complete set of financials. The owner credits the assistance she received with saving her day-care business for inspiring her to think about expanding.

Business networking organizations are an invaluable resource for people planning or running a business. For information about what's available in your community, do an online search and ask the members of your local chamber of commerce whether they have, know of, or intend to start a mentoring program.

Assembling Your Planning Team

The size of the team you bring together to develop your business plan depends on the size and structure of your company and on the complexity of the business plan you're developing:

- If your company is small, you don't need to worry about who's in charge of each piece of your written plan. Lucky you: You're in charge of it all! However, that doesn't mean you have to develop the plan alone. Your plan will be stronger if you bounce your thoughts around with someone who's willing to serve as a sounding board. Also, enlist someone you trust to read and critique your final draft before you print the final copy.

- If your company is moderately sized to large, the process of creating your written plan requires a certain amount of organization. Before you sit down and fire up your planning software or your word processor, consider the advice in the following sections.

Delegating responsibilities

If your company has a management team, you should divvy up the work involved in putting together your written business plan for several reasons. One reason is that it makes your job easier. Another reason is because different perspectives prove helpful as your team reads and reviews drafts, offers suggestions, and fine-tunes the document. Managed well, the group will arrive at a stronger plan, and you'll win group support and improve morale at the same time.

How many people you involve depends on the size of your company and how big and complicated your plan is. No matter how big you want your team to be, here are some tips to help you create a team that's both efficient and effective:

- **Keep your team lean.** Involve only the number of people you think you really need to get the job done. Too many planners — like too many cooks in the kitchen — can spoil the recipe for successful planning. A bloated team can mean endless meetings and too many points of view.

- **Appoint people who want the job.** There's no point in assigning a planning task to someone who really doesn't want to do it. To help win team interest, take time at the beginning to explain why creating a written business plan is so important. Select managers who really want to help and who are willing and able to complete the tasks you assign.

✔ **Organize your team around the plan.** By organizing your team around the major components of your business plan, you make sure that all team members know their tasks and how their work fits into the larger picture. Some of the assignments are pretty straightforward: Your financial person should take charge of the financial review, and your marketing head should put together the business environment and marketing sections. If certain pieces of the plan are more complex than others, think about assigning a small group to work on them.

✔ **Put one person in charge.** Every team needs a leader, and that's particularly true when putting together your business plan. Keeping track of the whole process can be a job in itself, especially if you have a larger team or a complicated plan. Name one person as project director, and make sure everyone on the team understands that he or she has ultimate authority.

✔ **Appoint a wordsmith.** If you're lucky, someone on your team is good at putting words down on paper. Name this person your senior plan editor. Among the tasks: Writing key sections of your plan, such as the executive summary; checking grammar and spelling; and making sure that the writing style is clear and consistent throughout the plan.

Setting the ground rules

As soon as you've selected your team, you need to establish procedures that spell out exactly how the team is to carry the work out. The clearer the ground rules, the smoother the process — and the happier your team. Make sure that your ground rules address these three points:

✔ **Identify key steps.** The process of writing a business plan usually includes five steps: research, first draft, review, revised draft, and final review. You may want more or fewer drafts and review opportunities, but make sure you specify the steps that fit your situation and spell them out upfront.

✔ **Establish a schedule.** The process of writing a business plan doesn't have to be long and drawn out. In fact, it shouldn't be. A business plan has to be timely, which means it needs to respond to the business environment as it is — not the way it looked six months ago. After the preliminary research is complete, the rest of the steps are fairly straightforward. To keep your project on track, set due dates for each component of the plan and each step in the process. Give the members of your team as much time as they reasonably need — but no more.

✔ **Assign duties.** Make sure that all team members know exactly what you expect of them, including which components or sections you want them to assemble and when drafts and reviews are due.

Putting first things last

Issues of timing are bound to come up as you try to put your plan on paper. How can you put together the executive summary, for example, before you have the rest of the business plan in place? And don't you need the company strategy written up before you can tackle the action plan?

Without a doubt, each component of your written business plan has to be in sync with the sections around it. For example, if you talk about the need to increase the subscriber base for your investment newsletter in the company strategy section, but you fail to say a word about it in your action plan, anyone reading your plan is bound to wonder if you really know what you're doing.

Follow these steps to make sure that everyone is working on the same page:

1. **Sit down with your team and hammer out an outline containing the key points that each section of the plan will address.**

   Refer to the checklist in Form 14-1 as a guide. You may need more than one meeting to create your outline, but consider it time well spent.

2. **With the outline in hand, team members can begin writing their parts with knowledge of what each section should include and how the information relates to the other plan components.**

   This allows team members to spot discrepancies or omissions early on.

3. **Write your executive summary last, because you can't summarize a plan you haven't written.**

   You'd be amazed at the number of business planners who've anguished over the executive summary simply because they tried to write it first. Save yourself the agony: The executive summary may come first in the finished plan, but it should be the last component you write — usually after your team completes and reviews the second drafts of each of the other components.

   When you write your executive summary, don't worry about repeating yourself. The whole point of the opening section is to capture the key points of your plan — using the same language you use in the plan. Don't grab a thesaurus hoping to find some colorful new way to express your mission or your strategy — you'll only confuse your readers and your team. Say what you mean the same way, only shorter.

Keeping track of it all

Two simple tools can go a long way toward streamlining the business-plan assembly process — and keeping everyone involved calm and happy. One tool is a simple tracking sheet that shows at a glance where every part of the process is at any given time. The other tool is as simple as a loose-leaf notebook. In fact, it is a loose-leaf notebook.

The master tracker

Use a master tracking sheet to track every piece of the plan, who's in charge of each piece, the key steps involved in completing them, and where each piece stands at any given moment. This is especially important when your plan has a large number of sections and appendixes.

You can create your master tracking sheet online, on a blackboard, or on paper. Whatever you choose, make sure you make it readily available to every member of your planning team and that you update it regularly.

Use the tracking sheet in Form 14-2 to customize a tracking sheet that matches the contents of your plan.

The old-fashioned loose-leaf notebook

All the razzle-dazzle online resources and state-of-the-art software tools are great, but you should also consider using an old-fashioned loose-leaf notebook to keep your project organized. You have to juggle a lot of information — versions of your mission and vision statements, biographies of your key managers, financial statements, charts and graphs, product specifications, and more — so each time you revise and reorganize, pop open the rings, slip an old section out, and pop a new one in.

A loose-leaf notebook is also one of the best — and most cost-effective — technologies around for capturing the big picture of your plan. As proof, try making sense of a long, complicated document as you scroll up and down on your computer screen.

If your planning effort involves a team of people, a loose-leaf notebook can serve as the master working document. Make sure that you make it easily accessible to everyone on your team, and be clear that the team leader must approve changes or additions before team members add them into the master document.

Targeting Your Plan to Key Audiences

Immediately after you decide who's going to write your plan, you need to think about who's going to read it. After all, your business plan should communicate your vision and strategy — what you plan to do, and how you intend to do it. But it can't communicate if the people who read it can't understand it. You wouldn't speak French to someone who only speaks Chinese, right? For the same reason, you don't want to fill your written business plan with technical jargon that your audience won't understand.

MASTER PLAN TRACKING SHEET							
Plan Components *(Fill in due dates)*	**Research**	**Outline**	**Draft I**	**Review**	**Draft II**	**Final**	**Done**
Executive summary							☐
Company overview							
Mission statement							☐
Vision statement							☐
Values statement							☐
Listing of key products and/or services							☐
Business model summary							☐
Major business goals							☐
							☐
Business environment							
Industry overview							☐
Barriers to entry							☐
Market segmentation							☐
Ideal customer profile							☐
Competitor analysis							☐
							☐
Company strategy							
SWOT analysis							☐
Business model							☐
Business goals							☐
Marketing plan							☐
Plans for growth							☐
Exit strategy							☐
Company description							
Introductory highlights							☐
Products and/or services offered							☐
Research and development							☐
Operations							☐
Sales and marketing							☐

Form 14-2: Use this form to customize a master tracking sheet that reflects the contents of your business plan.

If your business idea is based on something brand new, write your plan in such a way that the company overview section explains your new technology in terms that anyone can understand. Include all the technical details in an appendix.

Identifying your stakeholders

Your *stakeholders* include everyone who has a vested interest in your company, what it does, or how it operates. That includes employees, customers, suppliers, outside consultants, lenders, shareholders, regulators, competitors, and other interested parties.

Some of these groups may have direct stakes: You owe them money, for example, or they own a piece of your company. Others have less tangible interests: suppliers who want to continue selling to you or civic organizations that want to make sure you remain a good corporate citizen. Obviously, not all your stakeholder groups share the same interests or values:

✓ Someone who owns shares in your company is probably most interested in whether and when you plan to grow bigger.

✓ A local environmental group may want proof that you're following environmental regulations.

✓ Bankers look at your plan with a focus on your financial health — studying your cash flow, business assets, and forecasts to determine your prospects for solid, stable growth. They have to decide whether to finance your business, so they look for proof of your long-term prospects along with assurance that you're a good risk when it comes to repaying loans.

✓ Investors are interested in the factors that predict growth — especially rapid growth — so they turn a sharp eye to sections that describe your business opportunity, your management team, and your plan of action.

Form 14-3 lists various stakeholder groups along with the parts of the business plan and specific issues that are of special importance to each audience. Go through the list and put a check beside the groups of stakeholders you want your plan to address. Circle the issues that you feel are of greatest concern to each group. These target-audience guidelines will help you address all the key topics as you tailor your business plan to the interests of various audiences.

BUSINESS PLAN TARGET AUDIENCE GUIDELINES			
Intended Audience	**Key Plan Components**	**Issues to Emphasize**	**Ideal Length**
☐ **Bankers**	• Executive summary • Company strategy • Financial review	• Cash flow • Assets • Solid growth	10-20 pages
☐ **Investors**	• Executive summary • Business environment • Company strategy • Company description • Financial review • Action plan	• Assets • Business opportunity • Management team	10-20 pages
☐ **Strategic partners**	• Company overview • Business environment • Company description • Financial review • Action plan	• Synergy • Proprietary products • Management	20-40 pages
☐ **Customers**	• Executive summary • Company overview	• Stability • Service • Management team	5-10 pages
☐ **Employees**	• Executive summary • Company overview • Company strategy • Action plan	• Security • Business opportunity • Clear strategy • Goals and objectives	5-10 pages
☐ **Shareholders**	• Executive summary • Company overview • Company strategy • Financial review • Action plan	• Financial growth • Strategic opportunity • Management team	10-20 pages
☐ **General Public**	• Executive summary • Company overview	• Mission and vision • Values	3-5 pages

Form 14-3: Use this form on the CD-ROM to target the audiences for your business plan.

Addressing more than one audience

The following three parts of your business plan help different audiences to quickly access information that addresses their unique interests.

Table of contents

A well-designed table of contents offers a map that leads readers to the sections of your plan that most interest them in no time flat.

If your business plan is more than 10 pages long, consider including a table of contents that lists sections and subsections. Include page numbers so that you and your readers can quickly locate specific sections in the plan.

Executive summary

A solid, well-written executive summary gives a clear and concise description of your company and the key issues that the main body of your business plan will describe. Some of your readers may find out all they need to know in this summary. Others will decide to read the rest of your plan based on what they read in the executive summary. Either way, the executive summary is a critical piece of all but the briefest written plans.

To decide what to put into your executive summary, go through the revised draft of your plan and highlight all the critical points that you want everyone — including those who read only the executive summary — to know. Be ruthless here. Choose the one or two elements in each section that are absolutely essential. Remember, the executive summary is meant to give a very quick overview — the rest of your plan fills in the details.

After you highlight the critical points, organize them into the first draft of your executive summary. Try to express major ideas by using the same words that you use in the plan itself.

As you get started, think about the short speech you'd give if one of your stakeholders — a banker or potential investor, for example — asked you to describe your business on an elevator ride from the lobby to the 25th floor of a high-rise building. In those few seconds, how would you describe your business idea, your strategy, and how you intend to achieve success? Right now, write down your answer. (If you have a tape recorder handy, start talking.) Chances are good that you'll instinctively hit all the key points. (If you need help writing your "elevator speech," see Chapter 6.) Make sure that your executive summary hits all those same important points.

Ideally, you should keep the executive summary of your business plan to a single page. This section is a summary, after all. If it runs long, try tightening up the language or pruning out the least essential points.

The appendixes

Unlike your appendix, which sits in your body and does nothing, the appendixes in your business plan range from useful to absolutely essential — especially if you want your business plan to address several audiences at once. The appendixes are where you can stuff all the nitty-gritty details that flesh out your market analysis, your technology, or your product specs — details that may be essential to a full understanding of your business plan but are of interest to only a small number of your readers.

No one judges business plans by the pound, so don't fill your appendixes with absolutely everything you know just to make your plan look heftier. The material they contain should relate directly to your business plan and should provide important details about your markets, your strategy, your management team, your technology, or other key aspects of your business.

In fact, you should reference all documents that appear in the appendixes at some appropriate place within the main body of your plan. Here are two examples:

> *Our advanced Internet platform offers many competitive advantages over existing software, including higher speed, lower cost, and greater reliability. (For technical details, see the "Technical Specifications of ISP Version 6.1" in Appendix 2.)*

> *Our market analysis shows that many IT professionals are concerned about the speed and bandwidth of existing Internet software platforms, and they're willing to pay more for next- generation technology. Their chief concern is reliability. (For details, see the "Market Data Analysis Summary" in Appendix 3.)*

References alert readers to where they can find additional information. By putting supporting documents at the end, you ensure that the main body of your written business plan doesn't become bogged down with details.

Creating alternate versions of your plan

You may find that a single written plan can't cover all the bases — especially if you need to communicate specific information to a number of different audiences. Don't worry; no law limits you to just one version of your business plan. In fact, many companies write versions specifically targeted to different audiences — for example, one aimed at employees, another toward potential lenders or investors, and a third for more general interests.

Developing several versions of your business plan is basically an assembly job. Follow these steps down the line:

1. **Create a complete and comprehensive master plan — one that includes everything that's likely to be important to all your stakeholders (see Form 14-3).**

2. **Zero in on which special audiences you want to address.**

3. **Decide which parts of your master plan are important and which ones aren't relevant to each specific target audience.**

After you know your audience and its requirements, putting together an alternate version is as simple as cutting and pasting the relevant parts of the master plan together.

When creating alternate versions of your plan, make sure that they all mesh with each other. For example, don't write one mission statement for one audience and another for a second group of readers. And whatever you do, don't create different sets of goals and objectives for different stakeholders. At the very least, you'll confuse everyone — yourself included. At worst, you'll anger audiences if they discover that you're saying one thing to one group and something different to another.

The job of creating a targeted version of your business plan is really one of deciding which parts of the master plan to include and which to leave out. The wording should remain the same in all versions.

Fitting the Pieces Together

When you have a working draft in front of you, look at the document as a whole to make sure that all the pieces fit together. For example, your company overview should reflect your mission statement, your assessment of the business environment should be in sync with your business strategy, and your company strategy should support goals and objectives.

If your plan is a team effort, devote extra effort to a review of the overall document. Sometimes the right hand doesn't know exactly what the left hand is doing, even when you have a solid outline for everyone to work from. The best way to catch inconsistencies or omissions is to have all the members of your planning team read your draft plan in its entirety.

WORKING DRAFT CHECKLIST
☐ Is our executive summary clear and compelling?
☐ Do the major pieces of the company overview – our mission statement, values and vision, and major business goals and objectives – work together to explain who we are and what we believe in?
☐ Does the overview provide a strong sense of the nature of our business and the products and services we plan to offer?
☐ Do our goals and objectives match the company's mission?
☐ Does the plan offer a convincing analysis of the market we intend to enter?
☐ Does the plan give a clear description of who our primary customers will be?
☐ Does the plan adequately and objectively assess our strengths and weaknesses?
☐ Does the company's strategy make sense in light of our analysis of the business environment?
☐ Does our action plan match up with our strategic direction, as outlined in the plan?
☐ Does the plan's financial review reflect our business strategy and action plan?
☐ Does our action plan include enough specifics to create a road map for the near-term?
☐ Is the plan clearly written and easy to understand?
☐ Is there anything missing from the plan that should be added?
☐ Is there anything that should be cut from the plan?
☐ Are there other changes that would strengthen our written plan?

Form 14-4: When reviewing drafts of your business plan, use this checklist.

After the draft makes its way to a more polished version, enlist the help of people who haven't been involved along the way. Outside readers will see the document with fresh eyes and are more likely to catch discrepancies or places where the language isn't crystal clear. As you enlist help for this review, invite people who aren't afraid to tell it like it is — even if that means giving you a thumbs down on parts of your plan. Be clear that the plan is a working draft and that you welcome any and all comments, positive or negative.

To help with the review process, use the Working Draft Checklist in Form 14-4. The checklist covers key questions that you and other reviewers should ask when reviewing your written business plan.

Don't panic if your reviewers come back with all sorts of suggestions or constructive criticism. This just means that they're doing their jobs and helping you identify problems and fix them now — before your plan hits the desk of a banker, investor, or business partner. A little criticism won't hurt; it will make your business plan much more effective.

Forms on the CD-ROM

The following forms on the CD-ROM will help you put your written business plan together:

Form 14-1	**Business Plan Components Checklist**	A list of the major components of a business plan along with the elements that go into each section
Form 14-2	**Master Plan Tracking Sheet**	A tracking form that shows at a glance where you are in the process of writing your business plan
Form 14-3	**Business Plan Target Audience Guidelines**	A form that helps you tailor your business plan to various target audiences
Form 14-4	**Working Draft Checklist**	Questions to ask when reviewing the working draft of your business plan

Chapter 15

Putting Your Plan to Work

. . . .

In This Chapter

▶ Using your plan to organize your company

▶ Inspiring and leading employees

▶ Reviewing and revising your plan

. . . .

Congratulations! You've climbed a planning mountain. By now you've done the brainstorming, the research, and the analysis; you've come up with a solid business strategy, financial model, and a detailed plan of action; and you've pulled everything together into a written business plan. Take a minute to accept a well-deserved pat on the back — and then roll up your sleeves because you have to start the equally important job of putting your plan to work.

Ask successful entrepreneurs how they made it, and they'll usually list two reasons. Number one: They had rock-solid business plans in place. Number two: They stuck to them.

This chapter helps you follow their advice. We've packed it with ideas for putting your business plan to work. It shows how you can use your plan to organize your business, and it helps you choose the best organizational structure and the most effective procedures for getting the job done. It offers tips on how to use your plan to get all you can out of your most important resource: your people. Finally, it offers ideas for reviewing and revising your plan to keep it fresh and vital.

Organizing Your Company around Your Business Plan

A business plan is like a blueprint. It tells exactly what you're working to achieve, but the end result happens only if you hammer it into reality.

A blueprint guides every construction step down to a fraction of an inch, but a business plan is more of a success framework. It helps you organize your company around your mission and vision, your goals and objectives, and the strategy you've outlined to achieve success. Plus, it keeps everyone on the same sheet and working toward the same positive outcomes.

Form meets function

The first step in putting your plan to work is to configure your company to reflect your plan in every part of your organization, from the structure of your management team to the procedures you put in place to make your company work. As you shape your organization, pay particular attention to these three parts of your plan:

- ✔ **Company description:** Look at your company's capabilities and resources (see Chapter 6 for more information), and then develop your organization to fortify strengths and overcome weaknesses.

- ✔ **Company strategy:** Build programs and systems that support your plan for reaching, serving, and satisfying your customers.

- ✔ **Action plan:** Detail all the steps necessary to implement your business plan, including the priorities and timelines you'll follow as you make it all happen.

As you organize your company, know that most businesses are built around one of four common organizational models (see Chapter 6 for details):

- ✔ **The pack:** In this model, one person runs the show, and everyone else is an equal member of, well, the pack.

- ✔ **Function:** This model divides people into groups based on the functions they perform in the company.

- ✔ **Division:** This model divides distinct parts of the company's business into separate divisions, each with its own management structure.

- ✔ **The matrix:** In this model, employees can wear more than one hat and report to more than one supervisor, encouraging team members to share talent, expertise, and experience.

The most effective organizational format for your company depends on the kind of company you're running — big, small, formal, informal, online, manufacturing, retail, service, or a dozen other considerations. But most of all, it depends on your business plan.

Consider these questions and pointers as you shape the organizational structure that's best for your company:

- **Is one individual responsible for your company's vision and strategic direction?** If so, you may want to use the pack model, with one leader and a pack of team members.

- **Is employee creativity crucial to the success of your company?** If so, you may want to consider a loose organizational structure with relatively few management levels, giving your staff the freedom to be creative.

- **Are speed and flexibility crucial to your company's ability to remain competitive?** If so, think about a flat organizational structure with as few management levels as possible.

- **Does your company consist of several distinct functions, each with its own culture and kinds of employees?** If so, consider a functional organization.

- **Is much of your company's work conducted on a project basis, moving people and resources from one job to another?** If so, a matrix organization may work best for you.

You can alter the structure of your company at some point down the road, especially if your business is growing rapidly, for example, or your business environment has changed significantly.

Duties and responsibilities

After you've structured your organization, your next task is to assign duties and responsibilities to your key people. You may have made many or most of those assignments already, at least for your top management team. Even so, take time to review your assignments against your business plan. Be sure these assignments are closely aligned with your major goals and objectives, because if the work of your key employees isn't directly tied to your company's goals, those goals won't get accomplished.

Figure 15-1 shows how a secretarial-services company matched the duties and responsibilities assigned to key employees with the company's business goals and objectives.

By assigning responsibility for major goals and objectives, the company significantly improves the odds that its action plan will be carried out. What's more, the assignment chart confirms that senior managers will work closely together to accomplish the plan — supporting the company's decision to adopt a relatively flat, flexible management structure. As a bonus, the assignment chart provides guidelines the company can follow as it writes detailed job descriptions for key managers.

GOALS AND OBJECTIVES ASSIGNMENT CHART		
GOAL • **OBJECTIVE**	**WHO'S RESPONSIBLE**	**NOTES**
Enhance staff expertise	Director, H.R.	Must work closely with Director of Sales to determine key skills required by clients
• Schedule regular training seminars (by 5-1)	Training manager/ outside training consultant	
• Have all staff certified (by 12-15)	Director, H.R.	
Increase brand awareness	Marketing/Sales VP	Must work closely with direct reports to shape marketing strategy
• Create customer referral bonus program (by 6-15)	Director, Sales	
• Begin monthly newsletter (by 8-1)	Director, Marketing Communications/ outside contractor	Consult with Information Technology to determine feasibility of an online version
Improve customer service	Marketing/Sales VP	High priority–should involve input from all senior management
• Hire two new employees (by 7-15)	Director, H.R.	Consult with marketing
• Install new job-tracking software (by 9-15)	Operations VP/ outside consultant	Work closely with marketing staff to determine requirements

Figure 15-1:
Use an assignment chart to make sure management duties and responsibilities align with major business goals and objectives.

As you create your assignment chart, use the template provided in Form 15-1 on the CD-ROM. It helps you align assignments with your major goals and objectives to keep your plan on track.

Systems and procedures

In order to put your business plan to work, you must know how your business will operate on a day-to-day basis. Your knowledge leads to the development of systems and procedures for everything from product development to sales and customer service. If you're one of those people who finds the idea of systems and procedures a little dry, look at it this way: Good systems keep your company out of hot water and often mean the difference between business success or failure.

A rational set of procedures and well-defined systems ensure efficiency, quality control, employee productivity, and customer satisfaction. And, in the end, they protect your bottom line.

You don't have to reinvent the wheel to install systems and procedures. Consider these steps:

- ✔ Inquire with industry groups about standard operating procedures or basic business systems that may be well documented.

- ✔ Read trade publications and investigate third-party providers who may offer software or other packaged solutions that meet your operational requirements.

- ✔ Talk with people who run companies similar to yours outside your direct competitive arena. They likely have time-tested sets of procedures they can discuss with you.

- ✔ Hire managers with experience in businesses like yours. With these old hands comes expertise with procedures and systems that you can replicate to build an efficient operation and reliable quality control.

As you build your systems and procedures, look back over the company description, strategy, and action-plan sections of your business plan. Jot down all the systems and procedures you think you need to get the job done.

To make sure you don't leave anything out, Form 15-2 lists the business systems and procedures common to most businesses, along with slots for you to fill in procedures specific to your company.

After you go through the checklist, circle the two or three procedures most critical to your business strategy and plan. Break each down into a series of steps in an effort to identify potential gaps before they cause problems.

COMMON SYSTEMS AND PROCEDURES CHECKLIST

☐ **Research and development**
- ○ New product/service design
- ○ Existing product/service modification
- ○ Product testing and certification
- ○ Product specifications, manuals, users guides
- ○
- ○

☐ **Operations**
- ○ Facilities management
- ○ Supplies and raw materials procurement
- ○ Manufacturing processes
- ○ Quality control
- ○ Packaging
- ○
- ○

☐ **Marketing**
- ○ Advertising and promotions
- ○ Public relations
- ○ Sales force management
- ○ Customer contact management
- ○ Customer order tracking
- ○
- ○

☐ **Distribution and delivery**
- ○ Distributor relationships
- ○ Delivery systems
- ○ Inventory management
- ○
- ○

☐ **Customer service**
- ○ Help-desk procedures
- ○ Warrantee and service fulfillment
- ○ Customer complaints and returns
- ○
- ○

Form 15-2: This form lists areas that require business systems and procedures in most companies.

☐ **Management**
- ○ Business planning
- ○ Goal setting
- ○ Industry and market analysis
- ○ Strategy and tactics
- ○ Investor relations
- ○ Budgeting
- ○
- ○

☐ **Organization**
- ○ Employee recruitment
- ○ Salary, wages, and benefits
- ○ Employee training and development
- ○ Job descriptions and performance review
- ○ Employee complaints and terminations
- ○
- ○

☐ **Finance**
- ○ Business asset control
- ○ Cash flow tracking
- ○ Customer billing
- ○ Accounts payable and receivable
- ○ Payroll management
- ○ Financial reporting
- ○ Tax accounting
- ○
- ○

Page 2 of Form 15-2.

Getting Team Buy-In

Business buzzwords tend to have plenty in common with hula hoops and pet rocks: They achieve wild popularity one day and become clichés the next. But one buzzword has never gone out of fashion, and that's teamwork. Whether your company is a small shop or a sprawling multinational, if more than one person is responsible for the work, teamwork is critical to your success.

When your employees feel like they're part of a team, they have more incentive to work hard and work together instead of cruising on parallel tracks or even working against each other. As a result of teamwork, one plus one can actually equal three because team players often produce results that are greater than the sum of their individual contributions. Teams are inherently strong, so a business culture that encourages teamwork can help carry you and your employees through the bad times as well as the good.

Distributing your plan

Your plan lays out your company's mission, vision, and values (see Chapter 3). It also sets the ground rules and establishes your game plan, so you should share it with the people you count on to help you achieve victory. See that everyone on your team is familiar with your plan, clear about the strategy, comfortable with their roles, and in tune with exactly what has to be done to be successful.

Give each member of your management team a copy of your plan to read carefully. Distribute the most important parts of your plan to your entire staff — at meetings, in a newsletter, or on your intranet. By doing so, you

- ✔ **Promote teamwork:** If you want your employees to work together to make your business plan work, they need to know what's in the plan. That doesn't mean every employee needs to review every last detail, but each of your employees should know your company's mission, basic strategy, major goals, and plan of action.

- ✔ **Create a sense of ownership:** Your business plan serves as a blueprint for what you want your company to become. By sharing this information with employees, you show them how their personal involvement contributes to making the plan a reality. The result is a sense of ownership that goes a long way toward motivating everyone around you.

- ✔ **Link individual and company performance:** Too often, employee performance reviews can seem disconnected and rather arbitrary. By evaluating your people in relation to key goals and objectives in your business plan, you underscore why their performances really matter.

- ✔ **Generate feedback and new ideas:** At all levels of your organization, employees are a great resource — whether they offer new ideas or simply a reality check. Make sure they're familiar with what your company is working to accomplish and encourage their input.

You don't need to spring pop quizzes to test staff knowledge of your business plan. (Although it would be interesting to try one out on your top managers: "In 25 words or less, describe our ideal customer. Which of the following best describes our action plan?") But by giving the plan to employees and encouraging them to read it, you cultivate company-wide understanding of where your company wants to go and how you plan to get there. If your plan is more than 10 pages long, consider creating a shorter version to accompany your employee handbook.

Each time you revise your business plan, get the word out to everyone on your staff. While you're at it, highlight the changes that you've made and explain why. If your company has an internal newsletter, use it to describe the revised plan and its features. If you have an intranet, publish the new plan on it along with answers to a list of questions you think employees may have. (See the section "Keeping Your Plan Current" later in this chapter for more info on updating your plan.)

Leading effectively

Effective teams demand strong leaders who can see the future, communicate the vision, inspire and influence others, and make things happen. The best leaders are people who move easily among the following three management styles, laying down the law when they need to but also eliciting help or asking for advice when appropriate:

- ✔ **The boss:** Using this approach, the leader tells employees what to do, when to do it, and how to do it.

- ✔ **The advisor:** This style gives employees a fair amount of independence and responsibility while keeping the boss available to help or advice as necessary.

- ✔ **The colleague:** In this style, managers sit down with employees for a free exchange of ideas in which employees treat each other with equal respect and make mutual decisions.

Different kinds of companies and even different situations within each company call for the use of different leadership styles. If you run a design or advertising agency, for example, you need to serve as an advisor or colleague, giving people plenty of freedom to be as creative as possible, but you also need to be the boss who sets a clear vision and direction that everyone within the agency follows. If you start a local courier service, you need the ability to give instructions, direct people, and keep everyone on schedule, but you also need to remain open to ideas from your couriers regarding what could make the operation run more efficiently and effectively.

Use Form 15-3 as you weigh which management and leadership attributes most affect the success of your business plan. Always look for opportunities to practice those skills and traits. If tight deadlines are a fact of life in your business, develop ways to make colleagues aware of each deadline and make them comfortable meeting it. If creativity is the hallmark of your business, sit down with your colleagues to brainstorm the best ways to encourage it.

CHECKLIST OF MANAGEMENT AND LEADERSHIP TRAITS	
☐ Inspires people	☐ Promotes loyalty
☐ Wins trust	☐ Encourages creativity
☐ Communicates well	☐ Adapts to changing conditions
☐ Makes quick, confident decisions	☐ Delegates responsibilities
☐ Manages diverse projects	☐ Solves problems
☐ Sets specific goals and objectives	☐ Moves projects along on deadline
☐ Manages a tight budget	☐ Offers criticism without alienating
☐ Cultivates leadership in others	☐ Resolves conflicts
☐ Leads by example	☐
☐	☐

Form 15-3: Use the checklist to select management attributes that best match the needs of your business.

Sharing the vision

Your business plan presents the vision of what you want your company to become. By sharing it with everyone who has a stake in your company, you can create a sense of shared commitment and direction.

You don't have to allow everybody to read and reread your business plan on a monthly basis. You can use other methods to keep your vision, mission, and business goals front and center. The following are some examples:

✔ Reproduce your mission and vision statements in company newsletters, the employee handbook, and on the flip side of business cards.

✔ Refer to your business plan whenever appropriate — during marketing strategy meetings or new product development forums, for example.

✔ Use the plan as a yardstick when evaluating programs and initiatives.

✔ Use your business goals and objectives as a guide when conducting employee performance evaluations.

✔ Actively enlist feedback from everyone in the company when you prepare to reassess and revise your business plan.

Encouraging pride of ownership

People who own businesses usually work long hours, put up with tons of stress, and love every minute of it. They love it because they've built something of their own — a company that reflects their talents and inspirations — and they're motivated by a strong pride of ownership.

Good leaders find ways to motivate employees so that they feel the same way. Here are some ways that you can inspire your employees and give them pride of ownership:

✔ Give them a piece of the company, using stock-purchase plans that you tie to individual or team performance.

✔ Pay out year-end bonuses tied to company profitability.

✔ Without involving dollars and cents, you can foster entrepreneurial spirit by giving employees full control and responsibility for particular programs, including the freedom to make key decisions. Reinforce the sense that they own the successes of the projects by rewarding them for jobs well done.

Although a performance bonus is always nice, you should recognize contributions in other ways as well. Consider an employee of the month award, write-ups in the company newsletter, a round of applause at the next company-wide meeting, or a heartfelt gesture of thanks. When motivating employees, simple morale boosters can be more effective than money.

A major health-related Web site reorganized its writers and editors to create small editorial teams, each in charge of a specific content area or channel — men's health, diet and nutrition, children's health, fitness, and so on. The head honchos gave each team given creative freedom to shape the channel and develop new features. The company then set up monthly meetings to review channel performance and recognize important achievements, such as award-winning stories. By virtually every measure, the quality of the Web site improved dramatically over the next six months.

The Web company then tried to go one step further. To create competition among the channels, managers started tracking the number of *hits* (people logging on to the Web site) each channel received each month.

Although competition among teams can be a potent motivator, the approach can also backfire, creating resentment and hard feelings. When using team competitions as a motivating tool, make sure everyone plays on a level field. As you establish how you'll judge performance — profits, unit sales, Web-site hits, or other measurements — make sure you compare the work of the teams, not external factors that team members have little control over.

In the case of the Web company, the number of hits had little to do with the quality of a particular channel and much to do with the interests of the Web site's visitors, who tended to be women in their 30s and 40s. As a result, the men's health channel was always less popular than the women's health channel, regardless of the quality of stories or its special features. The result: Instead of motivating employees, the use of hits as a measure created a sense of frustration and unfairness among the teams. Fortunately, the company quickly abandoned the competition in favor of data reflecting the popularity of the entire Web site.

Developing employee skills

To a large extent, the success of your business plan depends on the quality of the people you attract and keep on your team. That means hiring qualified employees, of course, but it also means expanding the skills of people already on your staff.

Investing in your current team members is a win-win proposition. Employees get the opportunity to take on more responsibility, and your business gains an increasingly qualified (and loyal) staff.

To make the most of your investment in training, begin by defining which capabilities your company absolutely has to have in order to meet your goals and objectives. Study the company strategy and action plan sections of your business plan to identify skills your employees will need, including such general attributes as the ability to manage information, think independently, work in teams, and deal with change.

With your critical skills list in hand, explore education and training opportunities that are best suited to your needs and budget. To help you get started, Form 15-4 offers a checklist of some of the most common training options available. Check off the options that seem most promising given your situation and budget.

EMPLOYEE TRAINING RESOURCE CHECKLIST
☐ **Community college, university, and adult education courses**
☐ **Industry training courses**
☐ **In-house training programs**
☐ **Certification programs**
☐ **Internet-based education**
☐ **Independent learning programs**
☐ **Self-help business books and instructional guides**
☐ **Mentoring programs**

Form 15-4: Use this form on the CD-ROM as you investigate employee-training resources.

One of the most cost-effective ways to enhance the skills of your employees is mentoring. *Mentoring* occurs when experienced employees shepherd the careers of new hires or junior members of your team, and your business reaps the dual benefits of teamwork and company loyalty. If you decide to institute a mentoring program, realize that employees who serve as mentors make a personal investment of time and hard work. Plan to reward them accordingly. Among other options, free up their schedules in order to give them the extra time they need. Pick up a copy of *Coaching & Mentoring For Dummies,* by Marty Brounstein (Wiley), for the lowdown on mentoring.

Other terrific training resources include self-help business books and CD-ROMs, instructional guides, and educational Web sites. Subjects run the gamut from accounting and marketing to computer programming and customer service. Encourage continuous independent employee development by maintaining an in-house training library.

To increase involvement in employee training programs, consider offering job promotions, salary increases, bonuses, or other rewards to people who dedicate their personal off-the-job time to educational efforts that enhance their ability to contribute to your company's success.

Leading into the Future

If the vision for your company has anything to do with growth — especially rapid growth — you need to think about who's going to support your leadership and perhaps one day step in to fill your shoes.

Don't worry: No one's planning your retirement party quite yet. But as your company grows bigger, one person at the top can't do everything. Even with a strong management team, the time will likely come when you have to expand the leadership of your company and loosen your reins. That's what growing a company is all about. How well you manage the leadership transition determines how successful your company ultimately becomes.

Passing on the leadership mantle represents one of the most difficult transitions a leader can make. Relinquishing control is rarely easy; however, too many entrepreneurs fail to establish a transition plan or to cultivate next-generation leaders.

The issue of succession is doubly tricky for family-run firms because it brings up business and personal considerations. Some family members may not want to take over the family company; others may want to play a role but lack the training or experience. Planning is essential to ensure that the family member who assumes the helm is prepared and groomed for the job.

Although the best person to eventually take over your company's leadership may, in fact, be a family member or a member of your existing team, don't begin with any assumptions. Look beyond the usual question: "How do I identify the rising stars in my organization who are most likely to become leaders?" Instead, face the leadership transition issue by taking these steps:

1. **Ask yourself, "Where is my business likely to need strong leadership in the future?"**

2. **To answer your question, review your business goals and objectives and your action plan, which indicate areas where strong leadership is essential.**

3. **Get out your most recent SWOT analysis or conduct a new one (Chapter 5 provides all the details). Your assessment of your company's strengths and weaknesses helps you target the leadership capabilities your company needs to develop in order to take advantage of opportunities while sidestepping potential threats.**

4. **After you identify areas where leadership is critical, begin to consider people around you or recruit new hires that you can cultivate to take on future leadership roles.**

Keeping Your Plan Current

The only constant in business is change. Markets evolve; technologies emerge; customers and preferences change; and your company is bound to change as well. For these reasons, the business-planning process is never over, so your business plan will always remain a work in progress.

The pace of change varies depending on your industry. If you manufacture high-speed telecom switches, your world is in constant motion. If you run the corner hardware store, change may come more slowly. But no business sector is immune to change at some level or another.

The medical profession is a prime example. For years, a medical practice was one of the most secure (and lucrative) businesses around. Everyone gets sick, after all, and doctors thought they had a well-defined, stable market for their services. Along came managed care, and the business of doctoring changed dramatically — and some would say for the worse.

For further proof, consider the family farm. Farmers have always been at the mercy of the weather, but for generations, farming remained a pretty steady and predictable business in all other ways. Enter big agribusiness and new, sophisticated agricultural technologies — the business of farming changed forever from top to bottom.

Change isn't all bad, by any means. It creates opportunities. In fact, it's likely you wouldn't be planning to start or expand your company if markets, customers, and competitors weren't evolving in one way or another. However, change also poses threats — from the arrival of new competitors to the enactment of stringent new regulations — which is a big part of why you need to make business planning an ongoing process.

Monitoring your situation

Scheduling an annual review of your business plan is a good place to start, but you should also consider checking certain parts of your plan on a more frequent basis. For example, if new competitors are popping up all around you, take a close look at the competitive analysis and customer profile sections of the business-environment component of your plan. If sales are falling short of expectations, monitor your marketing plan more closely.

Chapter 16 presents 10 ways to know that your plan needs an overhaul, but even if your company is buzzing along precisely as planned, certain parts of your plan demand ongoing attention, perhaps on a semiannual or even a quarterly basis. Those sections of your plan include your

- ✔ SWOT analysis
- ✔ Company strategy
- ✔ Financial projections
- ✔ Goals and objectives
- ✔ Action plan

If you already have a business-planning team in place, consider asking the team members to assume the ongoing task of reviewing — and possibly revising — key parts of your business plan during the course of the year. If you're on your own, create a schedule at the beginning of the year that sets out which parts of your plan you'll review and when you'll review them.

In the rush of day-to-day business demands, you may be tempted to delay the review and revision of your business plan. Especially when your company is under pressure — from competitors, finances, and operational deadlines — you may want to postpone any kind of planning until your situation settles down. Don't. Giving your plan attention during critical times may well make the difference between pulling through or being pulled under.

Encouraging feedback

Your bottom line is the obvious place to look for proof that your plan is working. If your company is making money, your plan must be working, right? Well, yes, in a way. Your bottom line is critical, but it isn't a foolproof gauge of success.

Employee assessments of your company and its strategic direction are equally important. By listening to the people who actually carry out your plans — from top managers to entry-level hires — you can discover plenty about what's working and what isn't. Encouraging staff input taps a rich vein of ideas about how to revise and refine your business plan to make it even more effective. Some of the ideas you receive may be impossible to implement, and some may be downright wacky. But others are likely to be terrific and even invaluable.

In fact, employees can help you guide your company in the right direction. For instance, employees working on the front line may be the first to notice marketplace trends. They may be able to steer you toward prospective customers or customer groups worth pursuing. They may tip you off about competitors worth keeping an eye on or product problems that are worth analyzing. Employees working behind the scenes may have useful insights that lead to better processes or stronger strategic directions.

To solicit feedback from your employees, establish regular procedures that encourage employees to offer their comments and suggestions. Some companies install an old-fashioned suggestion box. Others use their intranets to create virtual suggestion boxes, chat rooms, and online question-and-answer areas. If your company is small enough, you can employ the best approach of all, which is talking face to face with employees doing the work to find out what's working, what isn't, and what the company can do differently.

Actively solicit suggestions and ideas each time you review and revise your business plan. You can do so by using memos, company-wide meetings, and employee questionnaires. In addition, invite employees to talk about the business plan during their performance reviews. Whatever methods you decide to use, consider asking for answers to the following questions:

- Is the company doing enough to communicate its vision, mission, and strategic plan to employees? If not, how would you suggest we do a better job?

- Are the business goals and objectives outlined in the plan clear and appropriate?

- Do your duties and responsibilities help support the company's goals and strategic direction?

- Can you suggest specific changes in the way you do your work that will help the company better meet its goals?

- Can you suggest ways to improve the company's overall operations?

- Do company procedures get in the way of you doing your best job? If so, how do you suggest changing them?

- Are you aware of changes in the industry — including our customers and our competitors — that our business plan should address?

- Can you suggest ways we can enhance the value we offer our customers?

- Can you think of additional ways to market our products and services?

- If you were in charge of revising the business plan, what other changes would you make?

By soliciting suggestions and ideas from people at every level of your company, you not only collect constructive information, but also enhance a sense of teamwork and shared mission, which go a long way toward making your business plan work and your business a long-term success.

Forms on the CD-ROM

The following forms on the CD-ROM help you put your business plan to work:

Form 15-1	**Goals and Objectives Assignment Chart**	An assignment chart designed to help you align management duties and responsibilities with major business goals and objectives
Form 15-2	**Common Systems and Procedures Checklist**	A list of business systems and procedures common to many companies
Form 15-3	**Checklist of Management and Leadership Traits**	A list of management skills and leadership traits you may want to develop to address future business needs
Form 15-4	**Employee Training Resource Checklist**	The most common training resources for developing employee skills

Part V
The Part of Tens

The 5th Wave   By Rich Tennant

In this part . . .

This final part sends you off with five super-quick chapters that you can turn to for at-a-glance advice now and in your business future.

Want to know ten signs that your business plan needs an overhaul? Turn to Chapter 16. Need ten ways to test the validity of a new business idea? Go straight to Chapter 17. If you're in search of funding, Chapter 18 outlines ten places to turn, along with pluses and minuses for each funding source. And if you decide to knock on venture capitalists' doors, Chapter 19 lists ten things to know before you make your case. Finally, Chapter 20 sums up why your business plan is worth its weight in gold, now and into what I hope is your long and lucrative business future.

Go put your plan to work, and enjoy success!

Chapter 16

Ten Signs That Your Plan Might Need an Overhaul

Giving your business plan a good once-over one time a year may not be often enough. An annual review is a fine schedule under most circumstances, but if your business environment is experiencing choppy conditions, or if you're facing major threats or opportunities, your plan should be the first place you turn. Chapter 11 offers help for companies in trouble; the first step is to see and recognize the warning signs. Here are 10 red flags to watch for as you monitor your business situation.

Costs Rise, Revenues Fall

The clearest sign of business trouble is that costs are going up and revenues are going down, yet many business owners ignore the warning. Why? Because these situations don't usually go wrong overnight. Costs creep upward while revenues drift downward, and too many business owners don't see what's happening because they don't watch (or maybe don't know how to watch) their financial margins.

The antidote? Study your financials, especially keeping an eye on

✔ **Gross profit trends** to see whether your costs of goods sold are slowly climbing out of control

✔ **Operating profits** to see whether your overhead and expenses are getting out of line

✔ **Profitability** to see how much of your original sales revenue is making its way to your bottom line

If any of these terms sound foreign, make a beeline to Chapter 8, which is like an introductory course on business financials. And promise yourself that at the first sign of a profit squeeze, you'll revisit your business plan — starting with a hard look at your financial projections.

Sales Figures Head South

If your sales for a product or service line aren't meeting your expectations — or if you see an unexpected drop in your overall sales revenues — move quickly to diagnose the problem. Take a look at your sales figures, and view them like a customer poll. If sales are sinking, you may have a disconnect between the features you offer and the benefits your customers seek, a problem with quality control, or a breakdown in customer service. Or perhaps the competition is simply tougher than you expected, or maybe your marketing message is off target. Your mission is to identify the reason that sales are slipping. After you spot the problem, revise the appropriate parts of your business plan — product design, operations, marketing strategy — to support your revised forecasts.

You Don't Meet Financial Projections

When your financial projections are off, your business plan needs attention — right now. Plenty of issues can knock even the most conservative financial projections out of whack, and you can't ignore a single one of them. Follow this plan:

1. **Start by reviewing the assumptions behind your original projections.**

2. **Make a detailed list of every internal and external force that may be responsible for the variances.**

3. **Fix what you can and plan around what you can't, but don't ignore what the black-and-white financial statements tell you.**

Don't just hope that things will change; in other words, don't wait until the crash to shore your projections up. Develop a revised set of financial statements based on the new reality and then revise your strategy and action plan accordingly.

Employee Morale Sags

The morale of the people who work for you isn't easy to measure, but it's absolutely critical to your company's success. If you sense that employee morale and motivation are on the skids, don't sit on your hands. Talk to key people around you to uncover what's wrong. Perhaps your goals and objectives are unreasonable, creating frustration rather than motivation. Or maybe you can spot a gap between the company's stated mission and your plan of action, creating confusion and indirection. When employee morale is at stake, you can't wait for the annual business-plan review; you have to address the problems immediately.

Key Projects Fall Behind Schedule

A serious business plan includes timelines for what needs to happen. If your company misses the deadlines, it can't move forward as planned. The minute you sense that important projects are falling behind schedule, sit down with all involved employees to assess the situation. Identify the source of the problem, including aspects of your current business plan that may not be playing out as expected. Brainstorm solutions for getting back on schedule. If you can't catch up and resetting timelines won't derail opportunities, amend your business plan, revise your action plan, and notify all involved.

New Competitors Appear

Even with careful planning, a competitive assault that you don't see coming can rock your company. If that situation occurs, take a deep breath and remember that competition isn't always a bad thing: It usually increases interest in your business sector, and it almost always forces you to focus on what you do best and how to do it as efficiently as possible.

If a big, predatory fish comes swimming into your little pond, revise the situation analysis in your business plan — immediately. Start with your SWOT analysis (see Chapter 5 for how-to information) to uncover areas where your capabilities lag behind or surge ahead of the capabilities of your competitors. Shore up the former and polish up the latter in order to overcome and even capitalize upon the changes in your business environment. Chapter 4 offers advice for sizing up and staying a step ahead of your competitors.

Technology Shakes Up Your World

In this age of constant technological innovation, no one needs to tell you that new products and processes can turn your company upside down, for better or worse. A shift in technology can make existing products obsolete and create markets for new products or services almost overnight. Technological change is often accompanied by a shift in customer preferences and demands. As a result, the competitive landscape is redrawn.

Meanwhile, business operations need revamping to address and incorporate the technological breakthroughs, including the installation of new equipment and processes that can affect your company *and* its financial statements. Therefore, when a new technology appears on your business horizon, reassess your business plan — fast. Ask yourself how the new technology may change the desires and demands of the markets you serve and how it may affect the way that you — and your competitors — do business. Lay out plans for how your business will incorporate the new technology and use it to your advantage.

Important Customers Defect

From time to time, good customers will switch allegiances to a new supplier. However, if you notice a trend in customer defections, something may be wrong. For instance, your competitors may be stronger than you anticipated, your efforts may be falling short, or the market itself may be changing.

The defection of important customers is an alarm signal that you can't afford to ignore. As your first step, look for deficiencies in your product or service offering. When possible, ask departing customers why they want to make a change, and talk to your salespeople and frontline staff for their insights. Get ready to retool your business plan, paying close attention to how your business strengths and weaknesses may have shifted and how those changes may be affecting your ability to compete in your market.

Business Strategy Does a 180

Slight course adjustments in your strategy are a normal part of doing business, but if your company does a 180-degree shift, something's very wrong. Instead of swinging wildly from one direction to another, sit down with your management team — business plan in hand — to figure out why your original strategic direction isn't working or isn't being followed. Take the time you need to do a complete diagnostic, and then plan a rational course change that will address the problems you identify.

Growth Is Out of Your Control

Entrepreneurs don't usually complain when business is booming, but your company *can* grow too fast — and that can mean trouble if you're not prepared. When business is booming, customer service can suffer or manufacturing may not be able to keep up with demand, for example. Some companies even find that their basic organizational structures no longer fit their new dimensions. If your business experiences similar growing pains, look at your business plan to identify the parts that need to change in order to accommodate the good news — and your increasing size.

Chapter 17

Ten Ways to Evaluate a New Business Idea

*E*very business venture starts with an idea. It may be as simple as opening a shop that features local artwork or as complex as creating a company that offers space vacations. Either way, your success depends on the strength of your idea, how well it fits your temperament, how well you can plan for success, and what resources you can bring to the effort.

Before settling and taking your first steps, consider this list of 10 questions that you absolutely, positively need to ask about your business idea before you take the big plunge.

Is This Something I Really Want to Do?

Running your own company is more than just a job. For most successful entrepreneurs, it's a full-time passion. The people most likely to succeed are ones who truly believe in their ideas, care about the products or services that they offer, and love what they do — even when the going gets tough. Take a moment to think about what it will take to turn your idea into a business and what running that business will be like. Is your heart in it? Is it something you really care about? Is it how you want to spend your time? If you answer all the questions with an enthusiastic "Yes!" read on. If not, maybe you need to go back to brainstorming (see Chapter 2).

Is This Something I'm Capable of Doing?

Thomas Edison called genius "1 percent inspiration, 99 percent perspiration." Your idea is a stroke of inspiration, but do you have what it takes to sweat out the details and do the hard work required to turn your inspiration into reality? Beyond desire, do you have the capability? In other words, *can* you do it? Do you have the resources, connections, skills, and experience to turn your idea into a success story? And if you don't have everything required to do the job well, do you have the knowledge and resources to assemble a team that does? Chapter 6 helps assess the capabilities necessary to make your business a success.

Does It Tap My Personal Strengths?

Not everyone can run a high-tech business — or a local gift shop, for that matter. Your strengths and weaknesses will go to work with you every day, so take time to consider whether your idea aligns well with your personal attributes or whether it requires talents in areas where you're a little weak. Successful entrepreneurs devote themselves to businesses that leverage their strengths and work around their weaknesses. How do your strengths and weaknesses match up to the business idea you're considering? If the business requires plenty of personal contact, for example, are you good with people? If the business requires you to move rapidly to seize an opportunity, are you prepared for long, sometimes stressful days? Chapter 2 helps you conduct a self-appraisal.

Can I Describe It in 25 Words or Less?

If your business idea is so complex that you need a half-hour and 20 flip charts to explain it, chances are it's too complicated. You can describe almost every great business idea in 25 words or less. Consider a few examples:

- ✔ A combination electronic organizer and wireless Internet device (8 words)
- ✔ A gift certificate that you can redeem online to contribute to the charity of your choice (16 words)
- ✔ A catering service that delivers meals based on The Zone, Atkins, or Weight Watchers diets (15 words)

As part of your evaluation, pare down your idea to its essentials and describe it as simply and concisely as you can. A simple, polished phrase can make your idea shine — or it may reveal a fatal flaw.

What's the Closest Thing to It in the Marketplace?

As the age-old saying goes, there's nothing new under the sun. In fact, refining or combining existing ideas generates most new business ideas. Here's a television, there's the Web — hey, how about WebTV? As you judge your idea, think about similar products or services already swimming in the marketplace, and then ask a tough question: How is your idea better?

Does It Meet a Need or Solve a Customer Problem?

Most customers don't plunk down hard-earned cash because they love spending money or love buying products. Customers spend money because they believe that what they buy can solve their problems, fulfill their needs, or satisfy their desires. If your business idea doesn't address a real problem, need, or desire, getting it off the ground will be doubly difficult, because instead of presenting your product as the best solution to existing needs, you have to create the sense of need and *then* present your product as the solution. That situation is a hard row to hoe. Turn to Chapter 4 for help defining your customers and what motivates them to buy.

Does It Take Advantage of a New Opportunity?

Often, business success hinges on having the right idea in the right place at the right time. The rise of the Internet — and the simultaneous passion in America for collecting — presented twin opportunities that helped turn the booming auction site eBay into a household word. And the nation's ballooning waistline was the opportunity that Weight Watchers rode all the way to a multimillion-dollar success story. Does your business idea stand a good chance of catching a similar wave of opportunity?

What's the Biggest Drawback or Limitation?

You have to take off your rose-colored glasses and admit that even the greatest business ideas have drawbacks and limitations. Maybe your idea is very easy for would-be competitors to copy, for example. Or maybe it requires a difficult-to-achieve change in some ingrained customer behavior. Perhaps your idea requires a long R&D phase, or maybe it poses difficult marketing challenges. By thinking long and hard about the potential drawbacks of your idea, you put your business opportunity in perspective. If the pluses far outweigh the worst-case scenarios you dream up, chances are your business idea stands a pretty good chance of succeeding.

Will It Make Money — and How Fast?

Oddly enough, this simple question is the one most likely to go unasked by wannabe entrepreneurs, maybe because it's one of the toughest questions to face up to. It goes well beyond your answer to the question of whether or not customers will be willing to pay for your product or service; this question takes you into the realm of forecasting:

- How long will it take before your business idea will generate profits?
- How long can you afford to wait?
- After the sales start rolling in, can you sustain profitability over time?

Take the time to give questions like these serious thought — sooner rather than later. Turn to Chapter 8 for help thinking through the numbers.

Am I Willing to Remortgage My House?

I'm not suggesting that you take out a second mortgage to fund your new business venture. But as a test of your passion and belief, ask yourself: If you had to do it, would you be willing? Even if you're planning on persuading outside investors to take on some of the risk for you, you need that kind of personal belief as you make the pitch. And if you decide to take a bank loan instead, you have to sign on the dotted line to pledge to repay the money, absolutely, positively. One way or another, you assume financial risk when you launch a business. If you're not willing to take on that risk, you may not be cut out for the business you're thinking about starting.

Chapter 18

Ten Ways to Fund Your Business Plan

In This Chapter

▶ Finding the cash you need

▶ Weighing the price of various forms of support

A great idea sparks most business start-ups, but money is the fuel that keeps those start-ups running. Even if you're launching a one-person freelance business, chances are you need cash to get off the ground. If you're starting a bigger company, and especially if you're founding a high-tech or manufacturing enterprise, chances are good that you need *lots* of cash. This chapter shares 10 places you can to turn to when searching for money to fund your company.

Your Own Pocket

Using your own funding for your start-up has its advantages and disadvantages. If you get your business up and running by using only your savings, you maintain 100 percent ownership and 100 percent control. But you also take on all the risk: If the company goes under, your money goes with it. If you link arms with investors, you still tap your own pocketbook, but you share the risk — and the rewards — with others. If you seek loans, banks require you to pledge personal assets as collateral to secure the debt. And if you go the venture capital route (see Chapter 19), most investors insist that you ante up some of your own cash, largely as proof of your commitment, before they'll add their own.

Friends and Family

Turning to friends or family members for help is a time-honored tradition when starting a small business. Some people borrow money in return for a simple IOU to be paid back in full when the company starts making a profit. Others set up a more formal loan along with an agreement for paying money back with interest on a specific schedule. Whatever arrangement you reach, make sure that everyone involved understands the terms and knows what to expect and when to expect it. To be on the safe side, put the terms in writing and ask all parties to sign the documents because disagreements over money can spoil even the closest family or friendly relationships.

A Bank Loan

Local branches of most banks are more than willing to consider loan requests from local businesses. The factors that influence a banker's yes-or-no loan decision include your personal credit history, your education, expertise, business experience, and the likelihood that you'll succeed in your business start-up or expansion. Before you consider approaching a banker, be prepared to make your case by presenting a formal written business plan along with a loan request that defines how much you want to borrow, how you plan to use the funds, and when you'll repay the money.

The simplest bank-loan arrangement is a standard commercial loan. In this case, the bank loans you the money, and you pay it back, usually in monthly installments and with interest. But you can find all sorts of variations on this theme, from real estate loans on commercial property to loans secured by your inventory or accounts receivable.

The advantage of getting a bank loan is that you gain business funding while maintaining all the equity in your company. The disadvantage is that loan payments are due on schedule, even if your business runs into hard times.

A Commercial Line of Credit

If you need access to money that you don't intend to need all at once, consider applying for a commercial line of credit. A *commercial line of credit* is an agreement from a financial institution to extend a specified amount of credit that your company can draw upon, as necessary, to finance inventory purchases or to provide working capital or funds for other cash needs. With a commercial line of credit, you pay interest only on the funds you actually borrow over the period between when you draw on the funds and when you pay them back. Banks don't usually require collateral to secure small lines of credit, but they may require that you secure larger lines of credit with your company's accounts receivable, inventory, machinery and equipment, or real estate.

Equipment Leasing

Another way to borrow money from banks is in the form of an *equipment lease,* which you can use to acquire anything from computers, printers, and copiers to manufacturing equipment, tractors, and trucks. Financial arrangements include lease-to-buy options, equipment upgrade options, and master leases, which cover a variety of equipment under one agreement.

The loan length for these options is usually tied to the lease term, and most banks base their leasing agreements on a company's established operating history.

A Small Business Administration (SBA) Loan

Bravo to the Small Business Administration (SBA), which is a government agency dedicated to helping small businesses that may otherwise have a tough time securing financing from commercial banks. The SBA has more than a dozen loan programs for small businesses. (See Chapter 10 and also check out www.sba.gov for more information.)

The primary program is the 7(a) Loan Guaranty Program, through which the SBA guarantees loans provided to small businesses by private lenders. The SBA also has a microloan program, which provides nonprofit community based lenders with funds to make very small loans to small businesses.

When seeking an SBA loan, realize that it isn't free money. Expect to pay fees and interest, and be ready for paperwork, oversight, and to personally guarantee loan repayment. The loans are actually made by banks or other lending institutions, but because the SBA provides the backup guarantee, loans that banks may otherwise turn down get extra attention.

Deep-Pocket Partners

It sounds like a marriage made in heaven: Entrepreneur with great business idea but no money finds like-minded entrepreneur with money in search of a great idea. In fact, many such partnerships go on to exist happily ever after. But if you're thinking about forming a financial partnership as a way to get the cash you need, establish an upfront agreement that defines how much control your partner or partners will exercise over the business strategy, planning, and day-to-day operations. And be sure that you get along. It may sound obvious, but a good working relationship with a business partner can help smooth the inevitable bumps on the road to success.

Venture Capital

Maybe you need more money than a bank is willing to lend you. Or maybe you're nervous about taking on all the risk of a major loan. If getting your business off the ground requires more money than you can or want to borrow, you may want to knock on the venture capital door. *Venture capitalists* are professional asset managers (in other words, investor groups) who seek a high rate of return on behalf of the investors they represent. When venture capitalists like a business concept and are confident that the management team has what it takes to make the business succeed, they fork over sizeable sums. The catch is that they want something in return, and usually that something is a big role in controlling your business, a major chunk of the ownership, and a clear way to recoup and realize a substantial return on their investment at a specified time in the future. For more information on how to go after venture capital, check out Chapter 11 and the 10 tips in Chapter 19.

Angel Money

Angels are successful and wealthy entrepreneurs who buy into up-and-coming companies, not only with their money, but also with their expertise and guidance. Angels make funding decisions more rapidly than venture capitalists largely because they operate independently rather than on behalf of a group of investors. Additionally, angels take greater risks than venture capitalists, funding businesses at earlier stages of their life cycles and entertaining smaller financing requests. Another difference between venture capitalists and angels is that angels are often more patient. Angels invest in start-up businesses that they believe will make it big at some unspecified point down the road, unlike venture capitalists, who get involved to catapult the firm to the next level of financial success. However, like venture capitalists, angels usually want a piece of the equity pie.

Prospective Customers

This option sounds counterintuitive, but you can turn customers into investors who can help your company get off the ground. For example, community-supported agriculture programs pair local farmers with consumers who pay a set fee in advance in return for a weekly load of produce during the summer growing season. And condominium projects often sell units to prospective owners before the builder ever breaks ground. When considering funding sources, think of people who use and benefit from your company's offerings. They may be willing to invest in your continued success.

Chapter 19

Ten Things to Know about Venture Capital

. . . .

In This Chapter
▶ Understanding what investors seek and require
▶ Targeting and approaching venture capitalists

. . . .

*F*ollowing what was famously labeled the irrational exuberance of the dot-com bubble, the flow of venture capital froze up. The funding environment has now thawed and investment dollars are once again flowing, but with way more scrutiny and only to businesses with unique and proprietary products, strong strategies, sound management, steady revenues, and proven, dependable markets. Because the arena of venture capital continues to evolve, I provide 10 important things to know in this chapter before you fully get your feet wet.

Three Sources of Investment Dollars

Chapter 18 outlines 10 ways to fund your business plan. When you decide to seek substantial investments in your company, however, here are the three places to turn:

- ✔ **The founders:** Your personal investment is essential for two reasons. One, the more money you invest, the more of your company you'll hold in your name. Two, your investment demonstrates your commitment to your business idea. Dedicating your hope and time isn't enough to convince outside investors to buy into your business. They need to see that your money is also on the line.

- ✔ **Angel investors:** These individuals invest their own money, expertise, and guidance. They often get involved with very young start-ups on the bet that the risk will pay off when the companies go public or sell to a third party. See Chapters 11 and 18 for more information on angels.

> ✔ **Venture capitalists:** Venture capitalists are professional investor groups that invest money on behalf of investors for whom they seek a high rate of return. Typically, venture capitalists invest from $250,000 to millions of dollars. In return, they usually require a share of ownership, an oversight role, and a timely and significant return on investment at the conclusion of their financial involvement.

What Venture Capitalists Look For

Unlike realtors, investors don't focus on "location, location, location." They want to invest in a great business idea wherever it exists. When deciding whether an idea is great, here are the factors venture capitalists consider:

> ✔ **People:** Starting with the founder and moving through your top managers, investors want to see that the people running your company have vision, leadership capability, and management experience that's relevant to the size and kind of business you want them to fund.
>
> ✔ **The business concept:** You need to persuade investors that your business will experience sustained growth. That means you need a product that's unique, proprietary, easy to protect, hard to replicate, faced with few competitors, and in high demand by a customer group with serious growth potential. Investors also want to see a strong business model, healthy revenue streams, high profit margins, and a management team that's capable of making it all happen.
>
> ✔ **Market opportunity:** Investors back businesses that serve fast-growing, untapped market segments with products that fill real and easy-to-defend market positions. Patents, trademarks, and other barriers that prevent competitors from eroding your market potential enhance the attractiveness of your market opportunity.

Don't approach investors until you've refined, produced, and sold your product, thereby proving that people will pay for what you're offering.

What Venture Capitalists Expect to Gain

A venture capitalist's main goal is to seek business opportunities that will provide a healthy return on investment. To achieve this goal, venture capitalists invest in companies with sound business plans, real and defensible strategic positions, healthy revenues and profit margins, and strong potential for going public or being acquired.

Most venture capitalists look for returns of at least three to five times their investments in five to seven years. Some venture capitalists even seek to recoup as much as 20 times their investments, and some set timelines as short as two years. Do your research before approaching venture capitalists because you want to be sure that their demands meet with your timelines. A good place to start your research is the Web site of the National Venture Capital Association at www.nvca.org. Go to the section About NVCA and click on Members to access links to the Web sites for member firms.

When to Raise Venture Capital

You want to approach venture capitalists only when you have a proven business model. A *proven business model* means that your product and its technology are fully developed and you have an established customer base, predictable streams of revenue, and a strong performance history. Until you can prove that your technology, production, sales strategy, and business model work, your chances of winning a venture capitalist's interest — and funding — are slim.

Aiming Your Proposals

When seeking venture capital, start by doing some homework:

- ✔ Study the *Pratt's Guide to Venture Capital Sources* or the *Venture Capital and Private Equity Firms* catalogs, both available at major libraries.

- ✔ Go online to www.vfinance.com to access lists of venture capitalists.

- ✔ Contact owners of venture-backed businesses to find out the names of investment attorneys, accountants, or advisors who can open doors on your behalf.

- ✔ Request literature or visit Web sites to find the philosophies and objectives of various venture capital groups.

When researching, create a short list of prospective venture capitalists, beginning with the ones that focus on your industry. Start with firms in your geographic area because the investors will want to be involved with your board, and proximity adds convenience and cost efficiency. See which firms fund at your stage of development and whether their upper- and lower-funding limits fit with your needs. Finally, know whether you want a *lead investor firm,* which serves as a strategic partner, or whether you want to attract more passive investors to provide follow-on rounds of financing. Different funds specialize in each realm.

Approaching Venture Capitalists

Like any introduction, an approach to a venture capitalist is best accomplished through a referral from a banker, lawyer, accountant, economic development executive, industry leader, or a venture-backed entrepreneur or another venture capitalist.

After you gain a meeting, be ready to give a quick, compelling introduction with the sole aim of making the investor want to know more. From there, be ready with a flawless copy of your business plan.

If the investor thinks that your business is worth a close look, the long process of evaluation — called *due diligence* — begins. Use this time to get to know the investing firm. Ask for references from other clients, and ask who in the firm would be your point person. You don't want to jump the gun, but you do want to find out all you can; if you reach an agreement with the firm, you enter into a close partnership, so assess whether you can establish trust and work well together.

Memorizing Your Elevator Speech

Venture capitalists coined the term "elevator speech" during the heyday of the Internet boom. Swamped with proposals, they listened to quick, people-language descriptions of business propositions before deciding whether or not to invest time reading full business plans. Today's investors are no different. Be ready to pitch your business idea in less than a minute. During those first few seconds, introduce your

- ✔ Vision
- ✔ Product
- ✔ Market
- ✔ Competitive advantages
- ✔ Value proposition
- ✔ Barriers to entry
- ✔ Expertise and ambition
- ✔ Unique advantages

You want to introduce these points in a way that prompts interest and makes your audience want to know more.

If you can't boil your explanation down or if you don't want to divulge your secrets, venture capitalists will cut you off at the pass. Chapter 6 includes advice and a planning questionnaire to help you put your precious few words together.

Tailoring Your Business Plan

Don't even think about seeking capital without a written business plan that defines a proven business model, strong capabilities, clear sales objectives, and the strategy that you'll follow to achieve success — including forecasts for how long it will take before your funding partners reap the reward of investing in your business.

Before presenting your plan, take special care preparing the executive summary. The truth is, the executive summary may be the only section the investor reads before he or she puts your plan into the go or no-go pile. Be sure that your summary describes

- ✔ **Your business:** Include your vision and mission, objectives, history, legal structure, and ownership.

- ✔ **Your product:** Include specifications and any patents, trademarks, or other proprietary positions.

- ✔ **Your competitive advantages:** Include management strength, business capabilities, business model, and market opportunity.

- ✔ **Your business strategy:** Include your operating and marketing plans and the role of any strategic partners.

- ✔ **Your funding request:** Include how much money your business needs, how you plan to use it, and how you'll structure the investment.

As they delve into your plan, venture capitalists will pay special attention to several sections, including the following:

- ✔ **Management section:** In this section, include inspiring bios of your founders, executives, and board members.

- ✔ **Marketing strategy:** In this section, discuss your market and competitive analyses and your promotion and sales strategies.

- ✔ **Business model:** Remember, this term is code for "show me the money," so in this section of your business plan, present proof that your product is completely developed, your market is sufficiently large, market response is strong, and your revenue model is capable of delivering a profit.

- ✔ **Financial strategy:** In this section, include financial statements, forecasts, capital requirements, valuations, and investor exit plans.

For more information on the components of a business plan, see Chapters 1 and 14.

The Importance of an Exit Plan

When making a proposal to a venture capitalist, include the proposed exit strategy in your business plan. Before venture capitalists will commit to investments, they want to see clear, timely, and profitable ways to recoup and realize returns on their investments. The most common exit strategies include an initial public offering (IPO), a merger with another company, an acquisition of the company, or a repurchase of the venture capital stake by the original founders of the firm.

The Red Flags

Following is a roundup of red flags that cause venture capitalists to push the brake pedal when reviewing investment proposals:

- Great product but no existing market
- Founders filling management positions for which they aren't qualified
- No clear organization chart
- No existing clientele or proof that people will actually buy the product
- Weak market and competitive analyses and an unclear marketing plan
- An unsustainable plan that will collapse under its own weight as the business achieves growth
- Inadequate attention paid to profitability timelines, profit margins, sales cycles and achievement milestones, or other financial realities

Chapter 20

Ten Ways to Use Your Business Plan

1 leave you with these 10 parting thoughts to reinforce your decision to write and use a business plan to bolster your success.

Put Your Business Idea to the Test

The business-planning process forces you to think about who's going to buy your product, who your competitors are likely to be, what it will take to get your company going, and how you'll achieve success.

Turn a Good Idea into a Viable Business

So where's the money? If you can't describe your business model, it's back to the drawing board rather than forward to a business mishap.

Determine Your Start-Up Needs . . .

Your business plan helps you get realistic about what it will take to launch your business, along with an action plan that serves as your marching orders.

. . . and What They're Likely to Cost

Your business plan provides an analysis of your financial situation and a funding forecast that allows you to have the cash available when you need it.

Uncover What You're Up Against

Writing a business plan forces you to scope out the competition and prepare upfront so you don't hit roadblocks later.

Find Funding

Whether you're trying to convince a local banker or a big-name venture capitalist to put up cash, you need to convey that you have a great idea and a solid strategy. In other words, you need a business plan. Period.

Gauge Progress

A business plan provides benchmarks to measure your progress. If you miss a milestone, use your business plan to determine where — and why — you fell short and how to get back on track.

Prepare for the Unexpected

If you hit a pothole or you find yourself on a dead-end street in need of a U-turn, your business plan will help you chart a turnaround. (See Chapter 11 for U-turn tips.)

Tell the World Who You Are

By defining your vision, your company overview, and your strategic plans, your business plan helps you communicate your business identity with everyone from investors and shareholders to regulators and media.

Inspire Your Team

Your business plan tells your employees what your company is, what it stands for, and how it will accomplish its mission through its goals and objectives. By sharing your plan — and, better yet, by involving employees in the planning process — you create a strong team and *esprit de corps*.

Appendix

About the CD

System Requirements

Make sure that your computer meets the minimum system requirements shown in the following list. If your computer doesn't match up to most of these requirements, you may have problems using the software and files on the CD. For the latest and greatest information, please refer to the ReadMe file located at the root of the CD-ROM.

- A PC with a Pentium or faster processor; or a Mac OS computer with a 68040 or faster processor

- Microsoft Windows 98 or later; or Mac OS system software 7.6.1 or later

- At least 32MB of total RAM installed on your computer; for best performance, we recommend at least 64MB

- A CD-ROM drive

- A sound card for PCs; Mac OS computers have built-in sound support

- A monitor capable of displaying at least 256 colors or grayscale

- A modem with a speed of at least 14,400 bps

If you need more information on the basics, check out these books published by Wiley Publishing, Inc.: *PCs For Dummies,* by Dan Gookin; *Macs For Dummies,* by David Pogue; *iMacs For Dummies,* by David Pogue; *Windows 95 For Dummies, Windows 98 For Dummies, Windows 2000 Professional For Dummies, Microsoft Windows ME Millennium Edition For Dummies,* all by Andy Rathbone.

Using the CD

To install the items from the CD to your hard drive, follow these steps:

1. **Insert the CD into your computer's CD-ROM drive. The license agreement appears.**

   Note to Windows users: The interface won't launch if you have autorun disabled. In that case, click Start ⇨ Run. In the dialog box that appears, type D:\start.exe. (Replace D with the proper letter if your CD-ROM drive uses a different letter. If you don't know the letter, see how your CD-ROM drive is listed under My Computer.) Click OK.

   Note for Mac Users: The CD icon will appear on your desktop. Double-click the icon to open the CD and double-click the "Start" icon..

2. **Read through the license agreement, and then click the Accept button if you want to use the CD. After you click Accept, the License Agreement window won't appear again.**

   The CD interface appears. The interface allows you to install the programs and view the sample forms with just a click of a button (or two).

What You'll Find on the CD

The following sections are arranged by category and present a list of the files and software you'll find on the CD.

Author created material: Business plan forms

All the business plan forms referred to in the book are included on the CD. The forms come in two file formats:

- **Microsoft Word files:** You can open these files if you use Microsoft Word 95 or later (for Mac or Windows).

- **Adobe Reader (PDF) files:** These forms can't be modified, but if you have Adobe Reader, you can view and print them. Adobe Reader for Mac and Windows is included on the CD.

All the forms are located in the Author directory on the CD and work with Macintosh, Linux, Unix, and Windows 95/98/NT and later computers. The form files are organized by chapter. Table A-1 lists them all by name and number.

Table A-1	Forms at a Glance
Form Number	*Form Name*
Form 1-1	Typical Business-Planning Situations
Form 1-2	Checklist of Common Business Plan Audiences
Form 1-3	Business Plan Target Audiences and Key Messages
Form 1-4	Major Components in a Typical Business Plan
Form 1-5	Business Plan Time Frame Questionnaire
Form 1-6	Business Plan Tracker
Form 2-1	The Idea Blender — Your Personal Traits and Interests
Form 2-2	The Idea Blender — Mixing and Matching Your Interests
Form 2-3	The Idea Blender — Your Business Ideas
Form 2-4	Business Opportunity Evaluation Questionnaire
Form 2-5	Business Opportunity Framework
Form 2-6	Personal Strengths and Weaknesses Survey
Form 2-7	Personal Strengths and Weaknesses Grid
Form 3-1	Basic Business Definition Framework
Form 3-2	Your Mission Statement Questionnaire
Form 3-3	Your Mission Statement Framework
Form 3-4	Examples of Real-World Mission Statements
Form 3-5	Our Mission Statement
Form 3-6	Goals and Objectives Flowchart
Form 3-7	Goals and Objectives based on ACES
Form 3-8	Checklist of Common Business Goals
Form 3-9	Our Major Business Goals
Form 3-10	Values Questionnaire
Form 3-11	Our Values Statement
Form 3-12	Examples of Real-World Vision Statements
Form 3-13	Our Vision Statement
Form 4-1	Industry Analysis Questionnaire

(continued)

Table A-1 *(continued)*

Form Number	Form Name
Form 4-2	Barriers to Entry Checklist
Form 4-3	Customer Profile Questionnaire
Form 4-4	Customer Intelligence Checklist
Form 4-5	Customer Snapshot
Form 4-6	Ideal Customer Questionnaire
Form 4-7	Distinguishing Traits of Ideal Customers
Form 4-8	Basic Market Segmentation Framework
Form 4-9	Business Customer Profile
Form 4-10	Our Biggest Competitors
Form 4-11	Competitive Intelligence Checklist
Form 4-12	Potential Stealth Competitors Questionnaire
Form 4-13	Stealth Competitor Tracking Form
Form 4-14	Biggest Competitors and Their Likely Moves
Form 5-1	Company Strengths and Weaknesses Survey
Form 5-2	Company Strengths and Weaknesses Grid
Form 5-3	Company Opportunities and Threats
Form 5-4	Company SWOT Analysis Grid
Form 5-5	Quick Financial Projection Worksheet
Form 5-6	Business Model Questionnaire
Form 5-7	Resources for Growth Checklist
Form 5-8	Planning for Growth Questionnaire
Form 5-9	Checklist of Common Exit Strategies
Form 6-1	Product/Service Description Checklist
Form 6-2	Elevator Speech Planning Questionnaire
Form 6-3	Operations Planning Survey (Location)
Form 6-4	Operations Planning Survey (Equipment)
Form 6-5	Operations Planning Survey (Labor)
Form 6-6	Operations Planning Survey (Process)

Form Number	Form Name
Form 6-7	Distribution and Delivery Survey
Form 6-8	Management Team Member Profile
Form 7-1	Positioning and Brand Statements Worksheet
Form 7-2	Product Strategy Checklist
Form 7-3	Distribution Strategy Checklist
Form 7-4	Pricing Strategy Checklist
Form 7-5	Promotion Strategy Checklist
Form 7-6	Customer Service Checklist
Form 8-1	Company Income Statement
Form 8-2	Company Balance Sheet
Form 8-3	Company Cash Flow Statement
Form 9-1	Is Self-Employment Right for You?
Form 9-2	Tasks and Time Survey
Form 9-3	Self-Employed Expense Checklist
Form 9-4	Evaluating Your Home Office Options
Form 9-5	Checklist of Business Networking Resources
Form 10-1	Start-Up Costs Worksheet For Small Businesses
Form 10-2	Job Description Profile
Form 10-3	Job Recruiting Checklist
Form 10-4	Employee Retention Checklist
Form 10-5	Tips on Promoting Teamwork
Form 11-1	Selling Your Business Worksheet
Form 11-2	Growth Strategies Worksheet
Form 11-3	Checklist of Common Warning Signs
Form 12-1	Not-for-Profit Planning Worksheet
Form 12-2	Examples of Real-World Not-for-Profit Mission Statements
Form 12-3	Ideal Individual Donor Questionnaire
Form 12-4	Checklist of Responsibilities for a Not-for-Profit Board

(continued)

Table A-1 *(continued)*

Form Number	Form Name
Form 12-5	Checklist of Typical Grant Proposal Sections
Form 13-1	Checklist of Key Steps in Planning an e-Business
Form 13-2	Online Customer Profile
Form 13-3	E-Business Value Proposition Worksheet
Form 13-4	E-Business Model Construction Worksheet
Form 14-1	Business Plan Components Checklist
Form 14-2	Master Plan Tracking Sheet
Form 14-3	Business Plan Target Audience Guidelines
Form 14-4	Working Draft Checklist
Form 15-1	Goals and Objectives Assignment Chart
Form 15-2	Common Systems and Procedures Checklist
Form 15-3	Checklist of Management and Leadership Traits
Form 15-4	Employee Training Resource Checklist

Other software

We've included the freeware software Adobe Reader from Adobe Systems for Mac OS and Windows on the CD. This program enables you to view and print Portable Document Format (PDF) files.

Trial, demo, or *evaluation* versions of software are usually limited either by time or functionality (such as not letting you save a project after you create it).

Troubleshooting

If you have trouble with the CD, please call the Wiley Product Technical Support phone number at (800) 762-2974. Outside the United States, call (317) 572-3994. You can also contact Wiley Product Technical Support at www.wiley. com/techsupport. John Wiley & Sons will provide technical support only for installation and other general quality control items. For technical support on the applications themselves, consult the program's vendor or author.

To place additional orders or to request information about other Wiley products, please call 877-762-2974.

Index

• *T* •

Notes

USINESS, CAREERS & PERSONAL FINANCE

0-7645-5307-0

Home Buying

0-7645-5331-3 *†

Also available:
- Accounting For Dummies †
  0-7645-5314-3
- Business Plans Kit For Dummies †
  0-7645-5365-8
- Cover Letters For Dummies
  0-7645-5224-4
- Frugal Living For Dummies
  0-7645-5403-4
- Leadership For Dummies
  0-7645-5176-0
- Managing For Dummies
  0-7645-1771-6

- Marketing For Dummies
  0-7645-5600-2
- Personal Finance For Dummies *
  0-7645-2590-5
- Project Management For Dummies
  0-7645-5283-X
- Resumes For Dummies †
  0-7645-5471-9
- Selling For Dummies
  0-7645-5363-1
- Small Business Kit For Dummies *†
  0-7645-5093-4

OME & BUSINESS COMPUTER BASICS

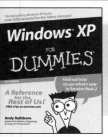

0-7645-4074-2

0-7645-3758-X

Also available:
- ACT! 6 For Dummies
  0-7645-2645-6
- iLife '04 All-in-One Desk Reference
  For Dummies
  0-7645-7347-0
- iPAQ For Dummies
  0-7645-6769-1
- Mac OS X Panther Timesaving
  Techniques For Dummies
  0-7645-5812-9
- Macs For Dummies
  0-7645-5656-8

- Microsoft Money 2004 For Dummies
  0-7645-4195-1
- Office 2003 All-in-One Desk Reference
  For Dummies
  0-7645-3883-7
- Outlook 2003 For Dummies
  0-7645-3759-8
- PCs For Dummies
  0-7645-4074-2
- TiVo For Dummies
  0-7645-6923-6
- Upgrading and Fixing PCs For Dummies
  0-7645-1665-5
- Windows XP Timesaving Techniques
  For Dummies
  0-7645-3748-2

OOD, HOME, GARDEN, HOBBIES, MUSIC & PETS

0-7645-5295-3

0-7645-5232-5

Also available:
- Bass Guitar For Dummies
  0-7645-2487-9
- Diabetes Cookbook For Dummies
  0-7645-5230-9
- Gardening For Dummies *
  0-7645-5130-2
- Guitar For Dummies
  0-7645-5106-X
- Holiday Decorating For Dummies
  0-7645-2570-0
- Home Improvement All-in-One
  For Dummies
  0-7645-5680-0

- Knitting For Dummies
  0-7645-5395-X
- Piano For Dummies
  0-7645-5105-1
- Puppies For Dummies
  0-7645-5255-4
- Scrapbooking For Dummies
  0-7645-7208-3
- Senior Dogs For Dummies
  0-7645-5818-8
- Singing For Dummies
  0-7645-2475-5
- 30-Minute Meals For Dummies
  0-7645-2589-1

NTERNET & DIGITAL MEDIA

0-7645-1664-7

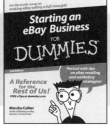

0-7645-6924-4

Also available:
- 2005 Online Shopping Directory
  For Dummies
  0-7645-7495-7
- CD & DVD Recording For Dummies
  0-7645-5956-7
- eBay For Dummies
  0-7645-5654-1
- Fighting Spam For Dummies
  0-7645-5965-6
- Genealogy Online For Dummies
  0-7645-5964-3
- Google For Dummies
  0-7645-4420-9

- Home Recording For Musicians
  For Dummies
  0-7645-1634-5
- The Internet For Dummies
  0-7645-4173-0
- iPod & iTunes For Dummies
  0-7645-7772-7
- Preventing Identity Theft For Dummies
  0-7645-7336-5
- Pro Tools All-in-One Desk Reference
  For Dummies
  0-7645-5714-9
- Roxio Easy Media Creator For Dummies
  0-7645-7131-1

Separate Canadian edition also available
Separate U.K. edition also available

vailable wherever books are sold. For more information or to order direct: U.S. customers visit www.dummies.com or call 1-877-762-2974.
K. customers visit www.wileyeurope.com or call 0800 243407. Canadian customers visit www.wiley.ca or call 1-800-567-4797.

SPORTS, FITNESS, PARENTING, RELIGION & SPIRITUALITY

0-7645-5146-9

0-7645-5418-2

Also available:

- Adoption For Dummies
  0-7645-5488-3
- Basketball For Dummies
  0-7645-5248-1
- The Bible For Dummies
  0-7645-5296-1
- Buddhism For Dummies
  0-7645-5359-3
- Catholicism For Dummies
  0-7645-5391-7
- Hockey For Dummies
  0-7645-5228-7

- Judaism For Dummies
  0-7645-5299-6
- Martial Arts For Dummies
  0-7645-5358-5
- Pilates For Dummies
  0-7645-5397-6
- Religion For Dummies
  0-7645-5264-3
- Teaching Kids to Read For Dummies
  0-7645-4043-2
- Weight Training For Dummies
  0-7645-5168-X
- Yoga For Dummies
  0-7645-5117-5

TRAVEL

0-7645-5438-7

0-7645-5453-0

Also available:

- Alaska For Dummies
  0-7645-1761-9
- Arizona For Dummies
  0-7645-6938-4
- Cancún and the Yucatán For Dummies
  0-7645-2437-2
- Cruise Vacations For Dummies
  0-7645-6941-4
- Europe For Dummies
  0-7645-5456-5
- Ireland For Dummies
  0-7645-5455-7

- Las Vegas For Dummies
  0-7645-5448-4
- London For Dummies
  0-7645-4277-X
- New York City For Dummies
  0-7645-6945-7
- Paris For Dummies
  0-7645-5494-8
- RV Vacations For Dummies
  0-7645-5443-3
- Walt Disney World & Orlando For Dummies
  0-7645-6943-0

GRAPHICS, DESIGN & WEB DEVELOPMENT

0-7645-4345-8

0-7645-5589-8

Also available:

- Adobe Acrobat 6 PDF For Dummies
  0-7645-3760-1
- Building a Web Site For Dummies
  0-7645-7144-3
- Dreamweaver MX 2004 For Dummies
  0-7645-4342-3
- FrontPage 2003 For Dummies
  0-7645-3882-9
- HTML 4 For Dummies
  0-7645-1995-6
- Illustrator CS For Dummies
  0-7645-4084-X

- Macromedia Flash MX 2004 For Dummies
  0-7645-4358-X
- Photoshop 7 All-in-One Desk Reference For Dummies
  0-7645-1667-1
- Photoshop CS Timesaving Techniques For Dummies
  0-7645-6782-9
- PHP 5 For Dummies
  0-7645-4166-8
- PowerPoint 2003 For Dummies
  0-7645-3908-6
- QuarkXPress 6 For Dummies
  0-7645-2593-X

NETWORKING, SECURITY, PROGRAMMING & DATABASES

0-7645-6852-3

0-7645-5784-X

Also available:

- A+ Certification For Dummies
  0-7645-4187-0
- Access 2003 All-in-One Desk Reference For Dummies
  0-7645-3988-4
- Beginning Programming For Dummies
  0-7645-4997-9
- C For Dummies
  0-7645-7068-4
- Firewalls For Dummies
  0-7645-4048-3
- Home Networking For Dummies
  0-7645-42796

- Network Security For Dummies
  0-7645-1679-5
- Networking For Dummies
  0-7645-1677-9
- TCP/IP For Dummies
  0-7645-1760-0
- VBA For Dummies
  0-7645-3989-2
- Wireless All In-One Desk Reference For Dummies
  0-7645-7496-5
- Wireless Home Networking For Dummies
  0-7645-3910-8

HEALTH & SELF-HELP

0-7645-6820-5 *†

0-7645-2566-2

Also available:
- Alzheimer's For Dummies
  0-7645-3899-3
- Asthma For Dummies
  0-7645-4233-8
- Controlling Cholesterol For Dummies
  0-7645-5440-9
- Depression For Dummies
  0-7645-3900-0
- Dieting For Dummies
  0-7645-4149-8
- Fertility For Dummies
  0-7645-2549-2

- Fibromyalgia For Dummies
  0-7645-5441-7
- Improving Your Memory For Dummies
  0-7645-5435-2
- Pregnancy For Dummies †
  0-7645-4483-7
- Quitting Smoking For Dummies
  0-7645-2629-4
- Relationships For Dummies
  0-7645-5384-4
- Thyroid For Dummies
  0-7645-5385-2

EDUCATION, HISTORY, REFERENCE & TEST PREPARATION

0-7645-5194-9

0-7645-4186-2

Also available:
- Algebra For Dummies
  0-7645-5325-9
- British History For Dummies
  0-7645-7021-8
- Calculus For Dummies
  0-7645-2498-4
- English Grammar For Dummies
  0-7645-5322-4
- Forensics For Dummies
  0-7645-5580-4
- The GMAT For Dummies
  0-7645-5251-1
- Inglés Para Dummies
  0-7645-5427-1

- Italian For Dummies
  0-7645-5196-5
- Latin For Dummies
  0-7645-5431-X
- Lewis & Clark For Dummies
  0-7645-2545-X
- Research Papers For Dummies
  0-7645-5426-3
- The SAT I For Dummies
  0-7645-7193-1
- Science Fair Projects For Dummies
  0-7645-5460-3
- U.S. History For Dummies
  0-7645-5249-X

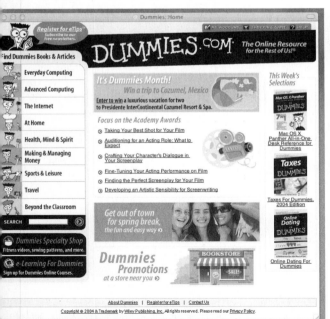

Get smart @ dummies.com®

- **Find a full list of Dummies titles**
- **Look into loads of FREE on-site articles**
- **Sign up for FREE eTips e-mailed to you weekly**
- **See what other products carry the Dummies name**
- **Shop directly from the Dummies bookstore**
- **Enter to win new prizes every month!**

* Separate Canadian edition also available
† Separate U.K. edition also available

Available wherever books are sold. For more information or to order direct: U.S. customers visit www.dummies.com or call 1-877-762-2974.
U.K. customers visit www.wileyeurope.com or call 0800 243407. Canadian customers visit www.wiley.ca or call 1-800-567-4797.

Wiley Publishing, Inc., End-User License Agreement

READ THIS. You should carefully read these terms and conditions before opening the software packet(s) included with this book "Book". This is a license agreement "Agreement" between you and Wiley Publishing, Inc. "WPI". By opening the accompanying software packet(s), you acknowledge that you have read and accept the following terms and conditions. If you do not agree and do not want to be bound by such terms and conditions, promptly return the Book and the unopened software packet(s) to the place you obtained them for a full refund.

1. **License Grant.** WPI grants to you (either an individual or entity) a nonexclusive license to use one copy of the enclosed software program(s) (collectively, the "Software") solely for your own personal or business purposes on a single computer (whether a standard computer or a workstation component of a multi-user network). The Software is in use on a computer when it is loaded into temporary memory (RAM) or installed into permanent memory (hard disk, CD-ROM, or other storage device). WPI reserves all rights not expressly granted herein.

2. **Ownership.** WPI is the owner of all right, title, and interest, including copyright, in and to the compilation of the Software recorded on the disk(s) or CD-ROM "Software Media". Copyright to the individual programs recorded on the Software Media is owned by the author or other authorized copyright owner of each program. Ownership of the Software and all proprietary rights relating thereto remain with WPI and its licensers.

3. **Restrictions on Use and Transfer.**

    (a) You may only (i) make one copy of the Software for backup or archival purposes, or (ii) transfer the Software to a single hard disk, provided that you keep the original for backup or archival purposes. You may not (i) rent or lease the Software, (ii) copy or reproduce the Software through a LAN or other network system or through any computer subscriber system or bulletin-board system, or (iii) modify, adapt, or create derivative works based on the Software.

    (b) You may not reverse engineer, decompile, or disassemble the Software. You may transfer the Software and user documentation on a permanent basis, provided that the transferee agrees to accept the terms and conditions of this Agreement and you retain no copies. If the Software is an update or has been updated, any transfer must include the most recent update and all prior versions.

4. **Restrictions on Use of Individual Programs.** You must follow the individual requirements and restrictions detailed for each individual program in the About the CD-ROM appendix of this Book. These limitations are also contained in the individual license agreements recorded on the Software Media. These limitations may include a requirement that after using the program for a specified period of time, the user must pay a registration fee or discontinue use. By opening the Software packet(s), you will be agreeing to abide by the licenses and restrictions for these individual programs that are detailed in the About the CD-ROM appendix and on the Software Media. None of the material on this Software Media or listed in this Book may ever be redistributed, in original or modified form, for commercial purposes.